FROM CONFLICT TO

International trade often inspires intense conflict between workers and their employers. In this book, Adam Dean studies the conditions under which labor and capital collaborate in support of the same trade policies. Dean argues that capital-labor agreement on trade policy depends on the presence of "profit-sharing institutions." He tests this theory through case studies from the United States, Britain, and Argentina in the late-nineteenth and early-twentieth centuries; they offer a revisionist history placing class conflict at the center of the political economy of trade. Analysis of data from more than one hundred countries from 1986 to 2002 demonstrates that the field's conventional wisdom systematically exaggerates the benefits that workers receive from trade policy reforms. *From Conflict to Coalition* boldly explains why labor is neither an automatic beneficiary nor an automatic ally of capital when it comes to trade policy and distributional conflict.

Adam Dean is an Assistant Professor of Political Science at Middlebury College, Vermont. He specializes in international relations with a focus on international political economy. His research interests include the political economy of trade, labor politics, and American Political Development. He earned his BA from the University of Pennsylvania, his MSc from the London School of Economics and Political Science, and his MA and PhD from the University of Chicago.

continued after the Index

FROM CONFLICT TO COALITION

*Profit-Sharing Institutions and the
Political Economy of Trade*

ADAM DEAN

Middlebury College, Vermont

CAMBRIDGE
UNIVERSITY PRESS

CAMBRIDGE
UNIVERSITY PRESS

University Printing House, Cambridge CB2 8BS, United Kingdom

One Liberty Plaza, 20th Floor, New York, NY 10006, USA

477 Williamstown Road, Port Melbourne, VIC 3207, Australia

4843/24, 2nd Floor, Ansari Road, Daryaganj, Delhi - 110002, India

79 Anson Road, #06-04/06, Singapore 079906

Cambridge University Press is part of the University of Cambridge.

It furthers the University's mission by disseminating knowledge in the pursuit of education, learning and research at the highest international levels of excellence.

www.cambridge.org
Information on this title: www.cambridge.org/9781316619735

© Adam Dean 2016

First published 2016
First paperback edition 2017

A catalogue record for this publication is available from the British Library

ISBN 978-1-107-16880-0 Hardback
ISBN 978-1-316-61973-5 Paperback

Cambridge University Press has no responsibility for the persistence or accuracy of URLs for external or third-party internet websites referred to in this publication, and does not guarantee that any content on such websites is, or will remain, accurate or appropriate.

Dedicated to Elana Dean
&
In Memory of Alvin Simonson

Contents

Figures

Tables

Acknowledgments

This book grew out of my Ph.D. dissertation at the University of Chicago, where I was lucky to have support from a wonderful group of advisers: Duncan Snidal, Will Howell, Dan Slater, and Jong Hee Park. The journey from dissertation to book would have taken many more years if not for encouragement from Jeffry Frieden, who hosted a book manuscript conference for me at Harvard in the spring of 2015. The generous feedback from Bill Clark, Jeff Colgan, James Ashley Morrison, Layna Mosley, David Singer, Dan Slater, and Dustin Tingley improved the final book immensely. I thank Middlebury College for the financial support that made that conference possible.

Numerous other scholars have offered feedback over the years. While studying in Chicago, I was fortunate to discuss my work with John Mearsheimer, John Padgett, Gerry Rosenberg, Alberto Simpser, Faisal Ahmed, Milena Ang Collan Granillo, Gene Gherzoy, Ethan Porter, Matthias Staisch, Felicity Vabulas, Tom Wood, David Burk, Carmine Grimaldi, and Andres Millan. A special thanks to Morgan Kaplan, whose constant support – often on every sentence I write – continues to be of enormous intellectual and emotional importance. I am also thankful for the help I received from several undergraduate research assistants, including Harsh Hiranandani, Katie Leu, Jamie Ocampo, and Joyce Oh.

While visiting Duncan Snidal in Oxford, I had the privilege to meet Desmond King, David Rueda, and Walter Mattli, all of whom offered much-welcomed interest and support. Visiting England also allowed me to re-connect with Ken Shadlen, my old advisor from the London School of Economics, who first encouraged me to pursue a Ph.D., and provided me with an attractive example of what an academic career might look like.

I owe perhaps my biggest intellectual debt to what we called the Gang of Four – a group of graduate students who met, at our best, once a week to discuss each other's work. Jonathan Obert, Anne Holthoefer, Nick Smith, and Chris Haid improved my writing and research incalculably. I owe a special thanks to Jonathan; it is hard to imagine having written this book without the hundreds of hours spent discussing our work over coffee, dinner, and the occasional whiskey. What a nice coincidence that we both find ourselves teaching at small liberal arts colleges in the mountains of New England.

This book project also benefited from continual feedback and critique from various workshops, conferences, and invited talks. I thank participants from multiple workshops at the University of Chicago, as well as audiences at Oxford, UMASS Amherst, and various APSA, ISA, MPSA, and IPES conferences. I also thank Robert Dreesen, from Cambridge University Press, whose early support for my research made finishing and publishing this book a pleasure.

Since joining the faculty at Middlebury College, I've received guidance from a wonderful group of colleagues, including Keegan Callanan, Kemi Fuentes-George, Chris McGrory Klyza, Sebnem Gumuscu, Bert Johnson, Peter Matthews, Jamie McCallum, Sarah Stroup, Jessica Teets, and Amy Yuen. Allison Stanger went above and beyond – she read the complete manuscript, came up with the title, and gave me the courage to finally declare the book finished.

I thank my family and my parents for their love and support throughout my education and career. I owe a special thanks to my grandfather, Al Simonson, whose enthusiasm for learning knew no bounds. I wish he were still here to see this book in print. Finally, I thank my wife, Elana, who read and discussed every draft of this project over the past seven years. She has kept me happy, motivated, and intellectually honest. With her help, this year will see the publication of my first book, and the birth of our first child.

Middlebury, VT
May 2016

I

Introduction

On November 21, 1882, the American labor movement abandoned its unified support for high tariffs. The momentous decision came after Frank K. Foster, an early leader of the American Federation of Labor (AFL), gave a rousing speech at the Federation's annual convention in Cleveland, Ohio.[1] According to Foster, high tariffs increased profits for employers in protected industries, but did nothing to increase workers' wages. "'Protection' does not protect labor," he explained, as "the rate of wages depends upon other causes than the tariff."[2] Foster went on to warn that employers used the benefits of "full protection" to form monopolies and crush labor unions. Trade protection, he told the convention, "only served to concentrate wealth in the hands of the few, to the disadvantage of the many."[3] Although many of the labor union leaders in attendance represented workers in tariff-protected industries, the Federation voted 17–1 to terminate its endorsement of trade protectionism. At the turn of the century, the AFL's Secretary-Treasurer looked back and explained, "we cannot afford to take a position on the tariff question, for our experience of the injury it wrought to the old Federation in 1882 is a sufficient lesson."[4]

Although the Federation ended its support for high tariffs, some American labor unions vehemently supported trade protection. For example, the steelworkers' union frequently appeared before Congress alongside their employers, lobbying in favor of the tariffs that protected the steel industry from foreign imports. In fact, the iron and steel workers

---

[1] The speech took place at the annual convention of the Federation of Organized Trades and Labor Unions, which changed its name to the American Federation of Labor in 1886.

[2] Federation of Organized Trades and Labor Unions 1882, 11.

[3] Federation of Organized Trades and Labor Unions 1882, 11.

[4] Letter from P.J. McGuire to Samuel Gompers, quoted in Foner 1998, 94.

were incensed over the Federation's 1882 decision not to support high tariffs and formally withdrew from the organization in protest.[5] As the union's President, John Jarrett, explained to the U.S. Senate in 1883, "Our organization is strongly a tariff organization, from the fact that we know that we do get better wages on account of the tariff."[6] However, the same Senate hearing also heard testimony from the textile workers' union, which denied the benefits of high tariffs. According to the union, high tariffs protected capital in the product market, but left workers unprotected in the labor market, where competition from immigrant workers held down wages. When asked about the benefits of high tariffs, the union's leader, Robert Howard, replied, "The benefit? Looking at the wages here compared with the wages in England I cannot see any benefit ... [manufacturers] will go over to Canada and bring over hordes of French people here to work in our mills at 50 or 75 cents a day."[7] While employers in the steel and textile industries consistently supported high tariffs, workers in these industries did not automatically join their employers in support of the same international trade policy.

This story presents a puzzle, the answer to which has the potential to reshape the way we think about economic history, as well as the political economy of contemporary globalization. Specifically, under what circumstances will workers actually share the same trade policy preferences as their employers? Although such capital-labor disagreement has shaped economic policy debates throughout the past two centuries, extant political economy theories are unable to explain the causes and cures of such class conflict. Canonical works in political science and economics predict that workers will automatically share the same trade policy preferences as their employers, and that capital and labor will therefore join together in favor of the same trade policy reforms.[8] When scholars do predict capital-labor disagreement over economic policy, they tend to envision economy-wide class conflict, and therefore offer no explanation for workers who do join their employers in support of the same policies.[9] In direct contrast, this book demonstrates that this conventional wisdom is based on a flawed theory of wage determination as well as a distorted history that ignores major instances of class conflict.

This book argues that labor's trade policy preferences depend on a previously omitted factor: the presence or absence of "profit-sharing institutions." Profit-sharing institutions are a set of rules that govern

---

5 McNeill 1887, 292.
6 United States 1885, 1, 122.
7 United States 1885, 655.
8 Brock and Magee 1978; Baldwin 1985; Gourevitch 1986; Frieden 1991.
9 Rogowski 1989; Hiscox 2002.

wage negotiations and create a credible link between an increase in profits and an increase in workers' wages. Profit-sharing institutions therefore entail more than just the existence of labor unions; the profit-sharing institutions at the heart of this book include formal union recognition, explicit agreements that wages will rise along with profits, and industry-wide wage contracts. For example, American steel workers in the late nineteenth century built an industry-wide labor union, gained formal recognition from their employers, and negotiated a sliding wage scale that explicitly indexed their wages to the profitability of the steel industry. When such profit-sharing institutions are in place, I predict that workers will be more likely to agree with their employers concerning international trade policy. However, when profit-sharing institutions are absent, I predict that workers will be more likely to disagree with their employers concerning trade policy.

In establishing the central importance of profit-sharing institutions for the political economy of trade, this book answers three related questions. First, how do profit-sharing institutions influence workers' trade policy preferences? This book demonstrates that, all else being equal, profit-sharing institutions make workers more likely to support the trade policy favored by their employers. Second, what explains the origin and evolution of profit-sharing institutions? This book describes the process through which wage bargaining and industrial conflict generates incentive for the creation of profit-sharing institutions. Third, what broader impact do profit-sharing institutions have on trade policy outcomes and international relations? This book argues that profit-sharing institutions lay the political foundation for cross-class coalitions of capital and labor in favor of the same trade policy, and thus create powerful interest groups that influence actual trade policy outcomes.

This book systematically tests my theory with a multi-method approach that includes qualitative case studies as well as large-N statistical analysis. The case studies explore trade politics in the United States from 1877 to 1945, Britain during the repeal of the Corn Laws in the 1840s, and Argentina during the development of import-substitution industrialization in the 1940s. In each of these cases, the field's conventional wisdom holds that workers joined their employers in support of the trade policies that benefitted their industries of employment.[10] In direct contrast, this book presents in-depth archival research that demonstrates that workers in each case frequently disagreed with their employers concerning international trade policy. Moreover, it demonstrates that my theory of profit-sharing institutions parsimoniously

---

[10] Rogowski 1989; Hiscox 2002.

explains this previously unrecognized variation in capital-labor conflict. Combined, these case studies demonstrate the generalizability of my theory across more than one hundred years, protectionist and liberalizing trade policy reforms, three continents, economies with four different types of factor endowments, and numerous political regimes.

This book complements these case studies with two quantitative tests of my theory. First, it tests my argument that profit-sharing institutions and workers' trade policy preferences have an important influence on trade policy outcomes. In order to do so it utilizes an original dataset on American labor union density to explore U.S. Senate voting on trade policy in 1945. The analysis demonstrates that U.S. senators were more likely to support free trade when lobbied by a cross-class coalition of capital and labor in favor of free trade. In contrast, when manufacturers lobbied without the assistance of their workers they were unable to influence senators' trade policy voting. Second, it uses data from 28 manufacturing industries, in 117 countries, from 1986 to 2002 to explore my theory's main causal mechanism – the link between trade policy and workers' wages. The analysis demonstrates that when workers lack bargaining power they are completely unable to capture a share of profits in the form of wages. In all of the above ways, this book challenges both the empirical and theoretical conventional wisdom regarding the political economy of trade.

Although this book focuses specifically on the political economy of international trade, my theory of profit-sharing institutions has broad implications for the study of many other economic issue areas. Contemporary political economy debates tend to assume that the benefits of various economic reforms are automatically shared between employers and their workers. This assumption pervades the study of economic globalization and shapes the way many scholars understand the politics of everything from international trade to foreign direct investment, and from exchange rate policy to immigration. This assumption is equally present in domestic policy debates concerning issues as diverse as education reform and the privatization of industry. In short, both domestic and international political economy debates often assume that workers will automatically benefit from any development that increases their industry's profitability. This book challenges this common assumption and argues that the degree to which workers benefit from – and join their employers in support of – economic policy reforms depends crucially on domestic labor market institutions.

Overall, this book makes four important contributions to the field of international political economy. First, it shows that the field's conventional wisdom overlooks major historical instances of trade policy disagreement between workers and their employers. Second, it establishes that the neoclassical models traditionally used in the political economy literature systematically exaggerate the benefits that workers receive from economic policy reforms. Third, it demonstrates that profit-sharing institutions are a previously omitted variable that determine workers' trade policy preferences, as well as their tendency to join their employers in support of the same trade policy. Fourth, it demonstrates that changes in profit-sharing institutions laid the political foundations for major trade policy reforms, such as the liberalization of American trade policy following World War II. For all of these reasons, scholars must think differently about domestic labor market institutions to understand the political economy of international trade.

CURRENT EXPLANATIONS

The political economy literature is dominated by the Ricardo-Viner (R-V) and Heckscher-Ohlin (H-O) models of international trade.[11] The R-V model assumes that there are two factors of production – capital and labor – both of which are unable to move between industries. According to this model, a trade policy that benefits a specific industry automatically leads to increases in both profits and wages. Based on the rational choice assumption that actors will hold a preference for the trade policy that benefits them economically, this approach predicts that capital and labor employed in the same industry will always share the same trade policy preferences.[12] As Gourevitch argues, international trade "is by no means a cleavage that brings capitalists and workers to confront each other. Rather, it joins the two groups together in conflict against another cross-class coalition."[13] For example, capital and labor employed in an import-competing industry, such as the contemporary U.S. steel industry, are both predicted to favor trade protection. In a similar way, capital and labor employed in an export-oriented industry, such as the contemporary Bangladeshi garment industry, are both predicted to favor free trade. Simply put, this popular model describes a world in which class conflict is theoretically impossible.

The H-O model assumes that there are three factors of production – capital, labor, and land – all of which are able to easily move between industries.[14] According to the H-O model, the distributive effects of trade

---

[11] Frieden 1988; Rogowski 1989; Hiscox 2002.
[12] Frieden 1991; Rodrik 1995; Frieden 1999; Lake 2004.
[13] Gourevitch 1986, 47.
[14] The original H-O model is based on only two factors of production – capital and labor – and therefore predicts that these two classes will always disagree with one another concerning trade policy. See, Stolper and Samuelson 1941.

policy depend on whether or not a country has relatively abundant or
scarce supplies of capital, labor, and land. When a factor of production is
scarce it automatically benefits from protectionist trade policies, whereas
when a factor of production is abundant it automatically benefits from
trade liberalization. The H-O approach therefore predicts that capital and
labor will share the same trade policy preferences when both represent
either scarce or abundant factors of production. Rogowski argues that
when "both capital and labor are scarce ... both are harmed by expanding
trade and, normally, will seek protection." In the opposite scenario, when
both capital and labor are abundant, "expanding trade must benefit
both capitalists and workers [both of whom] should favor free trade."[15]
When capital and labor do not share the same level of abundance or
scarcity, the H-O model predicts that all workers will join together
in opposition to the trade policy supported by capitalists. The H-O
approach therefore suffers from two different problems. First, the model
cannot explain trade policy disagreements between workers in different
industries, thus rendering it difficult to explain variation in class conflict
across sectors. Second, when applied to countries in which capital and
labor are both either abundant or scarce, the model predicts a world
devoid of class conflict. For example, Rogowski and Hiscox both use the
H-O model to incorrectly predict class harmony in the U.S. case discussed
below.[16]

How do scholars choose between these two trade models? According
to Hiscox, the applicability of these models depends on an economy's level
of inter-industry factor mobility. When both capital and labor mobility is
high, the predictions of the H-O model are more likely to be accurate,
whereas the predictions of the R-V model are more likely to be accurate
when both capital and labor mobility is low.[17] But why should we assume
that the inter-industry mobility of capital and labor must vary together?
In this vein, other scholars have explored the specific-factors (SF) model,
which assumes that capital is specific to its industry of employment while
labor is fully mobile between industries. According to this model, a

---

[15] Rogowski 1989.
[16] Rogowski and Hiscox agree that late nineteenth-century America had scarce
supplies of capital and labor. Both scholars therefore use the H-O model to predict
that capital and labor joined together in support of protection, and are thus
unable to explain the prominent instances of capital-labor disagreement discussed
in Chapter 4. Importantly, this shortcoming cannot be remedied by simply re-coding
the factor endowment of the United States during this period. If capital were scarce
and labor abundant – or vice versa – the H-O model would over-predict the extent
of disagreement between capital and labor. See, Rogowski 1989; Hiscox 2002.
[17] Hiscox 2001.

trade policy that benefits a specific industry will automatically increase profits for capital employed in the industry. The same trade policy will automatically increase nominal wages for all workers in the economy, but the overall effect of trade policy on real wages will depend on workers' consumption patterns. If the cost of the products that workers consume increases more than workers' nominal wages, then their real wages will decrease and they will oppose the trade policy reform. If these costs increase less than workers' nominal wages, then their real wages will increase and they will support the trade policy reform. The SF approach therefore allows for the possibility that workers will disagree with their employers concerning trade policy, but generally predicts that workers' trade policy preferences are ambiguous and indeterminate.[18] Since the SF model lacks clear predictions, the R-V and H-O models tend to dominate research on the political economy of international trade.[19]

Although scholars using "new" new trade theory (NNTT) have recently made important contributions to our understanding of the political economy of trade, this novel approach assumes that the benefits of trade policy are automatically shared with workers.[20] NNTT argues that only a small fraction of firms in export industries are actually productive enough to export. When trade expands, less-productive firms leave the market and highly productive firms increase output and expand. Overall, this leads to an increase in productivity throughout the industry, as less productive firms are replaced by more productive firms. According to NNTT, this increased productivity then leads to an increase in wages throughout the industry. Despite NNTT's innovative approach to heterogeneous firms, it still predicts that an increase in labor demand automatically leads to an increase in wages. In other words, NNTT is similar to the R-V and H-O models in omitting profit-sharing institutions and potentially overestimating the wage increases that workers receive from trade policy reforms.[21]

---

[18] Alt and Gilligan 1994. While the SF model allows for the possibility that workers will disagree with their employers concerning trade policy, it cannot explain the causal logic of the capital-labor conflict discussed below. As demonstrated throughout this book, such conflict is predominately motivated by workers' concerns regarding competition in the labor market.

[19] Gourevitch 1986; Rogowski 1989; Frieden 1991; Hiscox 2002; Milner and Kubota 2005; Rudra 2008; Oatley 2011; Chaudoin et al. 2015.

[20] Melitz 2003; Helpman et al. 2004.

[21] As Owen demonstrates in a recent study of foreign direct investment, NNTT also tends to ignore workers' concerns about unemployment, see Owen 2015.

While early research on the political economy of trade focused on the policy preferences of large groups (e.g. capital and labor), more recent scholarship uses these trade models to explore the trade policy preferences of individual people. This literature tends to accept the H-O and R-V models as accurate portrayals of how trade policy affects wages, and then identifies additional variables that influence trade policy preferences, such as home ownership,[22] patriotism,[23] education,[24] consumer prices,[25] risk tolerance,[26] as well as concerns for national economic performance,[27] fairness,[28] cultural 'westernization,'[29] and labor solidarity.[30] In this way, the literature has often focused on demonstrating that individual trade policy preferences are determined by "non-economic" factors. In contrast, this book suggests that before we rule out an economic basis for trade policy preferences, we should study the domestic institutional conditions under which the predictions of the H-O and R-V are likely to hold.[31]

When scholars challenge the distributional predictions of the H-O and R-V models, they tend to focus on specific developments related to contemporary globalization such as regional production sharing,[32] trade in services,[33] or skill-biased technology.[34] Implicit in these works is the argument that the H-O and R-V models correctly predicted the distributional consequences of international trade until recent changes altered the functioning of specific areas of modern economies. In contrast, this book argues that the uncertain connection between profits and wages is a generalizable characteristic of economic distribution, and one that applies to trade politics in the nineteenth century as well as the political economy of trade today.

The trade policy preferences derived from the H-O model also play a central role in the literature on the relationship between trade liberalization and democratization. A large body of literature has developed in recent years that explores both how democratization affects a country's

[22] Scheve and Slaughter 2001.
[23] O'Rourke et al. 2001.
[24] Mayda and Rodrik 2005; Hainmueller and Hiscox 2006.
[25] Baker 2005.
[26] Ehrlich and Maestas 2010.
[27] Mansfield and Mutz 2009.
[28] Ehrlich 2010.
[29] Margalit 2012.
[30] Ahlquist et al. 2014.
[31] For recent work that supports an economic basis for trade policy preferences, see Ardanaz et al. 2013.
[32] Chase 2003.
[33] Chase 2008.
[34] Hicks et al. 2013.

trade policies, as well as how changes in trade policy affect the probability of democratization. According to one argument, democratization enfranchises unskilled workers who then lobby the government for trade liberalization because of the automatic wage increases that workers receive from free trade.[35] According to the reverse argument, trade openness leads to democratization in developing countries because free trade automatically increases wages for unskilled workers who then use their increased incomes to lobby the government for democratic reform.[36] Central to the arguments running in each direction is the H-O model and the idea that the benefits of trade policy reform are automatically shared with workers.[37]

In these ways, the neoclassical trade models provide the underlying foundations for the literature on the political economy of trade. Despite new developments in trade theory, the literature has not explored how the distributional consequences of trade are filtered through domestic labor markets. In contrast, this book follows the insight that "economic laws ... work out differently under different institutional conditions."[38] In other words, profit-sharing institutions help explain the missing politics to the political economy of international trade. As will be made clear below, my theory of profit-sharing institutions has broad implications for how we understand the history of international trade as well as the political economy of contemporary globalization.

STRUCTURE OF THE BOOK

The book proceeds as follows. Chapter 2 develops my theory, which argues that we can understand workers' trade policy preferences by analyzing how the effects of trade are filtered through domestic labor markets. Trade policy directly increases profits, but whether or not these increased profits lead to an increase in wages depends on the outcome of wage bargaining between capital and labor. Since such bargaining is plagued by numerous uncertainties and enforcement problems, workers often doubt their ability to capture a share of increased profits and therefore tend to disagree with their employers concerning trade policy.

---

[35] Stokes 2001; Weyland 2002; Milner and Kubota 2005; O'Rourke and Taylor 2006; Chaudoin et al. 2015.

[36] Giavazzi and Tabellini 2005; Lipset 1959; López-Córdova and Meissner 2005; Rudra 2005.

[37] For the argument that trade liberalization increases income equality, lessens demands for redistribution, and therefore reduces elite resistance to democratization, see Acemoglu and Robinson 2006.

[38] Schumpeter 1994, 32.

Further, these same bargaining uncertainties also lead wage negotiations to occasionally collapse into costly strikes and lockouts. As labor becomes more powerful, such industrial conflict becomes increasingly costly and generates growing incentive for capital and labor to find ways to increase cooperation. Under such circumstances, capital and labor rationally create profit-sharing institutions which permit capital to credibly commit to increase wages along with profits. In short, when profit-sharing institutions are present, I predict that workers are more likely to share the same international trade policy preference as their employers.

Chapter 3 presents the research strategy for testing my theory empirically, using both quantitative and qualitative methods. Chapter 4 uses qualitative methods and original archival research to explore American trade politics during the late nineteenth century. This chapter explains the rise and fall of profit-sharing institutions, as well as the effect of such institutions on workers' trade policy preferences. First, it explores the relationship between profit-sharing institutions and the trade policy preferences of workers in the American textile industry hub of Fall River, Massachusetts. The analysis begins with a description of textile workers who lacked profit-sharing institutions and disagreed with their employers about the benefits of high tariffs. The chapter then shows how these workers slowly increased their bargaining power and established profit-sharing institutions with their employers. Following the creation of profit-sharing institutions, the textile workers changed their trade policy preferences and came to share their employers' support for high tariffs.

Second, it presents a similar analysis of workers in the American steel industry center of Pittsburgh, Pennsylvania. The analysis begins with a description of how profit-sharing institutions were established in the steel industry, and thus led steelworkers to join their employers in support of high tariffs. The chapter then shows how technological change decreased workers' bargaining power and contributed to the decline of profit-sharing institutions. Following the termination of profit-sharing institutions, the steelworkers changed their trade policy preferences and came to disagree with their employers' support for high tariffs. Overall, this chapter presents a structured, focused analysis that demonstrates the effect of profit-sharing institutions on workers' trade policy preferences.

Chapter 5 then uses a mix of qualitative and quantitative methods to explore the relationship between profit-sharing institutions and American trade policy outcomes. First, it uses qualitative methods to explore the effect of profit-sharing institutions on the trade policy preferences of the Congress of Industrial Organizations (CIO) during the 1930s and

1940s. Second, it uses quantitative methods to test the effect of the CIO's trade policy demands on U.S. Senate support for free trade and the Reciprocal Trade Agreements Act of 1945. The analysis uses a novel dataset of state-level CIO membership that I collected from the union's archival records. The analysis first demonstrates that the CIO did not support free trade in the 1930s. It then describes how the pro-labor legislation of the New Deal helped give rise to profit-sharing institutions that contributed to the CIO's endorsement of free trade in the 1940s. With profit-sharing institutions in place, labor joined capital and formed a cross-class coalition that successfully lobbied the U.S. Senate in favor of free trade.

Chapter 6 explores the generalizability of my argument with case studies based on archival research on trade politics in Britain and Argentina. It begins with an examination of Britain's repeal of the Corn Laws in the 1840s. During this time the working-class Chartists voiced their skepticism about free trade during hundreds of lectures and debates held throughout the country. The analysis draws on an original dataset of trade policy debates between the Chartists and the manufacturers' Anti-Corn Law League, from 1838 to 1846, which I compiled from the Chartists' newspaper, *The Northern Star*. This chapter then examines Argentina's development of import-substitution industrialization in the 1930s and 1940s. During the 1930s, Argentine labor unions faced severe labor market repression and vehemently disagreed with their employers concerning the potential benefits of high tariffs. In the 1940s, workers benefited from the rise of Juan Perón, whose pro-labor reforms strengthened labor unions and helped establish a credible link between profits and workers' wages. Following the creation of such profit-sharing institutions, workers quickly changed their trade policy preferences and joined their employers in favor of trade protectionism. The analysis draws on Spanish language documents from archival research in Buenos Aires, including the *Boletín* of the *Confederación General del Trabajo*, the main labor union federation, and the *Anales* of the *Unión Industrial Argentina*, the main manufacturers' association.

Chapter 7 further tests my theory by analyzing quantitative data from 28 manufacturing industries, in 117 countries, from 1986 to 2002. In order to greatly expand the scope of the analysis, this chapter uses a country's level of respect for labor rights as a proxy measure for labor's bargaining power. This large-N analysis avoids the selection bias that may influence the qualitative case studies, demonstrates the generalizability of my argument well beyond the American, British, and Argentine cases, and establishes the relevance of my theory for the study of contemporary political economy. This chapter also provides a rigorous test of my theory's causal logic by exploring how the effects of international trade are filtered through domestic labor markets. Most importantly, this chapter demonstrates that in the absence of labor bargaining power, an increase in profits does not lead to an increase in wages. In a similar vein, workers' ability to capture a share of profits in the form of wages increases as a country improves its protection of labor rights.

Chapter 8 concludes with a summary of the book's argument and evidence. The conclusion also briefly discusses the promising prospects for applying my theory to contemporary cases of trade politics, as well as political economy issue areas beyond international trade. In general, it suggests that scholars pay closer attention to domestic labor market institutions in order to understand the causes and consequences of globalization. Just as American workers were hesitant to join their employers in favor of high tariffs during the late nineteenth century, today, workers throughout the developing world are hesitant to join their employers in favor of free trade. In this way, this book's revisionist account of the history of international trade has clear implications for the study of contemporary political economy.

2

A Theory of Profit-Sharing Institutions

Sometimes workers join their employers in support of the same international trade policy. At other times, workers disagree with their employers and challenge the trade policy reforms that would benefit their own industry. What explains this variation in workers' trade policy preferences? When will labor share the same trade policy preference as capital? In order to solve this puzzle, I argue that we can understand workers' trade policy preferences by analyzing how the effects of international trade are filtered through domestic labor markets. Trade policy directly increases profits, but whether or not these increased profits lead to an increase in wages depends on the outcome of wage bargaining between capital and labor.[1] Surprisingly, the extant IPE literature tends to ignore this entire realm of political economy, overlooking how labor market institutions influence who wins and who loses from economic policy reform. This chapter opens the black box of domestic labor markets and explains the conditions under which workers expect an increase in profits to lead to an increase in wages. I predict that it is then, and only then that workers will join their employers in support of trade policies that benefit their industry.

This chapter presents my theory of profit-sharing institutions in three steps. First, it explains why workers' wages do not automatically increase

---

[1] Throughout this book, I refer to the economic benefits generated by favorable trade policy reform as "profits," rather than "rents." This has two main advantages. First, it allows me to use the same term when discussing the benefits from trade liberalization as well as trade protectionism. Some might insist that trade protectionism produces rents, not profits. However, most would agree that the export-oriented industries that benefit from free trade policies are indeed increasing their profits, not capturing rents. Second, the term "profit" allows for a clear connection between the theory and qualitative case studies. When discussing international trade policy, workers often refer to how policy reform will influence their employers' "profits," but never make reference to the more technical term "rents."

along with trade policies that benefit their industry. As part of this analysis, I unpack the causal logic of the neoclassical models that dominate research on the political economy of international trade. This exercise demonstrates that once we relax the models' assumption of full employment, capital captures all of the benefits of favorable trade policy reform. In this scenario, workers do not expect to receive a share of their industry's increased profits and therefore have no economic incentive to support the international trade policy favored by their employers. Or, as a prominent nineteenth-century American labor union newspaper explained, "unless the workmen were paid their share of protective tariff they could not be expected to support the party of protective tariff."[2]

Second, it introduces the possibility of workers developing bargaining power and negotiating with their employers for a share of increased profits. Broadly speaking, workers develop bargaining power by establishing the ability to launch costly strikes that stop production. This section presents a general framework for understanding the sources of such labor bargaining power, including high skills, legislation, and organizational capacity. In a fundamental sense, the outcome of wage bargaining depends on the balance of bargaining power between capital and labor. When workers are unorganized and weak they are unlikely to be able to bargain for a share of increased profits. However, when workers are organized and powerful they are more likely to successfully capture a share of increased profits.

Beyond this general relationship between labor power and workers' wages, however, actual wage bargaining is plagued by numerous uncertainties. Workers might wonder, how much power do we really have relative to our employers? Can our employers afford to pay higher wages? If they promise to increase wages in the future, how will we enforce such commitments? These uncertainties regarding the balance of bargaining power, privately held information, and the enforcement of commitments render the outcome of wage negotiations unpredictable.[3] Since workers remain uncertain about their ability to capture a share of increased profits they continue to disagree with their employers concerning trade policy. In other words, labor power is insufficient to establish a clear connection between profits and wages.

Third, it argues that these same bargaining uncertainties can provide clear incentive for capital and labor to develop profit-sharing institutions. Of course, the wage demands of a weak group of workers can be easily ignored by employers. However, when workers develop the ability to

[2] *National Labor Tribune*, October 29, 1892.
[3] Fearon 1995.

shut down production, capital's refusal to share profits with workers may come at a considerable cost. If workers' wage demands are not met, a strike can paralyze production, damage equipment, and lower employers' profits, as well as workers' overall incomes. The more costly these conflicts become, the more incentive capital and labor have to rationally develop labor market institutions – implicit or explicit rules, norms, or contractual arrangements – that will decrease uncertainty and thereby increase cooperation during wage negotiations.[4]

This book focuses on three specific labor market institutions that capital and labor can create to increase cooperation: formal labor union recognition, explicit agreement that wages will rise with profits, and industry-wide wage scales. Formal union recognition decreases uncertainty concerning the balance of bargaining power; agreement that wages will rise with profits requires that capital share private information regarding profitability; and industry-wide wage scales enable labor unions to enforce wage agreements. Importantly, none of these labor market institutions are individually sufficient to alleviate the multiple uncertainties that characterize wage bargaining. Rather, it is the simultaneous combination of all three of these labor market institutions that permit capital to credibly commit that an increase in profits will lead to an increase in wages. Therefore, when all three of these labor market institutions are present, capital and labor can be said to have created something greater than its parts, what I call "profit-sharing institutions." In turn, my theory predicts that workers are more likely to agree with their employers concerning international trade policy when profit-sharing institutions are in place.

INTERNATIONAL TRADE AND WAGES

How does international trade policy affect workers' wages? For the past twenty-five years, political economists have traditionally answered this question with recourse to one of two neoclassical models of international trade – the Heckscher-Ohlin (H-O) and the Ricardo-Viner (R-V) models. As explained in Chapter 1, these models predict that workers automatically receive the benefits of international trade policy reforms. Although these models are used to explain various aspects of the political economy of trade, scholars have thus far failed to critically explore the assumptions underlying their predictions. This section therefore carefully unpacks the causal logic of these models in order to demonstrate the important role played by the assumption of full employment. It shows that once we

[4] Menendez and Rueda 2015, 305.

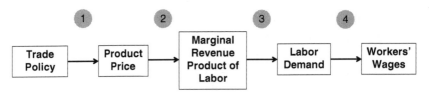

Figure 2.1. Causal Logic of Trade Models

relax this problematic assumption, the profits from trade policy are no longer shared between capital and labor. When the labor market contains unemployed workers, the benefits of trade policy accrue entirely to capital without any wage increases for workers. In this scenario, workers are predicted to disagree with their employers concerning international trade policy.

The H-O and R-V models both derive an automatic connection between trade policy and wages in four steps. The causal logic of the neoclassical trade models is displayed in Figure 2.1 and explained, step-by-step, below.

1. A trade policy change increases the relative price of a sector's output by either opening or closing the domestic economy.
2. An increase in the relative price of a sector's output increases the marginal revenue product of labor.
3. Since perfectly competitive firms hire workers until the marginal revenue product of labor is equal to the marginal cost of an extra worker, firms in the benefited sector seek to hire more workers. That is, demand for labor increases.
4. Under the assumption of full employment, hiring more workers requires these firms to offer higher wages in order to attract workers that are currently employed elsewhere.[5]

In these ways, a trade policy that increases an industry's relative output price leads to an increase in the marginal revenue product of labor, which automatically leads to an equal increase in wages.

The underlying causal logic is the same whether we use the H-O model's assumption of perfect inter-industry factor mobility, or the R-V model's assumption of zero inter-industry factor mobility. In addition,

---

[5] The scope of the wage increase depends on the models' assumptions concerning inter-industry factor mobility. According to the H-O model, a trade policy that benefits a labor-intensive industry will lead to wage increases for workers through the economy. According to the R-V model, the wage increases will be limited to workers in the specific industry benefited by the trade policy reform.

the same causal logic explains how both trade liberalization and trade protection affect wages. For example, consider the causal logic of how trade *protection* increases wages for workers. According to the R-V model, trade protection increases wages for workers in import-competing industries. This occurs because trade protection increases the relative price of such industries' output, which increases the marginal revenue product of labor, and therefore automatically increases wages. According to the H-O model, trade protection increases wages for workers throughout the economy in labor-scarce countries. This occurs because trade protection increases the relative price of labor-intensive industries' output, which increases the marginal revenue product of labor, and therefore automatically increases wages. The causal logic of how trade *liberalization* increases wages is analogous, only for workers in export-oriented industries and workers in labor-abundant countries, respectively.

However, this predicted connection between international trade policy and workers' wages relies on the assumption of full employment, or what John Maynard Keynes referred to as the "strange supposition" that underlies neoclassical economics.[6] Once we relax the assumption of full employment we can parsimoniously display that the relationship between trade policy and wages is conditional on the supply of labor. Large numbers of surplus workers, whether laid off by nearby firms or migrating from rural areas or foreign countries, create competition in the labor market that allows employers to hire additional workers without increasing wages.[7] That is, the fourth step of the causal logic of the neoclassical trade models (Figure 2.1) is disrupted, as firms can increase employment without increasing wages. In more technical terms, the presence of surplus workers in the labor market results in a labor supply curve that is perfectly elastic.

As can be seen in Figure 2.2, the elasticity of the labor supply curve conditions the degree to which an increase in labor demand leads to higher wages. As mentioned above, an increase in relative output price leads firms to hire more workers and thus increases the demand for labor. This is shown graphically in Figure 2.2a as an outward shift in the labor demand curve from LD1 to LD2. With an upward sloping labor supply curve, this increased labor demand leads to an increase in both employment and wages, as the firm's labor market equilibrium moves from point 1 to point 2. In contrast, the effect of trade policy on wages is very different in Figure 2.2b, where a labor surplus results in a perfectly

---

[6] Keynes 1936, 12.
[7] Lewis 1954; Peters 2015.

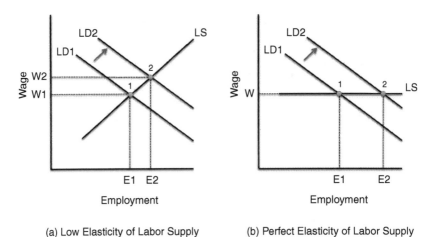

(a) Low Elasticity of Labor Supply   (b) Perfect Elasticity of Labor Supply

Figure 2.2. Unemployment, Labor Supply, and Wages

elastic (flat) labor supply curve. As the firm's labor market equilibrium moves from point 1 to point 2, the firm will increase employment but without increasing wages. The trade policy change will lead the firm to employ more workers, but the workers previously employed by the firm will not receive wage increases. In this way, relaxing the assumption of full employment completely severs the neoclassical models' prediction concerning the relationship between trade policy and workers' wages. A trade policy that benefits a specific industry will increase that industry's profits, but it will not increase the wages paid to workers in that industry. As demonstrated throughout the case studies below, workers often explicitly argue that influxes of migrant workers deprive them of their share of the benefits from trade policy reforms.

Some readers might insist that wages will rise along with profits, at least to some extent, even when workers face competition from surplus labor. Such concerns should be assuaged by the quantitative evidence presented in Chapter 7, which demonstrates that workers with low levels of bargaining power are incapable of capturing any share of increased profits. The chapter presents the results of a cross-national quantitative analysis of profit-sharing in 28 manufacturing industries, across 117 countries, from 1986 to 2002. Since it is difficult to observe workers' bargaining power independent from its effect, the analysis uses a country's level of respect for labor rights as a proxy measure for workers' bargaining power. When a state respects labor rights, it provides a permissive context in which workers can act collectively and therefore increase their bargaining power vis-à-vis their employers. The analysis demonstrates that when labor rights are not protected, what I call the "profit-sharing rate" is statistically indistinguishable from zero. Put simply, when workers lack bargaining power, their wages do not automatically rise along with profits.

Under such circumstances, workers do not expect to receive a share of their industry's increased profits and therefore lack economic incentive to support the international trade policy favored by their employers.[8] Instead, workers are more likely to express skepticism and doubt concerning the trade policy reforms advocated by their employers. Such skepticism is especially pronounced when employers argue that they are lobbying for trade policy reforms with the specific intention of increasing their workers' wages. In stark contrast, I predict that workers who lack profit-sharing institutions will repudiate such claims and explicitly deny that they receive a share of the profits generated by trade policy reform. In this way, the lack of profit-sharing institutions is associated with clear disagreement between labor and capital concerning trade policy.

In turn, such trade policy disagreement has an important influence on actual trade policy outcomes. When workers disagree with their employers concerning international trade they withhold their support from capital's favored trade policy. Trade policy disagreement therefore leaves employers to lobby the government on their own, without assistance from their workers. As discussed in Chapter 5, such capital-labor disagreement in the 1930s left American export-oriented manufacturers to lobby for free trade without assistance from their workers. It was not until the creation of profit-sharing institutions in the early 1940s that labor joined their employers in a cross-class coalition in favor of free trade. Only then, were capital and labor able to successfully pressure U.S. senators to support free trade. In this way, trade policy disagreement between capital and labor does not result in tacit labor support for capital's preferred policy. Influencing trade policy requires powerful domestic interest groups, and domestic trade policy coalitions are more powerful when profit-sharing institutions align the trade policy preferences of labor with capital.

As demonstrated throughout the following empirical chapters, the absence of profit-sharing institutions successfully predicts such trade

---

[8] Some might expect workers in import-competing industries to support high tariffs due to concerns about job security. This was certainly not the case for American labor unions in the nineteenth century, who often argued that high tariffs led to the consolidation of monopolies. According to workers, these industrial trusts then decreased employment, broke labor unions, lowered wages, and increased consumer prices. In this way, workers saw that tariffs generated super profits for employers, but did not save jobs in non-competitive industries. While concerns over job security may influence workers' trade policy preferences on the margins, the cases examined below suggest that such concerns are insufficient to establish trade policy agreement between labor and capital.

policy disagreement between labor and capital. However, there are also times when workers appear to go a step further and actually oppose the trade policy reforms supported by their employers. For example, in 1890, the leader of the American textile workers' union spoke out against the "evils of the McKinley tariff bill," despite the fact that it provided for high tariffs that protected the textile industry. While the absence of profit-sharing institutions can explain why the textile union did not support high tariffs, more is needed to explain such instances of actual opposition. The McKinley tariff might not have increased workers' wages, but why would these workers oppose a policy that merely failed to benefit them?

Understanding such cases of labor opposition requires attention to additional factors that influence workers' trade policy preferences, such as concerns over consumer prices and relative gains. In fact, it is exactly when profit-sharing institutions are absent that we should expect workers to be most influenced by factors beyond their wages. In contrast, when profit-sharing institutions are present, workers expect trade policy reforms to increase their wages, and the influence of other factors are less likely to matter. In this way, profit-sharing institution may help scholars identify the scope conditions under which non-economic factors influence trade policy preferences.[9]

From Disagreement to Opposition

This section discusses the causal logic of how consumer prices and relative gains may lead workers without profit-sharing institutions to oppose the trade policies favored by their employers. First, consider how workers' concerns over consumer prices might push them from skepticism concerning high tariffs to outright opposition. Without profit-sharing institutions, workers in import-competing industries do not expect to capture a share of the profits generated by high tariffs. In other words, they do not expect high tariffs to increase their nominal wages. However, since trade protection also increases consumers prices, high tariffs may actually decrease workers' real wages, as their cost of living increases more than their nominal wages. Under such circumstances workers have a clear economic rationale to actually oppose high tariffs.[10] Such concerns help us understand the American textile union discussed above, which argued that "in relation to the tariff, it is nothing more or less than a tax.

---

9 O'Rourke et al. 2001; Scheve and Slaughter 2001; Baker 2005; Mayda and Rodrik 2005; Hainmueller and Hiscox 2006; Mansfield and Mutz 2009; Ehrlich 2010; Ehrlich and Maestas 2010; Margalit 2012; Ahlquist et al. 2014.
10 Baker 2005.

The taxation by tariff is what is making all the millionaires. You do not have to go away from home to find examples of the evil effects of the McKinley tariff bill."[11] In other words, the textile workers opposed trade protectionism because high tariffs taxed the things workers consumed, but did not increase their wages.

In export-oriented industries, however, concerns over consumer prices might lead workers to join their employers in favor of free trade. Without profit-sharing institutions, free trade might not increase these workers' nominal wages, but it could lower their cost of living and therefore increase their real wages. Understanding why such workers might oppose free trade requires consideration of a second factor: concern over relative gains. Workers care about relative gains because of the foundational role of conflict and bargaining in wage negotiations. The key insight is that capital and labor can use their resources not only to increase their own bargaining power but also to decrease the bargaining power of the other side.[12] In terms of increasing their own bargaining power, workers can use resources to form a labor union, while employers can use income to form a manufacturers' association. In terms of decreasing the bargaining power of their negotiating partner, employers can invest their resources in new technologies that reduce their reliance on skilled labor, thus undercutting the bargaining power of their workers. Employers can also blacklist union organizers, coordinate anti-union campaigns, and hire private detectives to infiltrate and undermine union organizing. Similarly, workers may use their resources to enforce rules that limit employer prerogatives concerning hiring, hours, and output.

Most dramatically, capital and labor can translate their resources into the explicit use of force during strikes and lockouts. Workers use the threat of violence when they surround a workplace with a picket line, just as employers threaten the use of force when they seek to restart production using strikebreakers. In addition, capital and labor may use their resources to shift the balance of bargaining power by influencing government policy. Employers use increased profits to donate to political campaigns and fight against labor market regulations that might increase workers' bargaining power and wages.[13] In turn, workers can be a major political force behind the development of labor rights, which tilts the balance of bargaining power towards labor. As Tilly explains, it was "through intense struggles, incremental changes, and alterations in the

---

[11] *Fall River Daily Herald*, November 1, 1890.
[12] Scholars have long recognized that under such conditions, rational actors are concerned with relative gains. See, for example, Powell 1991.
[13] Hacker and Pierson 2011.

organization of states, [that] workers in capitalist countries acquired substantial collective rights."[14] Given the importance of the balance of bargaining power, capital and labor have reason to be deeply concerned about relative gains and losses. For this reason, workers may rationally oppose trade policies that increase profits without increasing wages. Otherwise, workers risk falling behind in the balance of bargaining power and fail to maximize their future income.[15]

In these ways, concern over consumer prices or relative gains may lead workers to oppose the trade policies which benefit their industry of employment. Despite the interesting theoretical difference between worker skepticism and worker opposition, however, it is important to note that the empirical distinction between skepticism and opposition is extremely difficult to identify in practice. For example, consider the trade policy preferences of the American textile union during the early 1880s. When testifying before the U.S. Senate, the union's leader was asked whether or not workers received any benefit from the high tariffs that protected the textile industry. Importantly, the inquiring Senator explained that textile manufacturers had just testified that they supported high tariffs because trade protection would benefit their workers. In testimony that certainly disappointed their employers, the union leader explicitly denied that workers received any benefit from high tariffs. However, how exactly should we characterize such trade policy preferences? Does this evidence suggest that the textile union was skeptical about the benefits of high tariffs, or that they actually opposed high tariffs?

The crucial point is that the union clearly *disagreed* with their employers concerning international trade policy, and that such disagreement cannot be explained by the neoclassical models conventionally used in international political economy. Since the subtle differences between skepticism and opposition are often ambiguous, this book therefore codes worker skepticism, as well as worker opposition, as instances of labor "disagreement" with capital. Ultimately, this book focuses specifically on explaining why some workers agree with their employers concerning international trade policy while others disagree with their employers.

---

[14] Tilly 1995.

[15] Workers in export-oriented industries that lack profit-sharing institutions might also oppose free trade due to concerns about downward pressure on labor rights. As Mosley (2010) and Kuruvilla (1996) have both shown, free trade and export-oriented industrialization are associated with decreased respect for workers' rights over time.

BARGAINING POWER AND UNCERTAINTY

The previous section argued that when workers' wages do not increase along with profits, workers tend to disagree with their employers concerning international trade policy. This section explores the possibility that workers can develop bargaining power in order to try and capture a share of their industry's increased profits. It introduces a general framework for understanding the various sources of labor's bargaining power, as well as changes in the relative balance of bargaining power between capital and labor over time. It then argues that wage bargaining is plagued by numerous uncertainties that result in unpredictable outcomes and continued trade policy disagreement between labor and capital. In other words, labor power is insufficient to establish a clear connection between profits and wages and therefore does not align the trade policy preferences of labor with capital.

The Balance of Bargaining Power

When we relax the assumption of full employment, and workers' bargaining power decreases, what options do they have to increase their power vis-à-vis their employers? In other words, what determines the relative balance of bargaining power between capital and labor? If workers find ways to augment their bargaining power, they may be able to negotiate for a share of the increased profits and re-establish the neoclassical models' positive relationship between profits and wages.

I argue that capital enjoys a large and natural bargaining power advantage over labor. Capital's natural advantage in bargaining power vis-à-vis their workers has long been recognized by even the most liberal of theorists. As Adam Smith explained:

It is not, however, difficult to foresee which of the two parties must, upon all ordinary occasions, have the advantage in the dispute, and force the other into a compliance with their terms. The masters, being fewer in number, can combine much more easily; and the law, besides, authorizes, or at least does not prohibit their combinations, while it prohibits those of the workmen ... In all such disputes the masters can hold out much longer. A landlord, a farmer, a master manufacturer, a merchant, though they did not employ a single workman, could generally live a year or two upon the stocks which they have already acquired. Many workmen could not subsist a week, few could subsist a month, and scarce any a year without employment. In the long run the workman may be as necessary to his master as his master is to him; but the necessity is not so immediate.[16]

In short, employers enjoy a natural advantage in bargaining power over their employees due to a combination of their smaller number,

[16] Smith 1776, Book I, Chapter 8.

ownership of the means of production, larger savings, and possible support from the state.[17] In late nineteenth-century America, employers often overcame the collective action problem, organized manufacturers' associations, and coordinated their attacks on nascent labor unions.[18] The common law tradition gave American employers tremendous autonomy in their relations with workers.[19] When that autonomy was threatened, employers often succeeded in demanding that the American court system issue injunctions to break up labor strikes.[20] While the exact relationship between these variables has been the source of much scholarly disagreement, there is no need to settle the debate in order to understand my theory of profit-sharing institutions.[21] The important point is that employers have a bargaining power advantage over their workers, who bargain individually and must work to live. As Polanyi explained, "the alleged commodity 'labor power' cannot be shoved about, used indiscriminately, *or even left unused*, without affecting also the human individual who happens to be the bearer of this peculiar commodity."[22]

How does capital's natural bargaining power advantage influence the prospects for profit-sharing? In a word, it permits capital to refuse to share profits. For example, consider the logic of wage negotiations following an exogenous increase in an industry's profitability. Workers seeking to maximize their incomes will demand a wage increase, as an increase in profits signals an increase in their employers' ability to pay.[23] How will employers respond to these wage demands? If workers lack the ability to strike and inflict costs on their employers, then employers clearly maximize their incomes by refusing to grant a wage increase.[24] Workers' demands for higher wages, even during periods of high profitability, can be easily ignored by employers. Far from sharing profits with their workers, many nineteenth-century American employers refused to even recognize the existence of their workers' labor unions. For example, when the textile workers requested the opportunity to formally negotiate wages with their employers during a short-lived strike in 1879, the employers did not even respond to the request. The textile workers' union had been founded and dissolved three times over the previous twenty years –

---

[17] Olson 1965; Acemoglu and Robinson 2008.
[18] Perlman 1922; Archer 2010.
[19] Orren 1991.
[20] Hattam 1993.
[21] Foner 1984.
[22] Polanyi 1944, 76. Italics added.
[23] Hayes 1984.
[24] Nineteenth-century American employers do not appear to have embraced the concept of "efficiency wages" whereby workers are paid above-market wages in order to increase productivity. See Krueger and Summers 1988.

a congenital weakness that failed to impress their employers. Simply put, employers do not increase their workers' wages unless there is a threat that there will be consequences if they refuse. To believe otherwise is to put our faith in wage increases that descend like manna from heaven.[25]

Sources of Labor's Bargaining Power

The prospects for workers to capture a share of increased profits improve if they manage to increase their bargaining power. In general, they do this by increasing their ability to launch costly strikes that stop production. According to Erik Olin Wright, workers can derive such bargaining power from two different sources – *association* and *structure*.[26] *Associational* power stems from the organization of labor unions, as well as workers' relationships with other groups. Workers who can act collectively are better able to sustain strikes that inflict costs on, and extract concessions from, their employers. In this vein, workers in nineteenth-century America struggled to form labor unions, build up large strike funds, and develop close ties with their surrounding communities.

Structural power is derived from workers' location within the economy, and can be broken down further into *marketplace* and *workplace* power. *Marketplace* power stems from the scarcity of the skills that workers possess. In order to increase marketplace power, workers can actively restrict the supply of labor for the firm or industry. Such "closed shops" decrease the elasticity of the labor supply and make it more likely that an increase in labor demand is translated into an increase in wages.[27] Similarly, some unions establish lengthy training or apprenticeship rules that seek to keep their craft skills in scarce supply. *Workplace* power stems from workers being employed in critical nodes of production, where a relatively small strike can shut down production for an entire factory or industry. For example, the skilled textile and iron workers discussed below were able to cripple production by cutting off the supply of key production inputs.

With this framework in mind, we can see how legislative reform, organizational innovation, migration, technological change, and the strategic use of violence can either increase or decrease workers' bargaining power. Legislation that decreases the number of hours in the work day or work week decreases the supply of labor and increases the marketplace power of workers. Alternatively, legislation that protects

[25] I thank Jeffry Frieden for this particular wording.
[26] Wright 2000.
[27] Oswald 1982.

workers' rights to organize can increase their capacity for associational power. Organizational innovation, such as labor unions' efforts to organize workers throughout an industry, can also increase the associational power of workers. Migration from abroad, as well as migration from rural to urban areas, can increase the labor supply and decrease workers' marketplace power. Similarly, technological change can make workers' skills suddenly obsolete, thereby decreasing their marketplace power. When new technology bypasses a critical node in the production process, technological change can also decrease workers' workplace power. Finally, both capital and labor may strategically use violence in ways that increase or decrease workers' associational power. As will be seen mostly clearly in Chapter 4, the outcome of strikes and lockouts often hinges on the ability of strikebreakers to overpower or outmaneuver striking workers and their allies in the community.

Using their bargaining power, workers can negotiate with their employers to establish wage and employment levels that surpass the logic of market forces.[28] Successful labor unions can establish a monopoly on the supply of labor, thereby decreasing the elasticity of their industry's labor supply. In general, the more labor unions are able to control the supply of labor into their industry the more they can influence the degree to which an increase in profits leads to an increase in wages. While there are important differences between the various bargaining models used in labor economics, all agree that wages increase along with the bargaining power of workers.[29] As Olson explains, "if a union has any real bargaining strength, it can force the unusually prosperous firm to raise wages well above the market level."[30]

In these ways, organized workers with bargaining power may be able to overcome competition from surplus workers in the labor market, and negotiate for a share of increased profits. But what does "real bargaining strength" look like, and how do workers know if they have enough of it to capture a share of profits? If workers go on strike, will they win their wage demands, or lose and possibly have their union destroyed? If employers promise to increase wages in the future, will workers be able to enforce such agreements? In short, just because workers can attempt to bargain for higher wages does not mean that they should expect to successfully capture a share of increased profits.

---

[28] Rosen 1969; Freeman and Medoff 1984; Rose 1987; Katz et al. 1989.
[29] For "right-to-manage" models in which a monopoly union sets the wage and the employer decides on employment levels, see Layard et al. 2005, chapter 2. For "efficient bargain" models in which a union and employer bargain over both wages and employment levels, see MaCurdy and Pencavel 1986.
[30] Olson 1965, 49.

The Limits of Bargaining

As discussed above, there is a general relationship between workers' bargaining power and their ability to capture a share of increased profits in the form of wages. However, this obscures a much more unpredictable bargaining process that renders the connection between profits and wages uncertain. This section argues that the outcome of wage negotiations are uncertain due to three distinct bargaining problems: uncertainty concerning the balance of bargaining power, the incentive to misrepresent private information, and enforcement problems.[31] Since bargaining workers face an uncertain connection between profits and wages, I predict that they will continue to disagree with their employers concerning international trade.

To be clear, my theory assumes that the state does not directly intervene in wage negotiations between capital and labor. The state provides the *context* in which negotiations occur, but does not provide the *content* of negotiated outcomes. Even when state regulations tilt the balance of bargaining power in one direction or the other, the state permits capital and labor to fight it out on their own and to enforce their own agreements.[32] This type of laissez-faire approach was clearly followed by the American state throughout the nineteenth and early twentieth centuries. As Orren demonstrates, American labor relations were regulated by the common law tradition of "master and servant relations," which held that the state should not intervene in negotiations between employers and their workers.[33] Beyond American history, this lack of state intervention into capital-labor relations is particularly common during periods of industrialization, when new working classes and labor unions are being formed.[34] In this way, my theory is most

---

[31] Fearon 1995.

[32] When the government does not intervene into industrial relations, capital and labor face bargaining problems that are similar to those faced by states in international relations. Although recent IPE research overlooks the role of conflict in capital-labor relations, early international relations theorists were keenly aware of such similarities. When Waltz analyzed the role of violence in international politics he explained that "the threat of force internationally is comparable to the role of the strike in labor and management bargaining ... [it] encourages labor and management to face difficult issues, to try to understand each other's problems, and to find accommodations" (Waltz 1979, 114). Building on this analogy, I argue that profit-sharing institutions increase worker certainty over profit-sharing in a way that is similar to how international institutions increase cooperation between states (Keohane 1984). Of course, Waltz himself did not believe that international institutions could reliably increase cooperation between states.

[33] Orren 1991. Of course, the American state was far from neutral; a conservative judiciary regularly used injunctions to end strikes and jail labor union leaders.

[34] Silver 2003.

applicable to the history of today's developed countries, as well as to the contemporary politics of present day developing countries.

Uncertainty Concerning the Balance of Bargaining Power

Bargaining workers continue to disagree with their employers concerning trade policy because they are unable to accurately measure the objective balance of bargaining power. This measurement problem stems from the fact that the balance of bargaining power depends on the unpredictable actions of other parties. According to Borjas, bargaining power depends on "such factors as the economic conditions facing the firm and the workers, the ability of unions to provide financial support to its members in the case of a prolonged strike, and the legal environment regulating the actions that firms and unions can take to 'convince' the other party to accept a particular offer."[35] For instance, it is often unclear, *ex ante*, if the state will help employers break a strike, or if it will protect workers from strikebreakers and privately hired police.[36]

In addition, the balance of bargaining power is uncertain because of the generally unpredictable nature of violence and the use of force. Whether force is used before negotiations, to deter unionization, or during negotiations in the form of lockouts and strikes, wage negotiations implicitly involve the threat of violence. As Greenstone explains, nineteenth-century American employers regularly used physical violence, anti-strike propaganda, and company informers to infiltrate unions and steal secret documents, amongst other tactics, to fight their workers' attempt to unionize and collectively bargain.[37] For a graphic reminder of how the use of force adds uncertainty to wage outcomes, consider the following description from an early scholar of industrial relations:

The trade union is then apt to show the militant character of its organization ... The works of the employer are beset by an angry crowd in the effort to keep non-unionists from entering, and a state of siege is practically declared. The employer erects a stockade around the works, and shelters and provisions there a force of workmen protected by private troops armed with rifles and revolvers. The works are destroyed, in whole or in part, by the efforts of the besiegers. The peace and order of the whole city are deranged during a great strike. A lawless mob threatens to bring about entire anarchy.[38]

Whether such violence and chaos will contribute to a victory for capital or labor is often impossible to predict. Worse yet, workers know that such

---

35 Borjas 2005.
36 Harring and McMullin 1975; Johnson 1976.
37 Greenstone 1969. See also, Friedman 1907.
38 Gilman 1904.

industrial conflict may end in the catastrophic destruction of their labor union.[39] The breakup of a labor union dismantles workers' associational power, tilts the balance of bargaining power towards employers, and leads to a reduction in expected future wages. Going on strike is a risky decision, and unforeseen setbacks may inspire employers to try and destroy the union once and for all. For instance, when the American iron and steelworkers' union demanded higher wages in the spring of 1892, their employer responded with a lockout that explicitly sought to terminate formal recognition of the union. As Henry Clay Frick, the company's chairman, explained, "Under no circumstance will we have any further dealings with the Amalgamated Association as an organization. This is final."[40] Overall, since workers are unable to reliably assess the balance of bargaining power they are uncertain of their ability to capture a share of increased profits. Given such uncertainty over profit-sharing, I predict that workers will continue to disagree with their employers concerning trade policy.

Uncertainty Concerning Profitability

Bargaining workers also continue to disagree with their employers concerning trade policy because of uncertainty regarding the profitability of their industry. This uncertainty flows from workers' knowledge that their employers have incentive to strategically misrepresent information regarding the industry's profits. Since workers are more likely to demand wage increases when their industry is profitable, employers have the incentive to obscure or deny that they are earning increased profits.[41] Since workers usually do not have access to their employers' records they cannot accurately assess whether or not profits are increasing. Moreover, capital may strategically threaten a lockout in situations where it would actually prefer to accept workers' wage demands rather than shut down production. Due to this informational asymmetry, workers are uncertain about their ability to capture a share of any future profits that result from trade policy reform.

This logic was clearly on display in the American textile industry during the late nineteenth century. The textile workers' union repeatedly offered to withdraw their wage demands if their employers would "open the books" and demonstrate their inability to afford higher wages. As demonstrated in Chapter 4, the opacity of such negotiations left the

---

[39] For a discussion of how the Pullman strike of 1894 led to the complete destruction of the American Railway Union, see Archer 2010.

[40] Brody 1960, 56.

[41] Hall and Lazear 1984.

union uncertain about profit-sharing and therefore contributed to its disagreement with their employers concerning the benefits of high tariff.

Enforcement and Commitment Problems

Even if workers were certain about the balance of bargaining power and the profitability of their industry, they would remain uncertain about their ability to enforce agreements. For example, employers faced with wage demands from their workers may promise to increase wages at some future point when profits are more propitious. When better days finally arrive, however, bargaining workers find themselves unable to force their employers to honor their original agreement. Such enforcement problems are especially dire for local unions that organize workers in industries that contain many non-unionized firms. The common experience of local unions was well described by Ulman: "if employers in strongly organized centers had to compete with nonunion employers elsewhere, how effectively could the strong union centers, with their flanks thus exposed, go about the business of pushing up wages and costs?"[42] The challenge for unions is therefore to adjust the conditions under which labor is sold throughout the industry, so that an improvement in the situation of all local groups can be made.

Local unions may attempt to punish their employers for reneging on such promises by going on strike. However, as discussed above, the outcome of such militancy is highly uncertain. Workers remain uncertain about the balance of bargaining power and are therefore unable to predict the likely outcome of industrial conflict. Moreover, workers are unable to monitor such agreements because they lack the information necessary to measure their industry's profitability. For all three of these reasons – uncertainty concerning the balance of bargaining power, uncertainty concerning profitability, and the inability to enforce commitments – bargaining workers without profit-sharing institutions do not expect to be able to bargain for a share of increased profits. Therefore, I predict that workers without profit-sharing institutions are likely to disagree with their employers concerning trade policy.

FROM CONFLICT TO COALITION: CREATION OF PROFIT-SHARING INSTITUTIONS

As discussed in the previous section, the uncertainties surrounding wage bargaining lead workers to disagree with their employers concerning trade policy. If this were the end of the story, we might never expect

[42] Ulman 1966, 21.

workers to join their employers in favor of the same trade policy reforms. However, the bargaining problems discussed above do more than simply cause uncertainty concerning the link between profits and wages; these same bargaining problems occasionally lead wage negotiations to collapse into strikes and lockouts. If labor is relatively weak, such industrial conflict is not terribly costly for capital and employers have little incentive to alter the status quo. As labor becomes more powerful, however, industrial conflict becomes increasingly costly and capital has a growing incentive to alter the status quo in a way that will increase cooperation. This section argues that such costly conflict leads capital and labor to rationally create profit-sharing institutions, which systematically alleviate uncertainty concerning the balance of bargaining power, asymmetric information, and enforcement problems. Profit-sharing institutions permit capital to credibly commit that wages will increase along with profits, and therefore lead workers to share the same international trade policy preference as their employers.

When workers develop the ability to shut down production, capital's refusal to share profits with workers may come at a considerable cost. If workers' wage demands are not met, a strike can paralyze production, damage equipment, and lower employers' profits. As North explains, "a change in the bargaining strength of parties may lead to an effective demand for a different institutional framework for exchange."[43] In a narrow sense, it is accurate to say that capital and labor devise profit-sharing institutions "to promote cooperation and make it more resilient."[44] Profit-sharing institutions enable capital and labor to settle wage negotiations without recourse to the destructive use of force. However, in a broader sense, it is important to keep in mind that cooperation, in and of itself, is not the ultimate goal of profit-sharing institutions. As Knight explains, "the primary motivation for social institutions cannot be achievement of collective goals ... If we want to ground explanations in terms of the intentions and actions of rational actors, we must look to the distributional consequences of those institutions."[45] In this vein, employers agree to establish profit-sharing institutions merely because refusing to do so would leave them worse off. Capital prefers a labor market with weak unions and a lack of profit-sharing institutions; employers only agree to create profit-sharing institutions when an increase in workers' bargaining power makes this

---

[43] North 1990, 47.
[44] Koremenos et al. 2001, 766.
[45] Knight 1992, 39.

preferred scenario untenable.[46] In this way, this book develops a theory that explains how the rise and fall of profit-sharing institutions are endogenously driven by bargaining dynamics between capital and labor.

Profit-sharing institutions systematically reduce uncertainty and alleviate commitment problems that plague wage bargaining between capital and labor. I define profit-sharing institutions as a set of rules that govern wage negotiations and create a credible link between an increase in profits and an increase in workers' wages. This book identifies three specific labor market rules that combine to produce profit-sharing institutions: formal union recognition, explicit agreement that wages will rise along with profits, and industry-wide wage scales.

Formal union recognition reduces workers' uncertainty about the balance of bargaining power because it represents capital's public acknowledgment that workers have sufficient power to launch costly strikes. Explicit agreement that wages will rise along with profits reduces workers' uncertainty about profitability levels because such agreements require employers to share private information. Industry-wide wage scales alleviate enforcement problems because they take wages out of competition and reduce competitive pressure from non-union firms. When profit-sharing institutions are in place, workers expect that an increase in profits will lead to an increase in wages.[47] Therefore, I predict that when profit-sharing institutions are present, workers are more likely to share the same international trade policy preference as their employers.

Union Recognition

Formal union recognition reduces uncertainty concerning the balance of bargaining power between capital and labor. As discussed above, capital enjoys a natural bargaining advantage over their workers. If unorganized workers demand a share of increasing profits, capital can easily refuse their request. In order to capture a share of increased profits, workers must first increase their bargaining power. But how much is enough? How

---

46 For a similar argument concerning capital's support for the welfare state, see Korpi 2006.

47 There is a long-standing debate concerning whether or not institutions have a causal effect that is independent of bargaining power (e.g. Keohane 1984; Mearsheimer 1994). This book argues that profit-sharing institutions have a causal effect on workers' trade policy preferences that cannot be reduced to the underlying balance of bargaining power between capital and labor. Profit-sharing institutions do not simply help scholars identify powerful labor unions; profit-sharing institutions also help workers identify themselves as sufficiently powerful to capture a share of increased profits in the form of wages.

can workers know when they have built up sufficient bargaining power to reliably capture a share of their industry's profits? Since it is difficult for workers to assess accurately their employers' power and resolve to resist union demands, subjective evaluations of the balance of bargaining power are fraught with uncertainty. In contrast, formal union recognition provides workers with external confirmation that their employers believe that labor has the ability to inflict costly strikes upon their employers. For this reason, formal union recognition reduces uncertainty regarding the balance of bargaining power between capital and labor.

However, even after workers win formal union recognition from their employers, labor will remain uncertain about their ability to capture a share of increased profits. The leaders of a formally recognized union may have the opportunity to sit down and collectively bargain with their employers, but uncertainty remains concerning whether or not the industry is enjoying increased profits that could be captured by workers.

Agreement that Wages will Rise with Profits

Explicit agreement that wages will rise along with profits reduces uncertainty regarding asymmetric information. As part of this agreement, employers must reveal private information regarding the industry's profitability. For instance, profit-sharing institutions provide an opportunity for workers to "examine the books" and determine whether or not their employers can afford to pay higher wages. When an employer holds this information privately, capital and labor can find themselves in a tragic situation; the only way for an employer to credibly prove that it is unable to afford to pay higher wages is to wait out a costly strike without increasing wages.[48] As demonstrated in Chapter 4, there are various ways in which employers can share pertinent information regarding profitability with their workers. In the iron and steel industry, employers agreed to index workers' wages to the price of iron; in the textile industry employers agreed to index wages to the margin between the price of cloth and the price of raw cotton.

Workers explicitly recognized that having access to such information helped avoid industrial conflict. As the steel union's newspaper explained,

There is less hope in fighting Mr. Carnegie than there is in conferring with him. If the workmen know they have facts and figures on their side that will win them this lockout, they should be able to persuade the company of this. If they think

---

[48] Hall and Lazear 1984; Keohane 1984; Fearon 1995.

they have, and have not, the company's representative should be able to convince them.[49]

The pacifying effect of such transparency was also noted by contemporary observers; as the U.S. Industrial Commission reported in 1901, "the familiarity with the conditions of production which comes to the representatives of the workingmen through the inspection of the accounts of manufacturers ... tends especially to promote intelligent negotiations as to the general wage scale."[50]

However, even after a union has been formally recognized by employers who explicitly agree that wages will rise with profits, workers often remain uncertain about their ability to capture a share of increased profits. Seen in a favorable light, employers may wish to increase wages along with profits, but may find themselves unable to do so if non-union employers in their industry do not agree to do the same. Seen in a more critical light, employers may agree to increase wages along with profits, but workers may find themselves unable to enforce such agreements if they renege.

Industry-Wide Unionization

Industry-wide wage scales reduce uncertainty about the enforcement of profit-sharing agreements. Such industry-wide contracts permit local employers to increase wages without facing downward wage pressure from non-union competitors. When workers establish industry-wide wage scales, they effectively "take wages out of competition." That is, they protect wages from downward "nibbling" from lower cost or more desperate firms in the same industry.[51] Of course, the difficulty of accomplishing this task varies significantly from industry to industry. Consider, for example, how the geographical concentration of an industry influences the prospects for industry-wide organization.[52] During the late nineteenth century, textile unions were faced with the task of organizing textile mills spread throughout New England, while iron and steel workers had the comparatively easy task of organizing steel mills that were predominately located in western Pennsylvania.[53]

Even when wage contracts are not enforced by the state, employers are deterred from breaking formal agreements by the near guarantee

---

[49] *National Labor Tribune*, May 5, 1888.
[50] United States 1901, 345.
[51] Bennett and Kaufman 2011, 61.
[52] Ulman 1966, 43; Belman and Voos 1993.
[53] Taussig 1915, 117–138, 261–278.

of a strike. When employers seek to alter the terms of profit-sharing institutions, they rationally wait until the end of the agreement to renegotiate terms.[54] For example, consider Weeks' description of profit-sharing institutions in the American iron and steel industry during the late nineteenth century: "they have in every instance been faithfully kept, the terms have been strictly adhered to, and, if any change in the terms of the agreement has been desired, the agreement has always been abrogated in the way named in its terms."[55] Although labor power is not sufficient to establish a clear connection between profits and wages, it certainly plays a role in contract enforcement; as Perlman explains, "the agreement is made by direct negotiation between the two organized groups and the sanction which each holds over the head of the other is the strike or lockout."[56] Repeated negotiations between employers and union leaders also increase the prospects for enforcement by permitting both parties to establish reputations that stabilize expectations.[57] Since union representatives and their employers continuously interact with each other, their relationship resembles one of iterated games in which each actor can punish the other side for reneging.[58]

In these ways, formal union recognition, agreement that wages will increase along with profits, and industry-wide wage scales are jointly sufficient for the creation of profit-sharing institutions. As discussed in Chapters 4 and 5, American labor unions and their employers established such profit-sharing institutions in the late nineteenth and early twentieth centuries, and then joined together in support of the same international trade policies. However, not all profit-sharing institutions are created through this endogenous process. As discussed in Chapters 5 and 6, profit-sharing institutions can also be exogenously created by direct state intervention into industrial relations. Such intervention was on clear display in the United States during World War II and in Argentina during Juan Perón's first presidency. In both cases, the state's pro-labor intervention during collective bargaining helped form a credible link between profits and wages and therefore established profit-sharing institutions in industries covered by such arrangements. Although the origin of profit-sharing institutions varied across these cases, the effect of such institutions on workers' trade policy preferences was exactly the

---

[54] For a related argument concerning the enforcement of non-binding agreements between workers and their employers, see McCallum 2013, 42–45.

[55] Weeks 1881, 18–19.

[56] Perlman 1922, 145.

[57] Keohane 1984.

[58] Axelrod 2006.

same; once profit-sharing institutions were created, workers joined their employers in support of the same trade policy.

CONCLUSION

In summary, my theory predicts that profit-sharing institutions make workers more likely to agree with their employers concerning international trade policy. When profit-sharing institutions are absent, my theory predicts that workers will disagree with their employers concerning trade policy. Such capital-labor disagreement cannot be explained by the conventional wisdom in international political economy, which is based on the distributional predictions of the neoclassical trade models. These models are based on the unrealistic assumption of full employment and incorrectly predict that wages automatically increase along with profits. In contrast, my theory of profit-sharing institutions places bargaining power and labor market institutions at the center of international political economy. With attention to these political factors, my theory helps explain the capital-labor conflict that has shaped the political economy of trade for the past two centuries, as well as the politics of contemporary globalization.

3

Evidence and Research Design

Chapter 2 developed my theory of how profit-sharing institutions influence workers' international trade policy preferences. The remainder of this book now seeks to test my theory using a multi-method approach and a variety of different types of empirical evidence. The goal is to combine qualitative and quantitative methods in a way that provides a more rigorous and compelling set of tests than would be possible using only one of these methodological approaches.[1] The qualitative case studies help explore the causal mechanisms that link the various pieces of my theory together. The rich historical evidence uncovered by my archival research helps explain the process through which workers augment their bargaining power, develop profit-sharing institutions, capture a share of increased profits in the form of wages, and come to share the same trade policy preferences as their employers. Overall, these cases demonstrate exactly *how* profit-sharing institutions alleviate the uncertainty-surrounding wage bargaining, and align the trade policy preferences of capital and labor. The large-N quantitative analyses, on the other hand, avoid the selection and omitted variable biases that may unintentionally influence the conclusions drawn from studying a small number of qualitative cases. Most importantly, the cross-national statistical analysis demonstrates that the underlying insight at the heart of this book – that the link between trade policy and workers' wages depends on wage bargaining between capital and labor – is a generalizable phenomenon that influences the political economy of trade far beyond the historical cases examined in this book.

The remainder of this chapter describes the details of this book's research design. It addresses four main issues: operationalizing the

[1] I thank Jeff Colgan for his helpful suggestions and advice concerning this chapter.

dependent variable, the unit of analysis, qualitative case selection, and testing causal mechanisms.

OPERATIONALIZING THE DEPENDENT VARIABLE

The main dependent variable in this book is capital-labor agreement concerning international trade policy. More technically, I seek to explain the conditions under which workers will share the same international trade policy preferences as their employers. In exploring this question, this book adopts the traditional international political economy approach which holds that "an actor's preferences rank the outcomes possible in a given environment."[2] International trade policy preferences, then, refer to an actor's rank of possible international trade policy outcomes. For example, do workers prefer protectionist or more liberal trade policies? In theory, trade policy preferences could vary on a continuous spectrum from pure protectionism, at one extreme, to pure free trade, on the other. Empirically, this book adopts a simplified framework in which trade policy preferences are coded as either pro-protection or pro-free trade. Since the book is ultimately interested in whether or not workers join their employers in support of the same trade policy, the dependent variable is operationalized as a dichotomous variable that takes the value of either "agreement" or "disagreement." If workers and their employers are both protectionists (or free traders) then I consider there to be capital-labor agreement. If workers and their employers have different trade policy preferences, then I consider there to be capital-labor disagreement. This dichotomous operationalization of the dependent variable is utilized to study trade policy preferences in Chapters 4, 5, and 6.

The empirical study of trade policy preferences poses a number of difficult methodological challenges. As Frieden explains, "preferences are not directly observable ... a particular public trade bargaining position is conceivably consonant with a wide range of preference."[3] Consider, for example, that we observe workers marching through the streets demanding an increase in tariffs. Is it safe to assume that these workers have protectionist trade policy preferences? What if we later discover that these workers have been paid by their employers to attend the march, and that the individual workers actually supported free trade? Surely, we must admit that the workers' underlying trade policy preference (pro-free trade) was not translated directly into their political behavior (pro-protection). In short, we would draw an incorrect inference if we concluded that the marching workers held a trade policy preference in

[2] Frieden 1999, 41.
[3] Frieden 1999, 45.

support of high tariffs. They did not. They were simply paid to say that they did.

Previous scholars have dealt with this methodological problem in various ways, each with their own advantages and disadvantages. Early research on the political economy of trade relied on evidence largely from the secondary literature.[4] Research along these lines identified broad political cleavages that often appeared consistent with the predictions of the H-O or R-V models. In this vein, Rogowski suggests that American workers and employers both supported the protectionist Republican party during the late nineteenth century, and therefore must have shared the same underlying trade policy preferences. On the positive side, Rogowski's methodological approach permitted him to cover a wide range of cases – from ancient Greece to the Vietnam war – and to provide sweeping evidence that international trade has played an important role in domestic politics for millennia. On the negative side, his study makes the tenuous assumption that voters' partisan affiliations were driven predominately by their underlying trade policy preferences. By focusing on broad political cleavages, Rogowski's work left a large inferential gap between trade policy preferences and political behavior.

Subsequent research by Magee and Hiscox moved the focus away from political cleavages and looked more closely at trade-related testimony before the House Ways and Means Committee.[5] In terms of closing the inferential gap between trade policy preferences and political behavior, their focus on statements regarding international trade policy certainly marked a step in the right direction. However, their focus on congressional tariff hearings introduced a strong selection effect that biased their results away from finding capital-labor disagreement. Unfortunately, such congressional hearings are likely to attract only the best organized and most powerful labor unions – precisely the unions we would expect to join their employers in support of the same trade policy. Not only is this approach unable to observe the trade policy preferences of unions that never testify, but it is equally unable to observe the trade policy preferences of testifying unions in years when the Ways and Means Committee did not hear testimony.

More recent research has addressed these methodological problems by analyzing the results of individual-level surveys.[6] These survey-based

[4] For two prominent examples of this early research, see Gourevitch 1986; Rogowski 1989.

[5] Hiscox 2002; Magee 1994.

[6] O'Rourke et al. 2001; Scheve and Slaughter 2001; Baker 2005; Mayda and Rodrik 2005; Hainmueller and Hiscox 2006; Mansfield and Mutz 2009; Ehrlich and Maestas 2010; Ehrlich 2010; Margalit 2012.

studies avoid selection bias by drawing on random samples of a population and close the inferential gap between trade policy preferences and
political behavior by asking people to anonymously share their private
opinion concerning trade policy. While there are laudable advantages to
this approach, there are three reasons why this book ultimately pursues a
different methodological approach.

First, many respondents admit that they have not thought much about
international trade issues, and thus call into question how much we
can learn from their responses.[7] Second, understanding individual trade
policy preferences is unlikely to help us understand actual trade policy
outcomes. Recent research suggests that international trade policy is
unlikely to determine an individual's voting behavior, and is therefore
unlikely to influence the policy decisions of elected officials.[8] In contrast,
Chapter 5 demonstrates that the trade policy preferences of organized
groups, such as labor unions, can have an important impact on
politicians' policy decisions. Last, for all of the potential methodological
benefits of survey-based research, it is clearly not possible to implement
new surveys to study the historical cases examined in this book.

Archival Research and Trade Policy Preferences

The approach taken in this book avoids many of the methodological
limitations of previous studies by using primary documents to trace
the trade policy preferences of labor unions over a series of decades.
This approach required extensive archival research and the analysis
of primary documents left behind by workers. Where possible, my
analysis draws on the meeting minutes and other publications of labor
unions, such as rulebooks, and union newspapers. To supplement these
sources, the analysis also draws on local newspapers that covered labor
politics, as well as trades journals, government reports, the records
of congressional hearings, and historical monographs. This in-depth
and across-time archival research has several important methodological
benefits.

First, it gets the history right. As discussed throughout this book, extant
political economy studies have often relied on cursory readings of the
secondary literature and come to mistaken conclusions about workers'
trade policy preferences throughout the past two centuries. The archival

---

[7] For an excellent example of research that overcomes these limitations by focusing
  on the informed opinions of members of the International Longshoremen and
  Warehouse Union, see Ahlquist et al. 2014.
[8] Guisinger 2009. According to Margalit (2012), individual trade policy preferences
  might be dominated by apprehensions about social and cultural openness.

evidence that forms the heart of this book necessitated identifying, locating, and carefully reviewing hundreds of primary documents. The American case draws on nineteenth-century newspapers, such as the *Fall River Daily Herald*, *Fall River Daily Globe*, *National Labor Tribune*, *The New York Times*, and the *Pittsburgh Dispatch*. Studying American labor unions also required analyzing the annual meeting minutes of the Amalgamated Association of Iron and Steel Workers, the American Federation of Labor, and the Congress of Industrial Organizations, as well as numerous government reports. The British case draws upon hundreds of articles from *The Northern Star*, the Chartists' early nineteenth-century newspaper.[9] The Argentine case required archival field work in Buenos Aires, where I studied documents in the *Banco Central de la República Argentina* and the national headquarters of Argentina's main labor federation, the *Confederación General del Trabajo*. Taken together, these primary documents reveal what is perhaps the most surprising and important insight of this book: the conventional wisdom in international political economy is based on a deeply flawed understanding of history.

Second, the use of multiple sources of primary documents allows me to triangulate workers' trade policy preferences and thus close the inferential gap between policy preferences and political behavior. For example, consider two different worker demonstrations that are further analyzed in the case studies below. One demonstration occurred in Pittsburgh, Pennsylvania in the immediate aftermath of the Homestead steel strike of 1892. Steelworkers marched through the city streets, declaring their opposition to the high tariffs that protected the steel industry. While this event, on its own, is insufficient to conclude that the steelworkers actually doubted the benefits of trade protection, we can corroborate this inference with evidence from the steel union's newspaper and meeting minutes. As discussed in Chapter 4, the steelworkers' *National Labor Tribune* was full of editorials, articles, and letters from union members proclaiming their opposition to high tariffs. By combining these various sources of evidence, we can more confidently conclude that the steelworkers' union did not support high tariffs in 1892.

Another demonstration occurred in Buenos Aires, Argentina during a 1933 debate about tariff protection for Argentine industry. Tens of thousands of industrial workers attended a downtown rally that demanded the Argentine government increase trade protection. While this event may suggest that Argentina's industrial workers supported high tariffs, a deeper analysis of the archival record suggests otherwise. The newspaper

[9] I thank Rana Abdelhamid, Roy Wang, and Michael Bernstein for their assistance with this research.

of Argentina's main labor federation declared the rally a farce, and claimed that workers were coerced into attendance by their employers. Moreover, the periodical of the manufacturers' association that planned the rally contains candid discussion of the group's propaganda campaign to convince workers to support high tariffs. By combining these various sources of evidence, we can more confidently conclude that Argentina's industrial workers did not support high tariffs in 1933.

Third, using multiple sources of information to trace the evolution of labor unions' trade policy preferences over time avoids the selection bias that plagues studies based solely on testimony before congressional hearings. Drawing on archival evidence, I am able to demonstrate that the labor unions that did not testify before Congress often disagreed with their employers concerning international trade policy. Fourth, focusing the analysis on the trade policy preferences of labor unions has the added benefit of helping us understand political behavior that has an important impact on trade policy outcomes. While the trade policy preferences of individuals are unlikely to lead to important political behavior, the trade policy preferences of labor unions result in organized lobbying that is more likely to influence actual trade policy. As demonstrated in Chapter 5, the trade policy preferences and lobbying of the CIO had a significant impact on U.S. Senate voting concerning American trade liberalization after World War II.

LABOR UNIONS AND METHODOLOGICAL BIAS

Although archival research and qualitative case studies have many advantages, this methodological approach also contains certain potential biases. Most importantly, my qualitative case studies use organized groups of workers, such as labor unions, as the main unit of analysis. Since labor unions only organize a fraction of the workforce, unions' trade policy preferences may not necessarily represent the preferences of unorganized workers. Unfortunately, there is no systematic record of unorganized workers' policy preferences, and it is therefore difficult to study the possible gap between the unions and unorganized workers. Moreover, some may even argue that the trade policy preferences of labor unions are dominated by labor union leaders. That is, labor union trade policy preferences may not even represent the preferences of rank-and-file union members. For these reasons, further research is needed to study the effect of profit-sharing institutions on individual workers, union and non-union, alike.

Despite these methodological concerns, the case studies presented below shed important light on the consequences of profit-sharing institutions. Most importantly, the trade policy preferences of labor unions matter for trade policy outcomes regardless of whether or not they faithfully represent rank and file members or unorganized workers. As demonstrated in Chapter 5, after the CIO formally endorsed free trade senators with powerful CIO constituencies were more likely to support free trade. Similarly, when the AFL endorsed trade protectionism senators with powerful AFL constituencies were less likely to support free trade. To the extent that we care about trade policy preferences in order to understand trade policy outcomes, the formal trade policy preferences of labor unions are clearly crucial.

Additionally, there are two reasons to believe that the trade policy preferences of labor unions do broadly represent the unions' rank-and-file members. First, each case study focuses on a period of major trade policy reform, during which trade policy was one of the most frequently debated policy issues. Workers therefore often had strong opinions on the matter, and it would have been difficult for union leaders to maintain power while expressing trade policy positions opposed by the majority of their union members.

Second, unions seeking formal recognition often sought to convince management that their organizations were conservative in nature. For example, union leaders frequently sought to calm their rank-and-file members in order to avoid strikes that would jeopardize the union's working relationship with their employers. Robert Howard, the leader of the American textile union "took extraordinary efforts to placate manufacturers in order to convince them that trade unionism was a positive good which alleviated industrial strife."[10] In such cases, it is likely that any divergence between rank-and-file workers and their union leaders concerning trade policy would have entailed the leaders agreeing with management, despite rank-and-file disagreement about the benefits of the given trade policy reform. In other words, studying the trade policy preferences of labor unions may actually make it harder to uncover the type of capital-labor disagreement explored throughout this book.

QUALITATIVE CASE SELECTION

The time-consuming research and detailed knowledge necessary to conduct historical case studies means that only a small number of cases can be examined in any one book. This book therefore carefully selected five different qualitative case studies to examine in varying depths. Chapter 4 focuses on the American textile and steel industries, respectively, during

[10] Silvia 1973, 514.

the late nineteenth century. Chapter 5 explores the politics of American trade liberalization during the 1930s and 1940s. Chapter 6 examines the repeal of the British Corn Laws in the 1840s, as well as the development of import-substitution industrialization in Argentina in the 1930s and 1940s. The remainder of this section explains the careful methodological rationale behind the selection of these cases.

Late Nineteenth-Century America

A large part of the qualitative evidence presented in this book focuses on the United States during the late nineteenth century. This American case study represents a "crucial case" in the technical sense that "a theory that passes empirical testing is strongly supported and one that fails is strongly impugned."[11] Correctly explaining the American case provides strong support for my theory because canonical works in the field explicitly disagree with my predictions. My theory makes the difficult claim that the field's conventional wisdom is based on a mistaken understanding of American history. Moreover, failing to explain the American case strongly impugns the main theoretical alternatives – the R-V and H-O models – for two reasons. First, the United States was at the height of its industrialization process during this period, and thus had the high inter-industry factor mobility that should make this an easy case for the H-O model. Second, the American case provides an example in which both the H-O and R-V models make the same predictions concerning capital-labor trade policy agreements. Both models predict that capital and labor would join together in support of trade protection. By showing that American workers who lacked profit-sharing institutions actually disagreed with their employers concerning trade policy, I am able to succinctly demonstrate the shortcomings of both traditional trade models.[12]

The American Textile and Steel Industries

Labor unions in the textile and steel industries were politically important, broadly representative of the mainstream American labor movement, and allow for a structured, focused comparison of most similar cases with different outcomes. This approach allows me to demonstrate that labor unions that were as similar as possible had different trade

---

[11] George and Bennett 2005, 9.
[12] The H-O and R-V models are often thought of as mutually exclusive alternatives – when one model is inapplicable, the other is assumed to be correct. For the clearest example of this manichean thinking, see Hiscox 2002.

policy preferences because of differences in the independent variable: profit-sharing institutions. Chapter 4 therefore focuses on labor unions representing workers in America's textile and steel industries in the 1880s and 1890s. These unions were politically important because they organized workers in the two "quintessential" sectors of industrialization; in 1880, the textile and steel industries were America's two largest industries, employing 12 percent of all men, women, and children working in American manufacturing.[13] These unions were broadly representative of the mainstream American labor movement in the sense that they were both founding members of the American Federation of Labor, a relatively conservative group of unions that eschewed radical critiques of capitalism and wage labor.

These unions represent most similar cases in the sense that both shared the same attributes identified by alternative explanations that focus on skill-level,[14] the global competitiveness of an industry,[15] regional location,[16] and economic ideology.[17] Both unions represented 1) highly skilled craft workers, 2) employed by import-competing industries, 3) located in the industrial, protectionist North, and were, 4) associated with the conservative, "pure and simple" craft unionism of the AFL. Despite these similarities, these two unions represent different outcomes; both unions held opposing trade policy preferences from each other throughout the late nineteenth century. While extant theories predict that both unions would consistently join their employers in support of protection, my theory parsimoniously explains the observed variation in workers' trade policy preferences. The textile workers disagreed with their employers and did not support high tariffs during the 1880s, yet joined their employers in favor of high tariffs in the 1890s. The steel workers followed the opposite trajectory. Workers joined their employers in favor of high tariffs during the 1880s, but broke with their employers and did not support high tariffs in the 1890s. These two cases therefore provide the opportunity to test my theory with cross-case, as well as within-case comparisons. Together, these case studies demonstrate that profit-sharing institutions led American workers to join their employers in support of *trade protection* during the late nineteenth century.

---

[13] United States 1895, 73–84.

[14] Rogowski 1987; Midford 1993; Hiscox 2001; Scheve and Slaughter 2001; Mansfield and Mutz 2009

[15] Frieden 1988.

[16] Bensel 2000; Sanders 1999.

[17] Hattam 1993; Mansfield and Mutz 2009; Ehrlich 2010; Ahlquist et al. 2014.

American Trade Liberalization Following World War II

However, it is important to clarify that profit-sharing institutions can also produce capital-labor coalitions in favor of *free trade*. Unfortunately, it is impossible to demonstrate this during the late nineteenth century because of the lack of export-oriented American industries favoring trade liberalization; America's "infant" industries supported high tariffs well into the twentieth century. In order to demonstrate the symmetry of my argument – profit-sharing institutions lead workers to join their employers in favor of whichever trade policy benefits their industry – Chapter 5 skips thirty years of American history and examines trade politics in the 1930s and 1940s. By this period several American industries were export-competitive, thus enabling us to examine how profit-sharing institutions affect capital-labor agreement concerning free trade. Although this case study necessarily allows the time period to vary relative to Chapter 4, the continued focus on American trade politics holds constant many other important factors.

The case of American trade politics in the 1930s and 1940s has three additional methodological advantages. First, it provides an additional test of my theory's causal logic. Chapter 4 demonstrates that organizational innovation and technological change influence workers' bargaining power and the development of profit-sharing institutions. Chapter 5 further demonstrates that national labor legislation can also influence bargaining power and profit-sharing institutions. In this way, it demonstrates an alternative causal pathway through which profit-sharing institutions can be created. Second, it provides qualitative, process-tracing evidence that complements the quantitative analysis presented in Chapter 7. Whereas Chapter 7 establishes a statistical correlation between respect for labor rights (e.g. the right to unionize) and profit-sharing, Chapter 5 demonstrates the causal mechanism through which the right to unionize (granted by the Wagner Act) leads to increased profit-sharing.

Third, American trade politics in the 1930s and 1940s provides a hard, and therefore ideal, case in which to test the effect of workers' trade policy preferences on actual trade policy outcomes. American trade liberalization after World War II is one of the most studied cases of trade policy reform in the political science literature, with explanations ranging from the H-O and R-V models, to the power of ideas, and influence of policymaking institutions.[18] Despite such scholarly attention,

---

[18] For arguments based on the H-O model, see Rogowski 1989; for arguments based on the R-V model, see Irwin and Kroszner 1999; Hiscox 1999; for an argument based on the power of ideas, see Goldstein 1993; for arguments based on policymaking institutions, see Bailey et al. 1997.

extant studies fail to acknowledge the important role that the newly pro-trade CIO played in securing bipartisan support for American trade liberalization. Studies that do explore the influence of interest groups on trade policy make the neoclassical assumption that industrial workers automatically joined their employers in favor of free trade. Moreover, by focusing on one of the most lauded trade policy reforms in the political science literature (American trade liberalization harbored the creation of the postwar multilateral trading system), Chapter 5 highlights the potentially "liberal" effect of pro-labor legislation that regulates labor markets and strengthens workers' bargaining power. In this way, it was increased regulation in the American labor market that provided the domestic political coalition necessary to decrease regulation in the global trading system.

Britain and Argentina

In order to test the generalizability of my theory beyond the America case, Chapter 6 presents additional historical case studies of trade politics in Britain and Argentina. Correctly explaining these two cases provides additional strong support for my theory because the field's conventional wisdom explicitly disagrees with my predictions. Whereas Hiscox and Rogowski both claim that workers in these cases joined their employers in support of the same trade policies (free trade in Britain; trade protection in Argentina), this book clearly demonstrates that workers strongly disagreed with their employers in both cases.[19] Combined with the American cases, these case studies present a "most different, similar outcome approach" to further demonstrate the relationship between profit-sharing institutions and workers' trade policy preferences. Together, these case studies cover over one hundred years, protectionist and liberalizing trade policy reforms, three different continents, economies with four different types of factor endowments, and various political regimes. Despite the multitude of differences between these case studies, the relationship between profit-sharing institutions and workers' trade policy preferences holds in each case. At the very least, these cases suggest that the inferences drawn from the American case were not based on a spurious correlation due to variables specific to the United States.

TESTING CAUSAL MECHANISMS

The qualitative case studies and statistical analyses presented throughout this book offer unique opportunities to test the causal mechanisms of

[19] Rogowski 1989; Hiscox 2002.

my theory. Taken together, the empirical chapters of this book test three different causal mechanisms. First, the link between profit-sharing institutions and workers' trade policy preferences. Second, the link between workers' bargaining power and the rise and fall of profit-sharing institutions. Third, the link between international trade policy and workers' wages. The remainder of this section discusses each of these causal mechanisms in turn.

Profit-Sharing Institutions and Workers' Trade Policy Preferences

The bulk of the qualitative analyses explores the causal mechanism that links profit-sharing institutions to capital-labor agreement concerning international trade policy. Throughout this book the case studies pay careful attention to the reasons why changes in profit-sharing institutions were followed by subsequent changes in workers' trade policy preferences. I demonstrate that when profit-sharing institutions were absent, workers pointed to labor market competition when explaining their trade policy disagreement with their employers. Moreover, when profit-sharing institutions were present, I demonstrate that workers explicitly argued that their trade policy preferences were conditional on profit-sharing institutions. The qualitative case studies follow a structured-focused approach, asking a set of standardized, general questions of each case.[20]

In general, the case studies start by examining the labor market conditions that workers faced at the beginning of the time period under consideration. If profit-sharing institutions were present, I describe the process through which they were developed. If profit sharing institutions were absent, I describe the factors that precluded their creation. The case studies then examine workers' trade policy preferences and note whether or not workers agreed with their employers and joined them in support of the same international trade policy. After evaluating whether or not workers held the trade policy preferences predicted by my theory, the case studies then examine subsequent changes in labor market conditions.[21] If profit-sharing institutions were discarded, I demonstrate the process through which this occurred. If profit-sharing institutions were created, I again describe the process through which they were established. The case studies then analyze whether or not this change in profit-sharing institutions was followed by the trade policy preference change predicted by my theory.

---

[20] George and Bennett 2005, 69.
[21] These subsequent changes in labor market conditions are examined in all qualitative case studies, with the exception of Britain's repeal of the Corn Laws.

This careful process tracing should also assuage any doubts concerning reverse causality. Chapters 4 through 6 repeatedly demonstrate that changes in profit-sharing institutions occur temporally prior to workers' trade policy preferences. In other words, profit-sharing institutions are not created in response to capital-labor agreement over trade policy. According to this reverse causal argument, an exogenous shock would lead to a change in workers' trade policy presences and a sudden alignment of preferences with capital. Following this preference alignment, capital would then agree to establish profit-sharing institutions in order to credibly commit to workers that wages would increase along with profits in the future. It is unclear why capital would seek to reassure workers in this way, considering that the sudden alignment of capital-labor trade policy preferences suggests that workers do not require any such reassurance.

Workers' Bargaining Power and Profit-Sharing Institutions

This book also examines the causal mechanisms that link workers' bargaining power to the rise and fall of profit-sharing institutions. The endogenous relationship between workers' bargaining power and profit-sharing institutions is explored throughout the qualitative case studies, with closest attention being paid in Chapter 4. That chapter carefully traces how changes in workers' bargaining power – increased by labor unions' organizational innovation or decreased by technological change – led to the rise and fall of profit-sharing institutions in the U.S. during the late nineteenth century. Chapters 5 and 6 further explore this relationship in the U.S. and Argentina during the 1940s, but also draw on exogenous factors such as pro-labor state intervention and tripartite bargaining.

Chapter 5 explains how the Wagner Act granted American workers the right to unionize, thus helping to increase their bargaining power during the late 1930s. Unions then fought for formal recognition and increased wages. However, profit-sharing institutions were not established until the National War Labor Board instituted tripartite bargaining that helped ensure workers a share of their industry's profits. Chapter 6 describes how profit-sharing institutions were established in Argentina in the 1940s, following the pro-labor reforms of Juan Perón. Labor unions were formally recognized, and the government created tripartite wage negotiations that helped workers establish industry-wide wage scales and a credible link between profits and wages.

These case studies also demonstrate that profit-sharing institutions have a causal effect that is independent from workers' bargaining power.

In order to do so, it takes advantage of three scenarios in which profit-sharing institutions and workers' bargaining power diverge. First, labor power does not automatically and instantly translate into the creation of profit-sharing institutions. Most importantly, the creation of profit-sharing institutions can be delayed by capital's ideological opposition to formally negotiating with a labor union. For example, American textile manufacturers' accepted many costly strikes before agreeing to negotiate with their workers because of their belief that such arbitration was "contrary to the mode of transacting business in this country."[22] This delay in union recognition allows us to compare the trade policy preferences of a powerful labor union before and after the creation of profit-sharing institutions. As demonstrated in Chapter 4, the textile workers were a powerful labor union for many years before their employers agreed to establish profit-sharing institutions. However, these powerful workers did not join their employers until these institutions had been created.

Second, profit-sharing institutions are not immediately discarded if workers' bargaining power decreases. As discussed above, technological change, migration, and the use of violence can all diminish labor's power over time. Since constantly renegotiating labor market rules is prohibitively costly, a gap can arise between the actual bargaining power of a labor union and the labor market institutions still in place.[23] The larger this gap grows, the more incentive there is for the stronger party to demand a favorable revision of the status quo. Although profit-sharing institutions and labor power are therefore highly correlated over time, there are periods during which profit-sharing institutions survive beyond the labor power needed to sustain them over the long term.[24] This delay in the destruction of profit-sharing institutions allows me to compare the trade policy preferences of a powerful labor union with profit-sharing institutions to a weak labor union with profit-sharing institutions.

This dynamic was on clear display in the American iron and steel industry in the late nineteenth century. The union established profit-sharing institutions as early as 1865, and regularly joined their employers in support of high steel tariffs throughout the subsequent decades. In 1886, the Carnegie Steel Company made major technological improvements to its mills that undercut the skills and bargaining power of the union

---

[22] Silvia 1973, 107.

[23] Keohane 1984.

[24] The relationship between the balance of bargaining power and profit-sharing institutions is therefore analogous to the difference between Gilpin's hierarchy of power and hierarchy of prestige. See, Gilpin 1983.

workers.[25] However, it was not until six years later that the company forced a revision of the status quo, by refusing to recognize the union, thus precipitating the Homestead strike of 1892. During the intervening years in which profit-sharing institutions remained formally in place, the union supported high tariffs despite their actual decrease in bargaining power. However, the union stopped supporting high tariffs and began to disagree with their employers concerning trade policy as soon as profit-sharing institutions were discarded.

Third, profit-sharing institutions can be exogenously created by the state in scenarios where workers do not have the bargaining power necessary to establish them on their own. This scenario is explored in Chapter 6, through a discussion of Argentina during the 1940s. Although Argentine labor unions lacked the independent bargaining power necessary for their employers to agree to profit-sharing institutions, the state directly intervened into collective bargaining and established a credible link between profits and wages. Following such state intervention, and despite a relatively weak labor movement, Argentine unions joined their employers in support of high tariffs.

International Trade Policy and Workers' Wages

This book also examines the causal mechanism that links international trade policy to workers' wages. According to the neoclassical trade models, favorable trade policy reform increases the marginal revenue product of labor, which automatically increases workers' wages. In contrast, this book argues that this connection between the marginal revenue product of labor and workers' wages – the causal mechanism that links trade policy to wages – depends on conditions in the domestic labor market. Specifically, it argues that workers without bargaining power are unlikely to capture a share of the benefits from trade policy reforms. Chapter 7 tests this causal mechanism by examining the relationship between the marginal revenue product of labor and workers' wages – what I call the "profit-sharing rate" – across 28 manufacturing industries, in 117 countries, from 1986 to 2002. The analysis demonstrates that when labor rights are not protected, the profit-sharing rate is statistically indistinguishable from zero. Moreover, as the protection of labor rights increases, so too does the ability of workers to capture a share of increased profits in the form of wages.

Taken together, the various empirical analyses work together to demonstrate the importance of profit-sharing institutions for the political

---

[25] Brody 1960.

economy of trade. The qualitative case studies demonstrate a correlation between profit-sharing institutions and labor-capital agreement, as well as evidence in support of my hypothesized causal mechanisms. When workers lack profit-sharing institutions, they point to competition in the labor market when explaining their trade policy disagreement with their employers. Moreover, when workers establish profit-sharing institutions, they explicitly refer to them when explaining their trade policy agreement with their employers.

The cross-national quantitative analysis then demonstrates that such worker concerns are based on a rational understanding of how trade policy is filtered through domestic labor markets. When workers lack bargaining power they correctly doubt their ability to capture a share of increased profits. These results should help convince readers that trade policy disagreement between labor and capital is not driven by idiosyncratic factors related to the historical case studies presented below. Rather, the argument made by American, British, and Argentine workers over the course of the last two centuries – that the link between trade policy and workers' wages depends on the presence of profit-sharing institutions – is still relevant for understanding the distributional consequences of contemporary trade policy reforms. Finally, the quantitative analysis of US Senate voting on the RTAA should assure readers that studying the trade policy preferences of workers and labor unions is vital to understand actual trade policy outcomes.

CONCLUSION

With this methodological discussion complete, we are now ready to test my theory of profit-sharing institutions. The chapters that follow combine historical case studies based on original archival research with large-N statistical analysis. This multi-method approach – combining both qualitative and quantitative approaches – makes possible a more rigorous test of my theory than would be possible by employing only one method or the other.

4

The Gilded Wage
Trade Politics in the American Textile and Steel Industries

This chapter presents a structured-focused comparison of two labor unions in the American textile and steel industries during the late nineteenth century. Overall, the analysis demonstrates that both unions joined their employers in favor of the same trade policy when profit-sharing institutions were present, but openly disagreed with their employers when profit-sharing institutions were absent. In examining the effect of profit-sharing institutions on workers' trade policy preferences, this chapter also demonstrates how changes in workers' bargaining power influenced the creation and destruction of profit-sharing institutions.

The first case study focuses on the textile industry in and around Fall River, Massachusetts, a city that dominated the American textile industry during the late nineteenth century. In 1883, Fall River's textile mills produced an astounding 60 percent of all print cloth produced in the United States, earning the city the nickname of the "Spindle City."[1] The analysis focuses on the highest skilled textile workers, the mule spinners, whose job it was to use mule spinning frames to turn raw cotton into yarn. These workers organized and formed the Mule Spinners' Association, a labor union that struggled for survival in the 1880s, but then grew and established profit-sharing institutions with their employers in the 1890s. Consistent with my theory, the textile workers disagreed with their employers and did not support high tariffs during the 1880s, but then joined their employers in favor of high tariffs in the 1890s.

The second case study focuses on the iron and steel industries in and around Pittsburgh, Pennsylvania, a city that dominated the American steel industry during the late nineteenth century and beyond. In the 1890s,

[1] Silvia 1973, 243.

the factories surrounding Pittsburgh accounted for roughly 40 percent of all iron and steel produced in the United States, earning the city the nickname of the "Steel City."[2] The analysis focuses on the highest skilled steelworkers, the puddlers, and boilers, whose job it was to stir molten iron. These workers organized the Amalgamated Association of Iron and Steel Workers, a labor union that maintained profit-sharing institutions throughout the 1880s, but then struggled for survival and lost their profit-sharing institutions in the 1890s. Consistent with my theory, the steel workers joined their employers in favor of high tariffs during the 1880s, but broke with their employers and did not support high tariffs in the 1890s.

These two labor unions represent most similar cases in the sense that both unions share the same attributes identified by alternative explanations that focus on skill-level,[3] the global competitiveness of an industry,[4] regional location,[5] and economic ideology.[6] Both unions represented 1) highly skilled craft workers, 2) employed by import-competing industries, 3) located in the industrial, protectionist North, and were, 4) associated with the conservative, "pure and simple" craft unionism of the AFL. These labor unions also shared the experience of organizing workers in America's two largest industries; in 1880, roughly 12 percent of all men, women, and children employed in American manufacturing were employed in either the cotton textile or iron and steel industries.[7] These "quintessential" industries were at the economic and political core of American industrialization.[8]

The only other three sectors that rivaled cotton textiles and iron and steel, in terms of employment, were those that produced lumber products, men's clothing, and machine tools. Since the lumber and clothing workers were not unionized during this period, it is not possible to systematically study their trade policy preferences. The machinists, who were organized by the International Association of Machinists starting in 1888, did not develop profit-sharing institutions during our period of study, and did not support high tariffs.[9] Their lack of support for high tariffs can be gleaned from their official periodical, *The Monthly Journal of the International Association of Machinists*. For instance, in 1893 it was reported that, "the

---

[2] Taussig 1915, 120.
[3] Rogowski 1987; Midford 1993; Hiscox 2001; Scheve and Slaughter 2001; Mansfield and Mutz 2009.
[4] Frieden 1988.
[5] Sanders 1999; Bensel 2000.
[6] Hattam 1993; Mansfield and Mutz 2009; Ehrlich 2010; Ahlquist et al. 2014.
[7] United States 1895, 73–84.
[8] Bensel 2000, 462; Silver 2003, 39.
[9] United States 1901, 217–222.

protective system protected one class, but there was nothing to protect the workingman. There was no duty to stop the immigrant who came to take his place in the workshop and factory at lower wages."[10] In 1894, the journal's editors concluded an internal union debate on the tariff by declaring that "the tariff is, in our opinion, a big bugaboo, and is like throwing sand in the people's eyes by the great political parties."[11]

Studying the trade policy preferences of the textile and steel workers' unions during this period also offers a unique methodological opportunity. These two labor unions changed their trade policy preferences in different directions during the early 1890s – the textile workers came to agree with their employers, while the steel workers came to disagree with their employers – permitting us to control for time-related shocks that may affect policy preferences, such as economic depressions or waves of immigration.[12] Moreover, the within-case variation allows for a longitudinal, process-tracing analysis that focuses on the sequencing of changes in trade policy preferences and allows each union to control for itself over time. Even when the trade policy preferences of these unions are consistent with the predictions of alternative theories, careful process tracing allows us to determine which of these explanations is most useful in explaining not only the final outcome but also how that outcome came about.[13] The opposite trajectories of workers in the American textile and steel industries are displayed below in Table 4.1.

The following case studies are both organized in the following way. First, each examines the labor market conditions that workers faced in the 1880s. Specific attention is paid to the absence of profit-sharing institutions in the textile industry and the creation of profit-sharing institutions in the steel industry. Second, each case study then analyzes workers' trade policy preferences and notes whether or not they are consistent with my theory's predictions. Third, each case study describes the major changes in labor market conditions faced by textile and steel workers during the 1890s. Specific attention is paid to the creation of profit-sharing institutions in the textile industry and the destruction of profit-sharing institutions in the steel industry. Fourth, each case study analyzes workers' trade policy preferences again to test whether or not they are consistent with my theory's predictions. After both industries

---

[10] International Association of Machinists 1893.
[11] International Association of Machinists 1894.
[12] As demonstrated at the end of this chapter, variation in these labor unions' trade policy preferences cannot be explained by the small differences in immigration patterns between Pennsylvania and Massachusetts.
[13] Slater 2009, 229.

Table 4.1. *Trade Policy Preferences of American Steel and Textile Unions*

Industry	Union	Years	Profit Sharing Institutions		Capital-Labor Agreement
Iron and Steel	Amalgamated Association of Iron and Steel Workers	1880–1891	Yes	→	Yes
		1892–1897	No	→	No
Textiles	Mule Spinners' Association	1879–1893	No	→	No
		1894–1897	Yes	→	Yes

have been analyzed, this chapter presents a cross-case analysis of workers' trade policy preferences in both the textile and steel industries. It then concludes with a discussion of immigration and the effect of workers' trade policy preferences on the presidential election of 1892.

THE POLITICAL ECONOMY OF AMERICAN TRADE POLICY

The tariff was one of the defining partisan issues in American politics throughout the 1880 and 1890s. Congress debated and revised the tariff schedule on four separate occasions, and trade policy played an important role in all national elections.[14] The Republican Party endorsed high tariffs and argued that trade protection shielded workers from the "pauper" labor of foreign countries. The Democratic Party endorsed downward revision of the tariff and argued that trade protection unfairly increased workers' cost of living. The Populists, in turn, sought to attract workers away from both parties by arguing that their focus on the tariff avoided more important political economy questions concerning monopolies, the railroads, and monetary policy.[15] Scholars have offered numerous explanations for labor's policy preferences during this period, but none have examined the profit-sharing institutions that provided the foundation for capital-labor agreement concerning trade policy. As will be seen below, even the most protectionist workers ceased to support high tariffs when profit-sharing institutions were destroyed.

Scholars of international political economy have frequently studied American trade politics in the late nineteenth century. According to both Rogowski and Hiscox, trade politics in this case were characterized by the

[14] Bensel 2000, 8.
[15] Sanders 1999, 139.

predictions of the H-O model.[16] Since the United States had an abundant supply of land, but a scarce supply of both capital and labor, both scholars predict that capital and labor supported trade protection. As Rogowski explains, "The details of the US experience are too familiar to require extensive discussion ... workers joined owners in support of a triumphant, highly protectionist, and increasingly imperialistic Republican party."[17] According to Hiscox, the American Federation of Labor was "internally unified on the trade issue" and endorsed high tariffs as well as the protectionist presidential campaign of William McKinley in 1896.[18] An alternative approach, based on the industry cleavages associated with the R-V model, also predicts worker support for high tariffs. According to Verdier, American workers joined their employers along industry lines and unanimously supported high tariffs; American workers were not well organized into labor unions, but "when they did organize, along trade lines, they took no independent position on the tariff, but assumed the position held by their respective industries."[19]

American trade politics during this period have also been studied by scholars of American Political Development (APD). According to Bensel, the tariff provided the political backbone that held the Republican Party together; industrial workers joined their employers in favor of the high tariffs that protected American industry, and thus helped to ensure Republican hegemony throughout the period. Bensel's otherwise magisterial account of American industrialization is based on the problematic assumption that workers automatically join their employers in favor of trade policies that benefit their industry. In contrast, Sanders argues that the benefits of high tariffs were often withheld from workers in protected industries.[20] She rightfully points out that tariff-protected trusts frequently broke labor unions, and that large waves of immigration likely competed away any potential wage gains. However, Sanders then uses this insight to motivate a puzzle regarding workers' false consciousness and continued political alliance with their employers. She does not explore cases in which workers disagreed with their employers concerning trade

[16] According to Hiscox, the H-O model is most accurate when inter-industry factor mobility is high. Importantly, trade politics during this period cannot be explained by revising the factor endowment of the United States. If capital were scarce and labor abundant, or vice versa, the H-O model would predict disagreement between capital and labor concerning trade policy. In this way, it cannot explain why some workers would join their employers in support of high not tariffs, but others world not.

[17] Rogowski 1989, 44.

[18] Hiscox 2002, 10.

[19] Verdier 1994, 108.

[20] Sanders 1999, 77.

policy, nor does she explore the profit-sharing institutions that led to the capital-labor agreement that occasionally existed. Even the in-depth historical research of APD scholars has overlooked the important role of profit-sharing institutions.

In contrast to both the IPE and APD literatures, the case studies presented in this chapter directly contradict this common portrayal of American trade politics. Studying the trade policy preferences of the textile and steel unions required extensive archival work and the analysis of primary documents left behind by workers. Where possible, both case studies draw on the meeting minutes and other publications of the two unions, such as rulebooks, and union newspapers. The Amalgamated Association of Iron and Steel Workers left behind annual meeting minutes, as well as their weekly newspaper, the *National Labor Tribune*. Since few records from the Mule Spinners' Association have survived, the analysis also draws on nineteenth-century newspapers that covered local labor politics, such as the *Fall River Daily Globe* and *Fall River Daily Herald*, as well as trade journals, government reports, the records of congressional hearings, and historical monographs. Since these labor unions tended to focus on the pressing issues of wages, strikes, and local labor market conditions, they often went long periods of time without discussing trade policy. The case studies presented below therefore required the analysis of thousands of pages of primary documents from the late nineteenth century.

TRADE POLITICS IN THE AMERICAN TEXTILE INDUSTRY

This section presents a case study of the American textile industry in and around Fall River, Massachusetts. First, it begins with an analysis of the absence of profit-sharing institutions during the 1880s. Second, it demonstrates how the absence of profit-sharing institutions led the Mule Spinners' Association to disagree with their employers regarding the benefits of high tariffs. Third, it describes the process through which organizational innovations allowed the textile workers to increase their bargaining power and establish profit-sharing institutions. Finally, it demonstrates how the presence of profit-sharing institutions led the union to change its trade policy preferences and to agree with their employers concerning trade policy.

Institutional Absence: Textile Workers, 1873–1884

This section analyzes the absence of profit-sharing institutions in the textile industry from the depression of 1873 through the Fall River strike of 1884. Moreover, it demonstrates the underlying logic of this institutional absence. Labor unions in the industry were short-lived and poorly funded, while employers coordinated anti-union actions through the Fall River Manufacturers' Board of Trade. Migrant workers flocking to Fall River put downward pressure on wages, and provided employers with ready strikebreakers. In short, the inability of workers to credibly threaten to strike and inflict costs on their employers resulted in the absence of union recognition and a lack of profit-sharing institutions.

Workers in the textile mills of New England were not well organized in the years after the Civil War. Despite frequent efforts to unionize, the depression of the 1870s led to wage cuts, job shortages, and pressure for workers to accept any employment they could find. Coupled with the anti-union philosophy of many textile manufacturers bent on "destroying labor solidarity," textile unions struggled to survive.[21] According to Norman Ware, from 1873 to 1876 all unions in cotton and woolen mills in New England were dissolved. For instance, the National Mule Spinners' Association was first founded in 1858, but disbanded and reorganized no less than three times before 1889.[22]

During this period, the textile industry was characterized by intense conflict between capital and labor. In 1879, the mule spinners lost a disastrous strike in the textile hub of Fall River, Massachusetts during which mill owners evicted the family members of strikers living in company tenements and provided strikebreakers with pistols. When the strikers sought to negotiate an "honorable end" to the strike, the mill owners insisted on an unconditional surrender and made no concessions. According to manufacturers, the union's efforts to influence wages represented illegal interference with the individual right of contract between employer and employee. As one representative mill owner proclaimed, "the despotism of the trades union is not surpassed by that of the Czar of Russia."[23]

During the strike of 1879, Robert Howard and the mule spinners made clear their aspiration for union recognition, collective bargaining, and a fair share of their employers' profits. As Howard proclaimed, "the interest of employer and employed is identical; and what we more eagerly desire at the present time is to get nearer to them."[24] However, Howard also made it clear that without formal recognition and wage negotiations, the mule spinners could not trust that increased profits would lead to increased wages. When the manufacturers refused to even acknowledge

---

[21] Silvia 1973, 255.
[22] United States 1901, 73.
[23] *Fall River Daily Herald*, May 7, 1879.
[24] *Fall River Daily Herald*, May 1, 1879.

the union's request for a meeting, Howard cautioned that the "refusal to do or say anything will do much to confirm the belief that workpeople are only looked upon in the light of serfs, to be used for money making at the lowest rate of wages by corporations."[25] In this way, the lack of recognition suggested to the textile workers that their employers had no intention of sharing profits with them.

Most importantly, the strike of 1879 demonstrates that employer promises to share profits with their workers are not credible without union recognition and collective bargaining. In fact, the strike of 1879 was fought precisely over what workers saw as broken promises to increase wages along with increased profits. The past decade had witnessed repeated wage cuts in response to the depression of the 1870s, with spinners' wages having been reduced 45 percent in the past five years.[26] In 1878, the Fall River mills cut wages by 15 percent, but promised that wages would be restored as soon as the depression ended and both cloth prices and mill profits rebounded. As one mill agent justified the wage cuts, "we are all sailing in one boat and if we go down you go down; we have to share alike."[27]

According to the union, the manufacturers promised that "with the first return of prosperity our wages would be advanced."[28] In 1879, the cloth market improved and the union sought their promised wage increase. As Howard explained,

We feel that we have weathered the storm, and there is fair weather and good sailing; and all that we request is to be allowed to remain in the same boat still and share with them in the apparent prosperity. We have shared with them in their adversity and we think our claims are just in asking to share with them in prosperity.[29]

Howard went on to claim that the union was confident that the present condition of trade enabled their employers to make the wage concession asked for. Furthermore, he explained that he was "willing to meet them in conference, and if they can prove, conclusively, that the present state of the markets are not such as to guarantee an advance, then we will willingly withdraw our application."[30]

However, the manufacturers did not even take the time to officially reject the mule spinners' request for a wage conference; the union received no response whatsoever. If the conditions in the cloth market did not

25 *Fall River Daily Herald*, May 6, 1879.
26 *Fall River Daily Herald*, May 8, 1879.
27 *Fall River Daily Herald*, May 8, 1879.
28 *Fall River Daily Herald*, May 8, 1879.
29 *Fall River Daily Herald*, May 8, 1879.
30 *Fall River Daily Herald*, May 8, 1879.

allow for a wage increase, the manufacturers' Board of Trade did not consider it necessary to "open the books" for the union. The need to strike for a wage increase in 1879, despite the return of prosperity, clearly demonstrated to the mule spinners that wages would not automatically increase with profits. Although the strike could have potentially ended with a wage increase, the inherent uncertainty of such a strategy meant that the union would not view policies that directly increased profits as an effective means of increasing wages.

In the early 1880s, manufacturers continued to refuse to collectively bargain with the Fall River Mule Spinners' Association and the union's leaders. According to Phillip Silvia, confrontation between capital and labor loomed during these years, "most especially over management's intransigent refusal to recognize officially Howard as representative, or to meet with spinner employees at individual mills."[31] Mill owners cooperated through a citywide board of trade to blacklist union organizers and destroy the union. In 1881, the union's Treasurer was fired and blacklisted, and the strike to have him reinstated was unsuccessful. Three years later, the union lost another strike against wage reductions, during which strikebreakers were armed with pistols, a union member was charged with murder, and a mill was burned to the ground by suspected arsonists.[32] According to Mary Blewett's careful study of this period, "the mule spinners' union struggled to survive in the early 1880s."[33]

While the union struggled for recognition and higher wages, the mill owners enjoyed increasing productivity and profitability. Despite tariff protection of approximately 40 percent on cotton textiles throughout the period, mule spinners' wages fell repeatedly from 1874 to 1879. According to the mill spinners' union Secretary, Fall River wages were cut by 10 percent in 1881 while the mills paid dividends that averaged 20 percent. Even the Granite Mills, which declared a 40 percent dividend that year, cut its workers' wages by the same 10 percent.[34] The disconnect between profits and wages was on glaring display before the 1884 strike when one Fall River corporation "announced the [10 percent] wage cut in the morning and the 5 percent quarterly dividend in the afternoon."[35] According to the editor of the local *Labor Standard*, workers were unable to wrench wage increases from their powerful employers because "when

---

[31] Silvia 1973, 255.
[32] For an account of the strike of 1884, see Blewett 2000, 304.
[33] Blewett 2000, 305.
[34] United States 1885, 656.
[35] Blewett 2000, 300.

trade is dull they cannot afford to pay, and when trade is good they can afford *not* to pay."[36]

Capital-Labor Disagreement: Textile Workers, 1873–1884

Given the lack of profit-sharing institutions in the textile industry during this period, my theory predicts that the textile union would disagree with their employers concerning trade policy. This prediction is in direct contrast to traditional international political economy theories, which predict that the textile workers would have agreed with their employers and held a policy preference in favor of high tariffs. Consistent with my theory, the union's lack of support for high tariffs can be clearly seen below in the testimony given by Robert Howard, the union's Secretary, before the U.S. Senate in 1883.

In the following testimony, Howard explained how competition in the labor market and a lack of profit-sharing institutions left workers unprotected by trade protection.

Q. Then, while this protective law is claimed to be and is passed in order that it may be a benefit to the operatives in our manufactories, I want to know how much benefit they do actually get from the increased prices which the protective tariff gives to the product. What share do the operatives receive when the product is sold and the proceeds are divided between them and capital?

A. The benefit? Looking at the wages here compared with the wages in England I cannot see any benefit.

Q. That is, the manufacturer takes the whole of the benefit; is that it?

A. Yes. They will go over to Canada and bring over hordes of French people here to work in our mills at 50 or 75 cents a day.[37]

Howard went on to claim that "nine-tenths of the intelligent operatives" understood that they did not receive the benefits of high textile tariffs. They believed that the tariff provided protection for capital, but that anti-immigration regulations were needed to protect workers; "if they think the tariff is going to benefit us any, and if they wish it to benefit us, let them do that [restrict immigration], and then the people might be generally more willing to concede the benefit of the tariff to the manufacturing corporations."[38] According to the union, the ability of

---

36 Blewett 2009, 325.
37 United States 1885, 655.
38 United States 1885, 656.

manufacturers to hire unemployed workers at low wages obviated any benefit labor received from tariff protection in the textile industry.

Howard and the union did not support high tariffs throughout the rest of the 1880s. In 1886 Howard explained that, "The friends of tariff reform [lowering tariffs] mean not to reduce, but to protect, the wages of workingmen."[39] Decreasing tariffs would lower consumer prices, and since the textile workers did not receive a share of tariff-generate profits, such trade policy reforms would increase workers' real wages. That same year, Howard clearly explained the union's doubts about the connection between high tariffs and wages: "the people do not have faith in the argument of the rich, that wages and prices are regulated by the law of supply and demand, but they are beginning to believe that prices are fixed by rings and monopolies, and that wages are regulated by the force and power of organized bodies of workers."[40] Howard went on to explain that it was not until employers respected "the right to meet organized capital with organized labor" that workers would have any chance of sharing in the profits of "a country which is walled in by tariff laws."[41]

Despite the incremental advances that the mule spinners' union made after 1886, profit-sharing institutions were not credibly in place until the mid-1890s. During the intervening years, the union continued to disagree with their employers concerning trade policy. In 1888, Robert Howard, still Secretary of the Fall River Mule Spinners' Association, campaigned for Massachusetts State Senate. In the days before the 1888 election, Howard gave a speech in which he endorsed the Democratic platform of tariff reform, as well as Democratic President candidate Grover Cleveland, and proclaimed that "the democratic party was the party to which labor must look for favors."[42] Two years later, in 1890, Howard explained that "in relation to the tariff, it is nothing more or less than a tax. The taxation by tariff is what is making all the millionaires. You do not have to go away from home to find examples of the evil effects of the McKinley tariff bill."[43]

Howard's opposition to high tariffs continued into the early 1890s. In November 1891, he rejected a journalist's assertion that operatives in Fall River who "earn their daily bread by labor in the different cotton mills were leaning toward Republicanism on account of the benefits

---

[39] *Fall River Daily Herald*, November 1, 1886.
[40] *Fibre and Fabric*, October 2, 1886, 243.
[41] *Fibre and Fabric*, October 2, 1886, 244.
[42] *Fall River Daily Herald*, November 1, 1888. For an account of Howard's support for Democratic candidates and tariff reform, see Silvia 1973, 739–740.
[43] *Fall River Daily Herald*, November 1, 1890.

that they were to derive from the passage of the McKinley bill."[44] As Howard explained, if the theory that workers supported high tariffs "is still believed by any politician in the United States, let him come to me. Why, we were never so solidly Democratic here in this Republican stronghold before."[45] The following year, Howard campaigned against the "superprotection" of the McKinley bill, which embodied an "unjust form of taxation" that "settles on the backs of the working people and stays there."[46]

Obviously, caution is needed in interpreting Howard's campaign speeches, which may not have faithfully represented the views of the Fall River mule spinners. Unfortunately, it is nearly impossible to study the tariff preferences of the union's rank and file, as the meeting minutes have not survived. For this reason, all extant historical research on the union has relied heavily on the newspaper accounts of its activities. Luckily, the *Fall River Daily Globe* and the *Fall River Daily Herald* each closely covered the mule spinners' monthly meetings and reported on significant decisions or debates that occurred. This newspaper coverage reveals that the union did not take action on the tariff issue during the McKinley tariff debates of 1889 and 1890.[47] Such silence, combined with Howard's public opposition to tariffs, suggests that there was little support for high tariffs amongst the spinners' rank-and-file members. Although Howard was a domineering figure within the union, it seems unlikely that members would have shied away from discussing the tariff simply because of his views; the union meetings throughout the period are full of rank-and-file disagreements with Howard and other union leaders regarding strike strategy.[48]

The union's silence on the tariff issue in the late 1880s and early 1890s must also be viewed in the light of the union's rule that "no political or religious issues are allowed to be introduced into the meetings."[49] However, what constituted a political issue was necessarily vague, as the union frequently discussed and endorsed important pieces of labor legislation, such as bills that would prohibit the fining of weavers for imperfect work, decrease the hours of work, require the weekly

---

44 *New York Times*, November 29, 1891.

45 *New York Times*, November 29, 1891.

46 *Fall River Weekly News*, November 2, 1892, quoted in Silvia 1973, 762.

47 For coverage of the mule spinners' meeting in the *Fall River Daily Globe*, see December 7, 1889; January 9, 1890; February 13, 1890; March 13, 1890; April 10, 1890; May 7, 1890; June 12, 1890; July 10, 1890; August 6, 1890; September 11, 1890, October 9, 1890; November 13, 1890; and December 11, 1890.

48 For examples of Howard and the rank and file openly disagreeing about union strike policy, see Blewett 2000, 329, 329 and Silvia 1973, 486.

49 Bureau of Labor of the State of New Hampshire 1894, 44.

payment of wages, or prohibit child labor. The National Mule Spinners' Association also debated clearly political issues during its 1890 annual meeting when it endorsed the labor measures advocated by the United Labor Alliance, a federation of labor organizations that pledged to "secure the defeat of all candidates for legislative positions who will not unqualifiedly promise to vote in the interests of labor."[50] The United Labor Alliance also advocated the free coinage of silver, which, along with the tariff, was one of the most heated political questions of the late nineteenth century.[51]

While Howard and the mule spinners denied that the tariff benefited workers, manufacturers from Fall River and other textile centers lobbied for higher tariffs. Throughout this period, the cotton textile manufacturers of Massachusetts coordinated their lobbying through an organization called the Arkwright Club.[52] In 1883, the Arkwright Club sent a petition to the U.S. Senate "praying that Congress will not reduce duties upon imported articles from foreign countries below the rates recommended by the Tariff Commission."[53] Admitting that the U.S. Treasury had accumulated an embarrassingly large surplus after years of high tariffs, the Arkwright Club proposed that the government do away with internal taxes on manufacturers, rather than decrease import duties![54] Five years later, the Arkwright Club argued that "A law to help the domestic trade is 15 times as useful as a law to foster foreign trade; and any law that promotes foreign trade at the expense of the home markets is the height of unwisdom."[55] In short, in the absence of profit-sharing institutions that credibly linked an increase in profits to an increase in wages, the textile workers disagreed with their employers concerning the benefits of high tariffs.

"A New and Brighter Era": Profit-Sharing in the Textile Industry

This section demonstrates how the mule spinners' union increased their bargaining power vis-à-vis their employers through innovations that increased the union's membership, strike fund, and geographical scope. These developments increased the union's associational power, and more than compensated for the technological change that threatened the mule spinners' marketplace and workplace power. The mule spinners' increased bargaining power enabled them to inflict costly strikes on their

[50] *The Daily Critic*, October 22, 1890.
[51] *Evening Capital Journal*, February 3, 1891.
[52] Blewett 2000.
[53] *Senate Journal*, 1883, 250.
[54] National Association of Wool Manufacturers 1883, 270–290.
[55] *The Tariff Review*, 1888, 122.

employers. The threat of such strikes led textile employers to slowly agree to three labor market institutions sufficient to establish profit-sharing institutions – formal union recognition, agreement that wages will rise with profits, and an industry-wide wage scale. In 1886, Fall River employers formally recognized the mule spinners' union and created a sliding wage scale that linked workers' wages to the profitability of the textile industry. In 1889, the mule spinners created a national labor union, which slowly gained recognition from firms throughout New England, and established an industry-wide wage scale in 1894. With profit-sharing institutions thus established, the mule spinners changed their trade policy preferences and joined their employers in favor of high tariffs.

The story of how the mule spinners came to be formally recognized by their employers begins with the failure of the strike of 1884. Although the mule spinners' union lost the struggle, returning to work without obtaining a restoration of their previous wages, the eighteen-week strike displayed the power of the union and their growing strike fund.[56] This fund, which permitted the union to pay workers while they were on strike, was slowly built up by a constitutional requirement that each member pays weekly dues of twenty-five cents.[57] This policy, combined with conservative rules that required a special general meeting to endorse a strike before benefits could be paid, allowed the mule spinners to amass significant savings. By 1889, the union had already deposited the maximum amount of money permitted by the union's by-laws in local Fall River banks and was contemplating investing their savings in real estate.[58] In 1891, Howard claimed that the mule spinners were the wealthiest union in the U.S. based on per capita savings.[59]

In addition to the bargaining power generated by a large strike fund and a credible threat to strike, the mule spinners worked in a critical node of textile production. Since the mule spinners produced the yarn needed to weave cloth, a mule spinner strike that curtailed the production of yarn could cripple cloth production.[60] In addition, the mule spinners carefully restricted competition in the labor market by limiting apprenticeships for the training of new mule spinners. This practice of "clannishly opposing the entrance of recruits into the trade" led manufacturers to accuse the mule spinners of being "a turbulent and unruly set [and]

---

[56] Silvia 1973, 274–308; Blewett 2000, 299–306.
[57] Fall River Mule Spinners' Association 1894.
[58] *Fall River Daily Herald*, September 12, 1889; *Fall River Daily Globe*, September 12, 1889.
[59] Silvia 1973, 475.
[60] Taussig 1915, 271.

of having a trade-union monopoly."[61] The skilled mule spinners also represented a small minority of the total textile workforce, which meant that wage concessions could theoretically be limited to a small group of favored union workers without significantly increasing the overall cost of production.[62]

The conservative leadership of the mule spinners, the large strike fund, the critical position of the skilled mule spinners in the production of cloth, and the small proportion of the workforce that they represented, all contributed to the formal recognition of the union. After years of blacklisting union members and ignoring their appeals for conciliation and collective bargaining, members of the Fall River Board of Trade finally agreed to hold a formal wage conference with Howard and two other union members on November 22, 1886. This formal recognition of Robert Howard as the bargaining agent for the union was a crucial break with the past period of capital and labor conflict. According to Philip Silvia, that day in late November was "the banner day in the history of Fall River textile unionism."[63]

Along with formal union recognition, Fall River manufacturers agreed to establish a sliding wage scale that linked their workers' wages to the profitability of the textile industry. Mule spinners' wages would rise and fall based on a formula that measured the margin between the price of raw cotton and the selling price of print cloth.[64] When the sliding wage scale was first adopted in 1886, manufacturers agreed to increase wages by 6.5 percent when cloth could be sold at $3\frac{5}{8}$ cents per yard, and by an additional 7 percent when the price of cloth increased to $3\frac{3}{4}$ cents.[65] According to David Montgomery, the sliding wage scale "marked a triumph of the version of 'political economy' for which the mule spinners had fought since 1858, by tying their fluctuating piece rates formally to the employers' profit margins, rather than to the prevailing wage."[66] As Silvia explained, "For the first time in the history of the textile industry in the United States, capital and a segment of the labor force of Fall River would attempt to avoid unnecessary friction by a rational recourse to statistics."[67]

---

[61] Taussig 1915, 272.

[62] For an argument that the wages of all textile workers in Fall River were highly inter-related, rising and falling in relative unison, see Segal 1956.

[63] Silvia 1973, 456. The wage conference was agreed to on November 22, 1886, and was held on November 24, 1886. For an account of the private conference, see *Fall River Daily Herald*, November 26, 1886.

[64] Blewett 2000, 310.

[65] Silvia 1973, 456. Also, see *Fall River Daily Herald*, March 9, 1887.

[66] Montgomery 1989, 163.

[67] Silvia 1973, 457.

While formal union recognition and the sliding wage scale marked important steps towards establishing a clear connection between profits and wages, the mule spinners still lacked an industry-wide wage scale. Without this, the Fall River mule spinners found it difficult to enforce their employers' original agreement to share profits. Although they had clearly established a powerful labor union, their lack of profit-sharing institutions left them uncertain about their ability to capture a share of their industry's profits. When explaining their decision not to increase their workers' wages, one Fall River manufacturer stated that competing mills in surrounding cities "have few powerful labor organizations to contend with and consequently are practically free to pay what they choose for work."[68] As the *Fall River Daily Herald* warned, "as competitors in a common market, the Fall River factories are at a considerable disadvantage."[69]

Despite local union bargaining power and formal recognition, the Fall River mule spinners found it difficult to raise wages above the level paid by non-union mills. If manufacturers in Lowell, Lawrence, and other New England textile centers did not increase wages along with increasing profits, then competitive pressures would provide incentive for Fall River manufacturers not to either. The disconnect between the manufacturers' focus on regional competition, and the Fall River spinners' focus on local prosperity can clearly be seen in the lament of one union member who claimed that "in the face of the large dividends the mills have been making lately, I feel that it is unnecessary to cut down wages at all."[70]

During the late 1880s and early 1890s, the Fall River mule spinners and their employers repeatedly struggled with the difficulty of enforcing a profit-sharing agreement that did not include an industry-wide wage scale. As Silvia explains, "the projected harmonious relationship began to disintegrate within a year because of technological changes."[71] These technological changes permitted the mills to diversify production away from the printed cloth that formed the basis of the spinners' wage agreement. Throughout 1887, the textile mills enjoyed increasing profits based on the production of various "odd" goods, while the price of printed cloth, and therefore spinners' wages, remained stagnant.[72] At the end of 1887, the union gave notice that it planned

---

[68] *Fall River Daily Globe*, October 10, 1889.
[69] *Fall River Daily Herald*, August 22, 1889.
[70] *Fall River Daily Globe*, October 10, 1889.
[71] Silvia 1973, 458.
[72] Blewett 2000, 311. In addition, the union accused their employers of providing false or "doctored" data.[73]

to "terminate the partnership" and demanded a 13.5 percent wage increase based on the state of the market and the profits of their employers.[74]

In early 1888, the manufacturers met with the union and agreed to a compromise 9.5 percent wage increase, that would, in the words of the *Fall River Daily Herald*, "avoid the objectionable features of past agitations of like character." In a sign of the mule spinners' growing influence and bargaining power, all other textile operatives were only granted a 4.5 percent wage increase.[75] Although the less skilled, and more numerous, weavers formed a union and demanded an equal wage increase "the manufacturers were more impressed by the number of weavers appearing at the mill gates throughout the city each morning seeking work than they were by this weaver union resolve."[76]

Even with this wage concession and clear favoritism relative to other textile operatives, the mule spinners were again disappointed with their wage agreement by the end of the year. Despite the high dividends paid by Fall River's Robeson Mill, the mill agents decided to cut spinners' wages over a technicality in the wage agreement. In addition, many spinners believed that the prosperity of the market warranted a wage increase, rather than a decrease. In November 1888, the union was once more on strike for higher wages.[77] As Silvia explains, "The men believed that the price list was unjust, and that they were not sharing in the year's soaring profits."[78] The union had been formally recognized and negotiated two separate wage agreement since 1886, but was still not convinced that their wages would rise along with the profits of their employers. Without an industry-wide wage scale, the Fall River manufacturers faced structural pressures not to increase their workers' wages above the level paid by non-union firms throughout the industry.

The mule spinners were not alone in their struggle to overcome the limitations of local union strength; all workers employed in national market industries faced similar economic forces. The common experience of nineteenth-century American unions was well described by

---

[74] Silvia 1973, 458.
[75] Blewett 2000, 311.
[76] Silvia 1973, 466.
[77] The technicality was related to the number of spindles contained in each mule spinning machine. It was discovered that spinners in the Robeson Mill were using machines with one less spindle than the number required for the wages they had been paid. As Silvia (1973: 462) explains, "this breakdown between labor and capital was caused by a reduction totaling less than seven dollars per week for eleven mule spinners!"
[78] Silvia 1973, 458.

Lloyd Ulman:

But if employers in strongly organized centers had to compete with nonunion employers elsewhere, how effectively could the strong union centers, with their flanks thus exposed, go about the business of pushing up wages and costs? Or, for that matter, how could unionized firms compete with nonunion establishments in their own localities?[79]

The task of the national union was therefore to adjust the conditions under which labor was sold throughout the industry in question so that an improvement in the situation of all local groups could be made. This required, amongst other things "a degree of organization throughout the jurisdiction high enough so that the competition of nonunion firms and workmen could not menace" union goals concerning higher wages, shorter hours, and better-working conditions.[80]

The lessons from these wage disputes were not lost on Howard and the Fall River mule spinners, who were well aware of the realities of regional competition. As Howard explained in 1883, he had gone to Lowell, Massachusetts "to start the men to ask for more wages, because we in Fall River could not do anything until Lowell made some advance."[81] As early as 1882, Howard had traveled to Rhode Island to lobby for a reduction in the weekly hours of work for textile operatives in an attempt to bring that state's labor legislation up to the standard established by the Massachusetts legislature in 1879. Once the Rhode Island law was passed in 1886, Howard went to New Hampshire to continue the struggle for regional coordination.[82] Discontented by the difficulty of raising wages, even after formal union recognition in 1886, the Fall River mule spinners responded by leading the effort to form the National Mule Spinners' Association in December 1889.[83] The union announced its intention to organize spinners throughout New England and New Jersey and that "an endeavor is to be made to obtain uniform wages throughout the United States."[84] The enforcement of such a uniform wage scale would decrease

---

79 Ulman 1966, 21.
80 Ulman 1966, 43. The limited ability of unions to translate local bargaining power into wage increases for workers in national product markets has also been demonstrated by contemporary labor economists. For example, see Belman and Voos 1993.
81 Garraty 1968, 25.
82 For Howard's lobbying efforts, see Fall River Mule Spinners' Association 1894; for an account of the ten-hour bill in Massachusetts, see Blewett 2000, 104.
83 *Fall River Daily Globe*, September 11, 1890.
84 *The Savannah Tribune*, December 21, 1889. For a history of the National Mule Spinners' Association, see United States 1901, 73–75; Bureau of Labor of the State of New Hampshire 1894, 42–44.

regional competition based on labor costs and facilitate the union's efforts to increase wages.[85]

During the early 1890s, the National Mule Spinners Association (NMSA) grew rapidly and systematically identified low-wage textile centers in which spinners strikes could equalize regional wage rates. Although the NMSA only had seven branches at its founding in 1889, by the end of 1890 the union had organized five additional branches. These twelve branches voted to focus their efforts on increasing the spinners' wage in Lowell, which the union determined to be the lowest paid in New England. As the union explained, "When the time for action comes the spinners of Lowell will be given an opportunity to make the first movement and begin the first strike, if a strike is necessary."[86] Two years later, the spinners of Pawtucket, Rhode Island asked for a 15 percent wage increase "in order to make prices for labor in that section and Fall River as uniform as possible."[87] This wage demand, and others throughout New England were "made in accordance with a plan outlined at the last meeting of the National Mule Spinners' organization."[88]

By February 1893, the union had equalized spinners' wages in the Massachusetts textile hubs of New Bedford, Lowell, and Fall River, and then ordered a strike by spinners to Lewiston, Maine to bring their wages up to the uniform wage scale.[89] In April 1893, the union was reported to have a membership of 3,000 spinners with an increase of 800 during the preceding six months. By 1894, the union had 40 locals and 4,000 members, having nearly doubled its membership in two years.[90] That same year, the Massachusetts Bureau of the Statistics of Labor reported that the union "has branches in all the large cotton manufacturing centres ... is steadily increasing in membership and has made great progress in its efforts to secure a uniform rate of wages."

The spread of an industry-wide wage scale eased the Fall River spinners' struggle to capture a share of their industry's profits. In 1892, the Massachusetts legislature passed a fifty-eight-hour bill, which decreased the weekly hours of work by two. Howard, in his role as State Senator, had such a significant influence over the passage of the bill that the governor of Massachusetts presented him with the gold-plated pen used to sign the bill into law.[91] To the astonishment of the local newspapers, the Cotton

[85] United States 1890.
[86] *Fall River Daily Globe*, May 7, 1890.
[87] *St. Paul Daily Globe*, May 7, 1892.
[88] *Burlington Weekly Free Press*, November 14, 1892.
[89] *Lewiston Evening Journal*, February 4, 1893.
[90] Brooks 1935, 22–23.
[91] Silvia 1973, 484.

Manufacturers' Association of Fall River decided to accept the new Massachusetts law without decreasing wages. Holding piecework wages constant, this shorter workweek was expected to increase productivity and thereby increase workers' weekly earnings by 3 percent. With the sliding wage scale's margin rapidly increasing in November 1892, the mule spinners then received an additional 7 percent wage increase for a total annual raise of 10 percent.[92]

Although some rank and file mule spinners advocated striking for even higher wages, Howard cautioned that such demands would only lead manufacturers to seek revenge during the next lull in the market. According to him, the union was finally being treated "on a plain of equality" by manufacturers, and a strike for an extra wage increase was not worth jeopardizing their new-found system of collective bargaining and profit-sharing. When the union decided to accept the wage increase without further demands, Howard announced that "a new and brighter era is beginning to dawn."[93]

The changes in the labor market that took place in the late 1880s and early 1890s completely changed the economic outlook of the mule spinners' union. Since the days of the blacklist and anti-union philosophy of Fall River manufacturers, the Fall River mule spinners' union had been formally recognized, created a sliding wage scale, and enforced a uniform rate of wages throughout the northeast. By the beginning of 1893, the Fall River mule spinners and their employers had finally created profit-sharing institutions. As Silvia explains the changes since 1884, "in the intervening years the Fall River mule spinners had come to enjoy the greatest power and influence of any cotton textile organization in nineteenth century United States history."[94]

Textile Workers' Support for High Tariffs

Following the establishment of profit-sharing institutions in the textile industry by 1893, I predict that the textile union would be more likely to agree with their employers over trade policy and hold a policy preference in favor of high tariffs. Of course, such pro-tariff policy preferences would represent a stark reversal of the union's previous position on the tariff, when they argued that tariffs increased profits without increasing wages.

As predicted, the establishment of profit-sharing institutions led the union to reverse its trade policy preferences and to support high tariffs

---

[92] Silvia 1973, 485–487.
[93] *Fall River Daily Globe*, November 29, 1892, quoted in Silvia 1973, 488.
[94] Brooks 1935, 513.

for the textile industry. In January 1894, the Fall River spinners held a meeting to discuss the Wilson tariff bill. According to one account of the meeting, "it was finally decided to send a delegation to Washington to ask for the retention of the McKinley tariff so far as it related to the cotton schedule."[95] The Fall River spinners were joined by the rest of the National Mule Spinners' Association; according to Blewett, "the national spinners' union lobbied successfully against any cuts in the tariff schedules on fine yarns made by the Democratic congress in the 1894 Wilson-Gorman tariff bill."[96] Even Howard, who had so forcefully denounced the tariff in previous years, admitted that he now "believed in protection to some extent."[97]

The mule spinners' support for high tariffs continued after 1894. When the tariff was revised again in 1897, Robert Howard joined two prominent Fall River manufacturers and testified at a Washington, D.C. hearing in favor of tariff protection. This testimony was incorporated into the Dingley tariff of 1897 and established a "superprotective" tariff rate that shielded fine yarn and thread from foreign competition. According to Silvia, "the new Fall River fine goods, thread, and yarn mills monopolized their field and were particularly well off during the late 1890s."[98] The high profits earned by these mills were shared with the mule spinners, whose union wage scale dictated higher wages for the production of finer quality yarn.[99]

This within-case analysis of the textile workers' union demonstrates that profit-sharing institutions shaped the union's trade policy preference. When employers refused to recognize the union or to formally negotiate wages during the 1880s, it did not support high tariffs. Testifying before the U.S. Senate, the union's leader argued that high tariffs did not lead to higher wages. When profit-sharing institutions were established in the 1890s, the union supported high tariffs. Testifying before the U.S. Congress in 1894 and 1897, the union reversed its previous trade policy preferences and argued that high tariffs would benefit textile workers. The next section now turns to a similar analysis of the American steel industry, where workers followed the exact opposite trajectory: workers joined their employers in favor of high tariffs during the 1880s, but broke with them and did not support high tariffs in the 1890s.

---

[95] Massachusetts Bureau of the Statistics of Labor 1894, 314.
[96] Blewett 2000, 313.
[97] *Fall River Daily Globe*, October 31, 1894.
[98] Silvia 1973, 583.
[99] Blewett 2000, 313.

TRADE POLITICS IN THE AMERICAN STEEL INDUSTRY

This section presents a case study of the American iron and steel industries in and around Pittsburgh, Pennsylvania. First, it begins with an analysis of the creation of profit-sharing institutions in the years after the Civil War. Second, it demonstrates how the presence of profit-sharing institutions led the Amalgamated Association of Iron and Steel Workers to agree with their employers and join them in support of high tariffs. Third, it describes the process through which technological change undercut the steelworkers' bargaining power and led to the destruction of the industry's profit-sharing institutions. Finally, it demonstrates how the loss of profit-sharing institutions led the union to change its trade policy preferences and to disagree with their employers concerning trade policy. This section is followed by a cross-case comparison of trade politics in the textile and steel industries during the late nineteenth century.

The Sons of Vulcan: Steel and the Civil War

Iron workers were completely unorganized until 1858, when a small group of highly skilled workers first formed a labor union in Pittsburgh. The union grew along with the iron industry's boom during the Civil War and was formally recognized by their employers in 1863. The iron workers' union established their first sliding wage scale in 1865, decades before the textile workers. In 1876, they formed a new national labor union that rapidly established an industry-wide wage scale. By 1880, the iron workers had established formal union recognition and an industry-wide sliding wage scale that linked their wages to the profitability of their industry. Once established, these profit-sharing institutions governed wage negotiations in the iron and steel industry until the devastating Homestead steel strike of 1892 marked the rapid decline of the union.

The gradual creation of profit-sharing institutions can be traced back to 1849, and the first "great strike" in Pittsburgh's iron mills. After a six-month long conflict, manufacturers succeeded in reducing their workers' wages by roughly 25 percent. According to Robinson, "the next decade was a period of frequent bickering between the men and the employers, due to mutual distrust and lack of cooperation."[100] Conflict between workers and their employers was particularly intense when wages were cut despite increases in the price of iron.[101] Such industrial conflicts continued into the crisis of 1857, a recession that drastically

---

[100] Robinson 1920, 11.
[101] Wright 1893, 404.

reduced output and wages in the iron industry throughout Pennsylvania. It was after these wage reductions that skilled puddlers and boilers in Pittsburgh first began to hold secret meetings to plan the formation of a union. On April 12, 1858, these workers formed the Iron City Forge of the Sons of Vulcan, a small group to which the modern day United Steelworkers can trace their origins.

Fearful of being blacklisted by their employers, this "secret circle" of iron workers did very little until the Civil War caused a revival of the iron trade.[102] The Sons of Vulcan then rapidly organized new local forges throughout eleven states and called for a national convention in September of 1862.[103] By 1863, the union had been formally recognized by their employers in Pittsburgh and representatives of capital and labor regularly met in conference to negotiate wages. As Commons explains, "puddlers enjoyed a bargaining advantage with their employers which seldom fell to the lot of other wage earners. The basis of this advantage was the high skill required of a puddler, and, second, the extreme localization of the industry which facilitated organization."[104]

With the benefit of associational and structural power, the Sons of Vulcan were able to demand wage increases when wartime demand increased the price of iron. With the price of iron increasing 230 percent from 1860 to 1864, the Sons of Vulcan were able to obtain nominal wage increases of 140 percent. With the general cost of living rising slower than the price of iron, this resulted in a 90 percent increase in real wages over the same period.[105] The frequent meetings needed to adjust wages along with fluctuations in the price of iron led both employers and employees to search for a new system of wage determination. As Joseph Weeks explained,

The fluctuations (of iron prices) requiring repeated conferences began to develop the propriety as well as the necessity of agreeing upon some general plan which would obviate frequent meetings and yet fix wages in accordance with the price of iron.[106]

An innovation came in 1865, when the Sons of Vulcan signed what was likely the first sliding wage scale in U.S. history. This contract indexed

---

[102] Robinson 1920, 11.
[103] Wright 1893, 402. The Sons of Vulcan founded forges in Eastern Pennsylvania, New Jersey, Delaware, Maryland, West Virginia, Ohio, Kentucky, Indiana, Illinois, Wisconsin, and Missouri.
[104] Commons et al. 1918, 80. Although the Sons of Vulcan organized workers in 11 different states, the union was still heavily concentrated in western Pennsylvania. In 1868, there were 76 total forges; 30 were in Pennsylvania, 17 in Ohio, and 29 in all other states combined, Robinson 1920, 13.
[105] Greenfield 1959, 87–88.
[106] Quoted in Greenfield 1959, 90.

wages to the selling price of iron, which workers presumably believed would continue to increase after the war. Accompanying the sliding scale was an agreement that either side could terminate the contract by giving ninety days' notice of their intention to quit the scale. As would soon become clear, the creation of cooperative labor market institutions required both learning and experimentation, as the original sliding wage scale did not result in sudden industrial peace and contentment.

Within less than six months the price of iron had plummeted, wages had fallen nearly 40 percent, and the union gave notice of its intention to withdraw from the sliding scale. As Greenfield explains, "for two years, after the demise of the first scale, the iron industry was beset with many industrial disputes and wage rates fluctuated with the bargaining strength of the contending parties."[107] During this period, the union's associational power was hampered by its uncoordinated strike behavior. The union customarily allowed strikes to be inaugurated solely by the men employed in the mill where a grievance arose, without any oversight or funding from the national union. This changed in 1867, when a new system of rules for legalizing and systematically supporting strikes was created.[108] Following a successful strike in May 1867 – which the union won despite close coordination amongst their employers – the Sons of Vulcan sent a formal letter to every iron firm in Pittsburgh inviting them to a wage conference to adopt a new sliding wage scale.[109]

Following this tumultuous period, the union and mill owners agreed to a new sliding scale, which now sought to address the workers' concerns about the potential for their wages to fall precipitously along with market fluctuations. This revised scale made important adjustments that limited the range of wage fluctuations and increased the degree to which workers shared in the industry's profits. Under this second sliding scale, wages fluctuated from a minimum of $6 to $8 per ton of iron produced, while under the first scale wages fluctuated from $4 to $9. Additionally, the ratio of wages to iron prices rose along with the price of iron in the second scale, whereas that ratio fell with the price of iron in the first scale.

The benefits established by this wage scale attracted additional members to the Sons of Vulcan, which by 1870, had unionized most puddlers in the city of Pittsburgh.[110] This second sliding scale was re-signed annually for seven consecutive years, until the panic of 1873

---

[107] Greenfield 1959, 92.
[108] Wright 1893, 403. According to Robinson, control over strikes was not centralized until 1870, Robinson 1920, 13.
[109] Weeks 1881, 11; Greenfield 1959, 92.
[110] Knowles 2013, 239.

sent iron prices plummeting.[111] The rapid decrease in the price of iron, below the lowest price listed on the sliding wage scale, inevitably led to its termination.[112] Over the next three years, the Sons of Vulcan responded to wage reductions and their employers' anti-unionism by going on strike nearly eighty times, mostly in the state of Pennsylvania.[113] The union led an especially long struggle from December 1874 until April 1875, during which "the memorable strike ... kept the many mills of Pittsburgh in an almost complete state of idleness."[114] Although the union members eventually won, the long strike of 1874 convinced iron workers of the necessity for further unionization to increase their bargaining power.

The main problem for the Sons of Vulcan was that they only organized puddler and boilers, which represented a small segment of the workforce in iron mills. During strikes, the union was hampered by the inability of various craft workers to act in concert. For example, when the puddlers went on strike, manufacturers could purchase iron bars that were already puddled and the heaters and rollers could continue producing wrought iron, the finished product.[115] As Wright explains, iron and steel workers believed that further organization was "a necessity, in order that they might obtain what they believed they were justly entitled to."[116] In order to better coordinate future strikes, the Sons of Vulcan decided to amalgamate their efforts with those of two other iron unions, the Associated Brotherhood of Iron and Steel Heaters, Rollers, and Roughers of the United States and the Iron and Steel Roll Hands Union. These three unions met, ratified a common constitution, and officially combined to form the Amalgamated Association of Iron and Steel Workers (AA) in 1876.[117]

The next year, the union quickly turned its efforts to establishing uniform wage scales throughout the industry. As discussed above, such industry-wide scales help take wages out of competition and lessen employers' incentive to renege on their agreement to share profits. At the AA's first annual convention, the President explicitly advocated for an industry-wide wage scale along these lines, explaining that such contracts

---

[111] Greenfield 1959, 93.
[112] Greenfield 1959, 94.
[113] Knowles 2013, 239.
[114] Wright 1893, 408.
[115] Robinson 1920, 17.
[116] Wright 1893, 409.
[117] Robinson 1920, 18. The puddlers from the Sons of Vulcan provided 85 percent of the initial membership and their former president, Joseph Bishop, became the first president of the AA, see Rees 2007, 1,287.

were needed "to prevent manufacturers forcing reductions on the ground that other mills in the district paid lower prices."[118]

The new iron and steel workers' union rapidly attracted new members. Though it started with only 3,755 members in 1877, by 1882 the union had grown to 16,000, and on the eve of the Homestead strike of 1892 had a membership of 24,000.[119] Even when there were periods of conflict between the union and their employers, the union won the majority of its demands.[120] Continuing the tradition of the Sons of Vulcan, the AA signed sliding wage scales in nearly all mills in which the union was recognized from 1876 until its strength declined at the end of the century. Although the first sliding wage scale in 1865 merely linked puddler's wages to the price of iron, these new wage scales became complicated contracts that contained different wage rates for various types of work and included dozens of pages of footnotes containing rules and regulations. In this way, the sliding wage scale and profit-sharing institutions in the iron and steel industry were developed through an iterative and experimental process. As Robinson explains, "the scale was not made; it grew."[121]

Contemporary observers praised these wage scales for contributing to industrial peace between capital and labor. According to the United States Industrial Commission, a government body that investigated economic issues from 1898 to 1902, "there has usually seemed to be very general satisfaction with the sliding scale system both on the part of employers and employees in the iron and steel trade."[122] As William Stanley Jevons, a prominent English economist, explained, the sliding wage scale was a "stepping stone to some still sounder method of partnership and participation in profits which a future generation will certainly enjoy."[123] Throughout this period, the combination of union recognition and the industry-wide sliding wage scale provided workers with a credible commitment that wages would increase along with the profitability of the industry.

In these ways, workers used a combination of associational and structural power to establish profit-sharing institutions in the iron and steel industry. Highly skilled workers in Pittsburgh, Pennsylvania organized their first union in 1858 and won a series of strikes and demands during the iron boom brought on by the Civil War. Although these workers had scarce skills that enabled them to shut down production,

[118] McCabe 1912, 130.
[119] Robinson 1920, 21.
[120] Robinson 1920, 19.
[121] Robinson 1920, 146.
[122] United States 1901, 344.
[123] Quoted in Robinson 1920, 157.

they augmented such structural power with extensive unionization drives and organizational rules that enabled them to build a large strike fund. The economic depression of 1873 weakened the union's power, but spurred it on to organize an industry-wide union. This new Amalgamated Association unionized roughly 25 percent of all eligible workers and maintained profit-sharing institutions in the iron and steel industry until the union's defeat in Homestead, Pennsylvania in 1892.

Capital-Labor Agreement: Steel and Profit-Sharing

This section analyzes the trade policy preferences of the iron and steel workers' union after the creation of profit-sharing institutions. Due to a lack of surviving records from the Sons of Vulcan, the analysis focuses on the trade policy preferences of the AA. As predicted, the AA agreed with their employers concerning trade policy and supported high tariffs throughout the 1880s.[124] For instance, the AA's first annual spring reunion in Pittsburgh, in 1880, included a public demonstration in favor of high tariffs.[125] As the union's President, John Jarrett, explained to the U.S. Senate in 1883, "Our organization is strongly a tariff organization, from the fact that we know that we do get better wages on account of the tariff."[126] At the AA's annual convention of 1883, the union reiterated its preference in favor of high tariffs by adopting a resolution that stated, "We therefore favor a tariff so adjusted as to give ... adequate protection against foreign competition, and place them upon, at least, an equal footing with foreign competition, in our home markets."[127]

Later in 1888, newly elected AA President Weihi and Secretary Martin both signed a letter sent to William McKinley, then Congressman from Ohio, voicing the union's support for high tariffs. According to the letter, although Democratic members of the House argued that "the tariff only benefits the manufacturer, and that they receive all the advantages from the protection given by the Government, *we know that we receive our share of the benefits of protection* on the industries we represent."[128]

---

[124] There is limited evidence on the trade policy preferences of the Sons of Vulcan, the union that joined with other iron workers' to form the AA in 1876. According to Jarrett, an early president of the AA, "the Sons of Vulcan were opposed to the free importation of the products of foreign labor in competition with those of their own labor. It needs no argument, therefore, to prove they were, as all iron workers now are, consistent protectionists." See McNeill 1887, 275. For an account that suggests that the Sons of Vulcan's concerns about immigration may have weakened their support for high tariffs, see Erickson 1952, 251.

[125] Montgomery 1989, 33.

[126] United States 1885, 1,122.

[127] Jarrett 1882.

[128] McKinley 1893, italics added.

Local lodges of the AA also participated in the lobbying effort, as dozens of lodges sent resolutions to the Ways and Means Committee in favor of maintaining high tariffs.[129] The AA also lobbied the Senate Finance Committee during its hearing on tariff revision, explaining that, "While every member in our organization is free to and does exercise his political preference, *we are Protectionists, and have unanimously declared ourselves such as an organization at almost every recurring annual convention.*"[130]

In 1890, the AA sent a delegate to Washington to lobby in favor of high tariffs and the passage of the protectionist McKinley bill.[131] With the passage of the bill, the AA was optimistic about the future; "With the metal tariff as it is … there is no reason why the labor of the mills should not have part of the plum of profits that the ownership has been enjoying."[132]

The AA's pro-tariff preferences were clearly on display in 1891, just one year before the devastating Homestead steel strike of 1892. In April 1891, the union's newspapers explained:

Now, we are having our own homes, getting good wages, able to live as workingmen ought to live, therefore I say *let us keep the protective policy* as our leading star in the progress in which we glory, and our organization to protect us and to get our share of the products and prosperity to which it brings.[133]

In short, in the presence of profit-sharing institutions that credibly linked an increase in profits to an increase in wages, the AA joined their employers in favor of high tariffs. Moreover, it is clear that the AA's pro-tariff position was predicated on the presence of profit-sharing institutions, and not a belief in an automatic connection between high tariffs and high wages. As AA President Jarrett explained, "the majority of them [manufacturers], where they have the workingman in their power, the tariff or anything else will make but very little difference as to the wages they pay … Hence I favor organization among the workingmen of our country."[134] Given the AA's conditional support for high tariffs, it should not come as a surprise that their support for high tariffs ended with the destruction of profit-sharing institutions in 1892.

---

[129] United States 1888a.
[130] United States 1888b, 1823, italics added.
[131] Amalgamated Association of Iron and Steel Workers 1890, 3, 473.
[132] *National Labor Tribune*, June 7, 1890.
[133] "Letter from Cleveland," *National Labor Tribune*, April 18, 1891, italics added.
[134] United States 1885, 1127.

Institutional Destruction: Homestead and Steelworkers, 1889–1892

This section illustrates both the maintenance and eventual destruction of profit-sharing institutions in the American steel industry. Throughout the late nineteenth century, technological change in the steel industry gradually eroded the AA's structural power. While this decrease in workers' bargaining power generated a growing incentive for capital to discard the industry's profit-sharing institutions, such institutional change did not come immediately. Following major technological improvements in 1886, the Carnegie Company locked out their workers and made a first attempt to discard profit-sharing institutions. The AA then drew on its remaining bargaining power and creative tactics to convince the company to re-sign a new three-year sliding wage scale. Unhappy with the settlement, the Carnegie Company spent the subsequent years preparing to defeat the AA. The final confrontation came three years later, when a similar lockout devolved into the infamous Homestead steel strike of 1892. This section demonstrates how the company carefully learned from its failure in 1889 and strategically undermined every source of the AA's bargaining power in preparation for its rematch with the union in 1892. The union was totally defeated, the profit-sharing institutions that had governed wage negotiations since the Civil War were discarded, and the AA rapidly faded from the American steel industry. Importantly, this section also highlights the potential stickiness of profit-sharing institutions. Although technological change gradually eroded the AA's bargaining power throughout the 1880s, profit-sharing institutions were maintained until 1892.

Homestead 1889. As discussed above, the AA used its associational and structural power to establish profit-sharing institutions in the iron and steel industry in the years following the Civil War. In the subsequent years, however, the AA's bargaining power was gradually undermined by technological improvements. The union was particularly weakened by the spread of the Bessemer converter, which generally reduced demand for highly skilled workers.[135] The Bessemer converter and other technological developments also weakened the ability of a small group of puddlers and other skilled workers to shut down production. At Carnegie's steel mill in Homestead, Pennsylvania, technological improvements drastically improved efficiency and output. According to the company, it would not be possible to amortize the cost of such improvements without

---

[135] Marcus et al. 1987, 62; Montgomery 1989, 27. The first Bessemer converters were in use in the United States by 1868, see Knowles 2013, 237.

revising the AA's wage scale and lowering the wage paid per ton of steel produced. Although the union recognized the need for an adjustment, the AA chafed at the company's proposed reduction and harsh ultimatum; wage negotiations quickly broke down and led to a lockout in July 1889.

Although the union's structural power was being eroded by technological improvements in the steel industry, the union maintained its overall power through increased associational power. The union spread throughout the industry, and by 1892, had organized 292 lodges and roughly 24,000 dues-paying members.[136] The union's membership allowed it to amass a large strike fund with which to compensate workers during prolonged lockouts or strikes. From the AA's founding in 1876 until 1892, the union paid out roughly $600,000 to workers engaged in strikes and lockouts, the present-day equivalent of roughly $16 million. Despite the United States' legacy of weak labor movements, by 1892 the AA was the largest iron and steel workers' union in the world.[137] Beyond the strength of the union itself, the AA also gained associational power from its close relationship with the community surrounding steel mills, as well as other labor unions. As will be shown below, it was the AA's associational power that allowed it to prevail in the Homestead lockout of 1889.

On July 9, 1889, the Carnegie Company began an open confrontation with the AA employed at the Homestead steel mill. After the union refused to accept a proposed 35 percent wage reduction, the company responded by placing advertisements for new, non-union workmen to run the mill. Clearly aware that the AA would resist being replaced by non-union strikebreakers, the company's advertisements promised "permanent positions, steady employment, and *ample protection*." The potential for violent conflict was obvious to contemporary observers; as *The New York Times* reported the next day, "the gauntlet of defiance to the powerful organization of iron and steel workers is therefore thrown down."[138] With the Carnegie Company set on breaking the union through the hiring of non-union workers, the outcome of the lockout would hinge on the union's ability to stop workers from entering the mill.

Carnegie's advertisement received a quick response from unemployed workers in nearby Pittsburgh. On July 11, a party of 31 non-union men took the train from Pittsburgh to Homestead with the intention of

---

[136] Robinson 1920, 9.
[137] Montgomery 1989, 35; Foner 1998.
[138] "Carnegie's Defiance," *New York Times*, July 10, 1889.

restarting the steel mill. Upon their arrival at the Homestead train station, they were "surrounded by a crowd of strikers which frightened the new men so badly that only three succeeded in getting inside the mill."[139] The rest were chased away by strikers screaming "Scab!" but "no stones were thrown or blows struck and no one was injured."[140] Sensing the potential for violence and destruction, Homestead's Sheriff McCandless directed the strikers to keep away from the company's property under penalty of arrest.

The following day, Sheriff McCandless recruited a small army of 124 deputized sheriffs to help preserve order in Homestead. These deputized sheriffs were then sent by train to Munhall, Pennsylvania, the closest station to the Homestead mill. Upon their arrival, the deputies were greeted by "at least a thousand men, women, and children [who] were assembled about the station."[141] The deputies were completely surrounded by strikers and their families, and another large group of strikers blocked the gates to the Homestead mill. The deputies "drew their clubs" and awaited instructions from their leader; according to one reporter, "It was evident that at the movement to advance war would commence in dead earnest."[142] The AA's President, William Weihi, elbowed his way to the front of the crowd and cautioned the strikers to be calm: "the success of our struggle depends in a large measure on how you conduct yourselves today. These men did not come here to work, and have the right to enter the mill."[143] The AA and their supporters yielded to Weihi's request for non-violence, but quickly sought to stop the deputies from entering the mill.

Weihi's speech was soon drowned out by "deafening cheers," as the strikers and their families pleaded with the deputies to go home. One deputy later told how "a poorly-dressed woman with a babe suckling at her breast came up to me and said, 'For God's sake go home. If you men stay here and help the company to beat the men you will drive us to starvation.' "[144] Another deputy, who was a Civil War veteran, explained that "I went all through the war; I was in at least a dozen battles, and did my share of fighting, too; but I candidly confess that, as I stood in front of the body of strikers this noon, I felt my heart come up in my throat. I don't want any more service in Homestead."[145] All but fifteen of the

---

[139] "Carnegie's New Men Driven Off," *New York Times*, July 12, 1889.
[140] "Carnegie's New Men Driven Off," *New York Times*, July 12, 1889.
[141] "A Big Conflict On Hand," *New York Times*, July 13, 1889.
[142] "Is There a Remedy?" *Pittsburgh Dispatch*, July 13, 1889.
[143] "A Big Conflict On Hand," *New York Times*, July 13, 1889.
[144] "A Big Conflict On Hand," *New York Times*, July 13, 1889.
[145] "Is There a Remedy?" *Pittsburgh Dispatch*, July 13, 1889.

deputies returned to Pittsburgh, telling how "they could not withstand the pathetic appeals of the women and children."[146]

Although newspapers reported that there was no violence between the strikers and the deputies, apparently some deputies "had their coats, hats, and badges torn from them."[147] Strikers then used this clothing to create an effigy that was hung from a freight car at the Munhall station outside the Homestead mill. According to the *Pittsburgh Dispatch*, the effigy was pierced with dozens of bullet holes and "was cited as an example of what would happen to anyone who attempted to go into the mill yard."[148] With the deputized sheriffs chased away, the Sheriff attempted to deputize the clerks from the Homestead mill. They refused to wear badges or be sworn in and claimed that "their lives would not be safe."[149] The Homestead Town Council then appointed ten special policemen to maintain law and order in the town. All ten were AA union members currently on strike.[150]

With the town in the hands of the AA, and Carnegie unable to re-start production at the mill, the company hired one hundred Pinkerton detectives to travel from Philadelphia to Homestead. The movement of these detectives was closely watched by newspapers, as well as local unions sympathetic to the AA. *The New York Times* reported the arrival of the Pinkertons in Pittsburgh on July 12, armed with "rifles and revolvers" and under the command of Captain R.J. Linden, "who achieved fame during the Molly Maguire disturbances in the anthracite coal region of Pennsylvania." The same article reported that the Pinkertons brought their own chef and ate all their meals onboard their train, having been poisoned by townspeople during previous strikes.[151] John W. Hayes, the General Secretary of the Knights of Labor, sent a telegram to the AA to warn them of the Pinkerton's approach; "Fifty of the worst characters in Philadelphia left last night for Pittsburgh ... Fifty more leave tonight. I have wired your Chief of Police."[152]

In response to the Pinkerton's movements, the AA guarded "every approach to town" to warn "the whole army of strikers" as soon as

---

146 "A Big Conflict On Hand," *New York Times*, July 13, 1889.
147 "A Big Conflict On Hand," *New York Times*, July 13, 1889.
148 "Peace is at Hand" *Pittsburgh Dispatch*, July 14, 1889.
149 "A Big Conflict On Hand," *New York Times*, July 13, 1889.
150 Henry Clay Frick, in testimony before the Congress' Committee on the Judiciary in 1892, would later accuse Sheriff McCandless of failing to protect the Carnegie Company's property. While Frick was surely criticizing McCandless in order to justify his use of Pinkerton detectives in 1892, it should be noted that the Sheriff was democratically elected to serve a county dominated by steel workers.
151 "A Big Conflict On Hand," *New York Times*, July 13, 1889.
152 "A Friendly Tip," *Pittsburgh Dispatch*, July 13, 1889.

the Pinkertons arrived.[153] According to the AA, the Pinkertons would not just tilt the balance in this one struggle, but would have important consequences for all future relations between the union and the company. As one reporter explained, "The impression has gained ground that the strike will do much to regulate the workingman's position in the future ... If it is within the power of these men to prevent it, no non-union workmen will ever gain admittance to the mill."[154] The AA guarded the town, required men to carry passes in order to approach the mill, and set up "a perfect code of signals" by which union workers could be summoned in the "shortest possible time."[155]

In addition to the AA's efforts in Homestead, the union drew on its associational and workplace power in nearby steel mills. At the time of the lockout, the Carnegie Company was reportedly "crowded with orders at the Homestead mill, and some of them must be filled at once."[156] With production at the Homestead mill shut-down, the company attempted to fill these orders by producing extra steel at their mills in Pittsburgh. However, the production of steel in these mills required the cooperation of two high-skilled "boss rollers," both of which were "good Amalgamated men." When the Carnegie Company attempted to have these union workers increase production, they answered: "We will not work a pound of steel on Homestead orders, or on work to relieve Homestead, until the trouble with the men there is settled."[157] In addition to the support of these two irreplaceable workers, the AA also made preliminary preparations to call an additional 6,000 workers from these mills out on strike.

In these ways, the union used a mix of associational and structural power to improve its bargaining power vis-à-vis their employers. In terms of associational power, the union's large membership, as well as support from family, townspeople, and sympathetic labor unions, allowed the AA to block strikebreakers from entering the Homestead mill. In terms of structural power, the union benefitted from the ability of just two highly skilled union members to thwart the Carnegie Company's attempts to fill Homestead's steel orders at nearby mills. Although the skills of AA members were gradually being made obsolete by technological change, at this critical juncture two AA members appear to have significantly altered the outcome of a major industrial conflict. In the

---

[153] "A Big Conflict On Hand," *New York Times*, July 13, 1889.
[154] "Is There a Remedy?" *Pittsburgh Dispatch*, July 13, 1889.
[155] "Is There a Remedy?" *Pittsburgh Dispatch*, July 13, 1889.
[156] "Peace is at Hand," *Pittsburgh Dispatch*, July 14, 1889.
[157] "Peace is at Hand," *Pittsburgh Dispatch*, July 14, 1889.

face of the AA's opposition and impending violence between the union
and approaching Pinkerton detectives, the company became anxious to
settle the lockout. As the local newspaper explained, "Although they
[the Company] have issued what was termed an ultimatum, it has
been withdrawn. This action has been caused by the serious outbreak
before them, and they have evidently discovered that a fight with the
powerful Amalgamated Association means a fight in every sense of the
word."[158]

Following these developments, the AA and Carnegie Company both
agreed to attend a wage conference mediated by Homestead's Sheriff
McCandless. According to a local reporter, the company agreed to revise
its bargaining position once the Sheriff "explained the fearful results
that might follow an adherence to the original proposition."[159] The final
settlement included concessions from both sides, but was heralded as a
major victory for the union.[160] The Pinkerton detectives were halted at
the doorstep of the Homestead mill, and were sent back to Philadelphia
without confronting the union. The company formally recognized the
union, signed the AA's sliding scale for an additional three years, and
the Homestead mill became the "keystone in the structure of ninety-four
lodges in the district, which constituted one-third of all lodges in the
union."[161]

By the end of 1890, nearly all American iron mills had signed the
AA scale and the closed union shop was strictly adhered to.[162] The
successful Homestead strike of 1889 also attracted new members to
the union, with membership peaking at approximately 25,000 in 1892.[163]
The union was able to dictate working rules to their employers, and to
demand wages that were higher than the wages paid in nearby, non-union
mills. The wage scale signed after the 1889 strike at Homestead included
fifty-eight pages of footnotes and rules meant to protect its members.[164]
As Carnegie explained in a speech after the union victory of 1889, "An
amalgamated association has compelled us to pay one-third more ... than
our great competitors pay in Pittsburgh. I know that for the success
of the Homestead Works ... the present system at Homestead must be
changed."[165]

---

158 "Peace is at Hand," *Pittsburgh Dispatch*, July 14, 1889.
159 "Peace is at Hand," *Pittsburgh Dispatch*, July 14, 1889.
160 Marcus et al. 1987, 64.
161 Montgomery 1989, 36.
162 Hoagland 1917, 675.
163 Robinson 1920.
164 Brody 1960, 53.
165 *New York Times*, July 7, 1892.

In these ways, the Homestead lockout of 1889 ended in a tense truce, with both sides preparing for future confrontations.[166] The union sought to increase membership, but could do little to stem the tide of technological change that was gradually undercutting their structural power and weakening their bargaining power vis-à-vis their employers. As described below, the Carnegie Company set out to defeat the union by systematically overcoming every source of bargaining power that the AA used to prevail in the contest of 1889. As one of Carnegie's partners explained the company's new approach to the union, "the Amalgamated placed a tax on improvements, therefore the Amalgamated had to go."[167] And the Amalgamated would go, but only after one of the most violent labor disputes in American history would unfold in Homestead, Pennsylvania in the summer of 1892.

Homestead 1892. The Homestead strike of 1892 has been written about at length elsewhere.[168] The July 6 battle between the locked-out workers and Pinkerton detectives, in which at least four people were killed and more than twenty injured, received immediate recognition as a major event in American history.[169] Six days after the battle, 8,000 members of the Pennsylvania National Guard arrived in Homestead to begin a ninety-five day military occupation that eventually allowed the company to re-open the mill with strikebreakers.[170] In short, the union ultimately lost the strike and the AA was no longer recognized at Homestead. Its defeat marked the beginning of the end of unionization in the steel industry. In 1897, Carnegie's main competitor, Jones and Laughlin, refused to sign the AA wage scale, and by 1900 not a single important steel mill in Western Pennsylvania recognized the union.[171]

The difference in outcomes between the 1889 and 1892 Homestead strikes offers an ideal opportunity to examine how variation in the balance of bargaining power influences the rise and fall of profit-sharing institutions. While technological change continued to reduce the AA's structural power, the most important difference between the 1889 and 1892 confrontations was the company's ability to undermine and overcome the AA's associational power. One-hundred-and-twenty-five years ago, the Carnegie Company underwent an analysis that was very similar to the discussion presented above. While I asked, "how did the AA maintain profit-sharing institutions despite technological change that

---

[166] Werner and Yuen 2005.
[167] Hogg 1943, 242.
[168] Hogg 1943; Burgoyne 1979; Krause 1992; Krooth 2004.
[169] Krause 1992.
[170] Montgomery 1989, 38.
[171] Brody 1960, 57.

weakened its bargaining power?," the company asked, "how can we defeat the union in 1892?" Just as I identified the ways in which the AA strategically used its associational power to block entry to the Homestead mill, the company identified ways to outmaneuver the union in future industrial conflicts.

In preparation for 1892, the company hired Henry Clay Frick, a manager with a history of brutally defeating labor unions in the coal industry. Frick carefully studied the company's defeat in 1889 and identified various mistakes. His strategic thinking was preserved in a report from the U.S. House Committee on the Judiciary, which sent investigators to Homestead during the violent strike of 1892.[172] First, Frick concluded that the county sheriff could not be trusted to protect company property. As Frick explained,

The sheriff assured the members of the firm [in 1889] that there would be no difficulty, that he would give them ample protection and see that men who were willing to work were not interfered with. What was the result? The posse taken up by the sheriff – something over 100 men – were not permitted to land on our property; were driven off with threats of bodily harm, and it looked as if there was going to be great destruction of life and property. That frightened our people.[173]

Frick concluded that the company must hire its own security force to protect its property, as well as strikebreakers. In Frick's own words, "it was necessary for us to secure our own watchmen to assist the sheriff, and we know of no other source from which to obtain them than from Pinkerton agencies, and to them we applied."[174] Second, Frick also knew that the AA was on guard for Pinkerton detectives in 1889, and was notified of their movements by sympathetic labor unions, as well as the press. Frick therefore sought complete secrecy in recruiting and transporting the Pinkertons to Homestead. In a personal letter to Robert A. Pinkerton, Frick wrote that "we think absolute secrecy essential in the movement of these men so that no demonstration can be made while they are en route."[175] Third, Frick clearly understood that the AA's 1889 victory was made possible by their guarding and control of local train stations. In 1889,

---

[172] Of course, Frick's testimony was carefully calibrated to justify the company's violent actions during the strike of 1892. Regardless, this report contains valuable information that corroborates my analysis of how the AA won in 1889, as well as how the Carnegie Company systematically outmaneuvered the union in 1892.

[173] U.S. House Committee on the Judiciary 1892, 31.

[174] U.S. House Committee on the Judiciary 1892, 32.

[175] A copy of this letter is included in U.S. House Committee on the Judiciary 1892, 34.

crowds of strikers and their families surrounded the train station and easily stopped strikebreakers and deputies from entering the Homestead mill. In 1892, Frick instructed the Pinkerton detectives to travel to the Homestead mill on barges, under the cover of night, along the Monongahela River. Frick described how the company planned to "land the men by taking them up by water so that they would not pass along any railroad, through any streets, but would be landed right on our property from the river, so as not to interfere with anybody."[176] In addition to avoiding Homestead's train stations, Frick sought to ensure that strikers would not be able to stop the Pinkertons from landing their boats on shore; Frick constructed a fence – topped by barbed wire and with holes for guns – constructed around the mill and down to the water's edge.[177]

Last, Frick understood that the AA had pressured the company in 1889 by refusing to let union members work on steel orders that were coming due. In order to eliminate the effectiveness of such sympathy strikes, Frick carefully stockpiled steel ahead of the 1892 strike. Any pressing orders could be filled from the company's inventory, even if the Homestead lockout dragged on or spread to other Carnegie mills.[178] With these strategic adjustments in place, Frick and the Carnegie Company systematically undermined the associational and structural sources of bargaining power that had helped the AA prevail in 1889. Perhaps the most important aspect of the conflict's outcome was the complete breakdown of collective bargaining and the company's commitment to re-opening the Homestead plant as non-union. After wage negotiations failed, the company announced its refusal to recognize the AA. As the company's Secretary made clear two days after the expiration of the AA wage scale agreed to in 1889, "Hereafter, the Homestead steel works will be operated as a non-union mill ... such a thing as a union will not be recognized. There will be no further conferences with the Amalgamated Association."[179] As Frick explained, "Under no circumstance will we have any further dealings with the Amalgamated Association as an organization. This is final."[180]

In short, technological change gradually eroded the AA's ability to inflict costly production stoppages. This decrease in labor's bargaining

---

[176] U.S. House Committee on the Judiciary 1892, 32.

[177] Marcus et al. 1987, 65; During the 1889 lockout, AA members were concerned about their ability to defend the shoreline of the Monongahela. The night before the lockout was settled, the AA reportedly sent a boat filled with strikers down the river to protect the shore around the Homestead mill, "Is There a Remedy?" *Pittsburgh Dispatch*, July 13, 1889.

[178] Marcus et al. 1987, 65.

[179] Quoted in Burgoyne 1979, 39.

[180] Quoted in Brody 1960, 56.

power generated growing incentive for capital to discard profit-sharing institutions. After a failed attempt in 1889, the Carnegie Company finally defeated the AA in 1892 and destroyed the profit-sharing institutions that had governed wage negotiations in the iron and steel industry since the end of the Civil War. As Frick explained after the defeat of the union, "Before, decision had been reached by 'an agreement,' now it was brought about by our fixing the wages that we felt we could afford to pay, and they agreeing individually to accept them."[181] According to Brody, "the employees' bargaining power ended with the union. Now the determination of labor expenses rested solely with the steel men."[182] The end of union recognition and the industry-wide sliding wage scale had profoundly negative effects on the workers' position in the labor market, and predictable effects on their international trade policy preferences.

Steelworkers' Lack of Support for High Tariffs

Given the termination of profit-sharing institutions in the steel industry, my theory predicts that the steelworkers' union would start to disagree with their employers concerning the benefits of high tariffs. As predicted, the AA rapidly began to critically evaluate the benefits they received from high tariffs. As wage negotiations stalled in the spring of 1892, the union's newspaper, the *National Labor Tribune (NLT)*, printed numerous articles denying the connection between tariffs and high wages. As early as June 4, the *NLT* printed a letter claiming that since it was impossible to ensure that workers benefit from the tariff, "laboring men should advocate free trade ... A protection that but half protects us must get out of the way. A full protection is the only thing we want."[183] The following week the *NLT* would complain of "the indisposition [of employers] to divide fairly with the workmen the results of protective tariff."[184] Another article argued that tariff protection only benefited their employers; "what farce is such protection to the working man when as many foreign workmen are allowed to arrive each year as would run all the iron and steel works for this country!"[185] Without profit-sharing institutions, steelworkers now clearly believed that competition in the labor market would break the link between trade policy and wages.

As the tensions of the stalled wage negotiations grew, workers began to consider the looming industrial dispute and its political consequences.

---

[181] Quoted in Brody 1960, 78.
[182] Brody 1960, 77.
[183] *National Labor Tribune*, June 4, 1892.
[184] *National Labor Tribune*, June 11, 1892.
[185] *National Labor Tribune*, June 11, 1892.

According to the *NLT*, "there is quite a feeling among a number of our Republican workmen that if the manufacturers force a reduction ... they will vote the Democratic ticket this fall, claiming that promises made in the event of Republican success have not been fulfilled."[186] In response to continued Republican arguments that tariffs led to higher wages, the *NLT* explained that "the only argument that will have effect is that of the withdrawal of the unfair scale proposed and the substitution of propositions that will be as fair to the workman as to the employer."[187]

On June 19, the AA held a public meeting in the Homestead opera house to discuss the strike. As the AA annual convention was then in session in nearby Pittsburgh, the meeting was attended by many of the union's leaders from around the country. Vice President Jere Doherty explained that the trouble at Homestead would be a test of the protection guaranteed to labor by the Republican Party.[188] The meeting's most memorable speech was given by John McLuckie, the Burgess of Homestead, and a member of the AA. According to McLuckie, the high tariffs of the McKinley bill failed to protect workers. In lines that resonated with the strikers, McLuckie claimed that "you men who voted the Republican ticket voted for high tariff and you get high fences, Pinkerton detectives, thugs and militia!"[189]

After the July 6 battle with the Pinkertons, the *NLT* letters written by AA members only become more critical of the tariff. According to one letter, the unfortunate trouble at Homestead "has caused the men of the AA to consider the part they have taken in making tariff a law, and aware that 'protection to American industries' has enriched manufacturers, the present action of the employers in attempting to reduce our wages has fanned that revulsion."[190] The letter went on to acknowledge that the tariff had enriched the country, before asking "but what does it avail a working man who voted for this system to feast his eyes upon a pyramid of gold when his family can starve beneath it, and can call none of it his?"[191]

As the strike wore on through the summer of 1892, the intransigence of the Carnegie Company continued. In August, the company reiterated that it would not negotiate with the workers or recognize the union; "We have announced our ultimatum, and there will be no deviation from our policy as has been previously outlined. No arbitration, no conferences,

---

[186] *National Labor Tribune*, June 18, 1892.
[187] *National Labor Tribune*, June 25, 1892.
[188] Burgoyne 1979, 24.
[189] Burgoyne 1979, 25; Krooth 2004, 104–107.
[190] *National Labor Tribune*, July 16, 1892.
[191] *National Labor Tribune*, July 16, 1892.

nothing but what we have stated."[192] Following this announcement and three months of military occupation in Homestead, the *NLT* succinctly explained the union's views on trade policy;

It is folly for employers to insist upon protective tariff and expect workmen to aid them in this, except they shall agree to labor organization. There cannot be Frickism and protective tariff too, for if the basis of good wages (which is protection) is to live, assuredly the workmen must insist that *labor organization, which secures them their share of the benefits of protection,* must live and flourish.[193]

A union member from Conshohocken, Pennsylvania added that "high tariff is an addition to the employers; but do they divide with their men? No, they keep it themselves. The employers want high tariff on product and free trade on human freight."[194] Such statements not only provide evidence that the AA changed its trade policy preferences after Homestead, but also provide evidence for the causal mechanism of my theory. The AA did not end its support for high tariffs on a whim of disagreement inspired by class conflict. Instead, the AA clearly articulated that it did not favor high tariffs unless its employers used profit-sharing institutions to credibly commit that an increase in profits would lead to an increase in wages. Moreover, union members explicitly noted how competition in the labor market severed the potential connection between trade policy, profits, and wages. In the words of the *NLT*, "The reduction of wages at Homestead is not because the business under protection is not profitable, but because the employers insist upon having all the profits themselves."[195] Importantly, workers did not simply lament their lack of bargaining power – they specifically inveighed against their employers' unwillingness to formally recognize the union, or "agree to labor organization." What changed abruptly at Homestead in 1892 was not the union's objective bargaining power, it was their loss of profit-sharing institutions.

The most dramatic expressions of the union's new trade policy preferences were on display during parades in Pittsburgh and Homestead in October 1892. In Pittsburgh, 600 AA strikers joined a Democratic parade that carried signs attacking the Republican promise of high tariffs and high wages. One sign read,

Show us a man in a Pittsburgh mill
Who had his wages raised by the McKinley bill.[196]

---

[192] *National Labor Tribune*, August 6, 1892.
[193] *National Labor Tribune*, October 1, 1892, italics added.
[194] *National Labor Tribune*, August 13, 1892.
[195] *National Labor Tribune*, August 20, 1892.
[196] Burgoyne 1979, 213.

According to one observer, "it looked on that October night very much as though Pittsburgh, the headquarters of high tariff sentiment, had become suddenly inoculated with free-trade virus."[197] Two weeks later, the strikers' Advisory Committee, the members of which had all previously been Republicans, headed a Democratic parade in Homestead.[198] Three thousand steel workers marched amongst floats that decried the failures of tariff protection.[199]

The apparent failure of trade protection to protect workers was lamented well beyond the steelworkers' union. According to Brecher, the plight of Homestead's workers led to an overnight hit folk song titled "Father was killed by the Pinkerton men!"[200] The most relevant stanza goes as follows:

Hear the orphans tell their sad story
"Father was killed by the Pinkerton men!"
Ye prating politicians, who boast protection creed,
Go to Homestead and stop the orphans' cry.
Protection for the rich man ye pander to his greed,
His workmen they are cattle and may die.
The freedom of the city in Scotland far away
'Tis presented to the millionaire suave,
But here in Free America with protection in full sway,
His workmen get the freedom of the grave.[201]

The Homestead strike, and the termination of profit-sharing institutions, proved to be a turning point for the union's trade policy preferences. The union's anti-tariff letters, speeches, and demonstrations were not instances of short-lived animosity bred from the violent conflict. At the AA's 1894 annual convention, the union announced that due to internal disagreement over the benefits of tariff protection, the national union would leave future trade policy lobbying to local union lodges to decide for themselves.[202] In 1897, the AA did not lobby the Congress in favor of iron or steel tariffs, despite the continued protectionist requests made by iron and steel manufacturers.[203]

---

[197] Burgoyne 1979, 213–214.
[198] Hogg 1943, 162.
[199] Burgoyne 1979, 212–214; Montgomery 1989, 39–40.
[200] Brecher 2014, 67.
[201] Lyrics available at http://historymatters.gmu.edu/d/5322/
[202] Amalgamated Association of Iron and Steel Workers 1894, 4678. It should be noted that the AA leadership did testify in favor of high tariffs before the Ways and Means Committee in September of 1893. However, that testimony was at the center of the union's 1894 debate about the benefits of the tariff and its final decision to curtail future trade policy lobbying by the national union.
[203] Sanders 1999; Bensel 2000.

A decade later, the dwindling AA stood idly by as the AFL denounced high steel tariffs.[204] At the AFL's 1909 annual convention, the Federation petitioned the U.S. Congress to "appoint a special committee to investigate the methods employed by corporations in this [steel] industry: and if it is found that the tariff, instead of being used to maintain American industrial conditions, is entirely turned into the pockets of the owners, the tariff on steel be suspended."[205] When the AFL questioned the benefits of high steel tariffs back in 1882, the AA angrily withdrew from the Federation in protest. A quarter century later, the AA delegates attending the AFL's 1909 convention did not even comment on the anti-tariff resolution, which appears to have passed without any opposition.

This within-case analysis of the steelworkers' union demonstrates that profit-sharing institutions shaped the union's trade policy preferences. When profit-sharing institutions were in place in the 1880s, the AA clearly supported high tariffs. The union held pro-tariff rallies, adopted internal resolutions in favor of high tariffs, and lobbied the U.S. Congress in favor of tariff protection for the steel industry. However, when these profit-sharing institutions were terminated during the Homestead steel strike of 1892, the AA quickly re-evaluated its trade policy preferences and ended its support for high tariffs. Articles in the *NLT*, AA speeches and demonstrations, and the meeting minutes of their annual conventions, all demonstrate that profit-sharing institutions shape workers' trade policy preferences.

CROSS-CASE COMPARISONS – TEXTILES AND STEEL

In addition to within-case analysis of the textile and steel workers' unions, it is also helpful to consider cross-case comparisons of the two unions. Since the unions represent most similar cases, sharing the same attributes identified by alternative explanations, we can draw inferences by comparing them at the same time. Such comparisons are especially worthwhile because of the mirror image nature of the two cases; the textile workers did not support high tariffs in the 1880s but then supported them in the 1890s, while the steelworkers supported high tariffs in the 1880s but then did not support them in the 1890s.

---

[204] By 1909, the AA only had 6,295 members and 114 lodges, down from the 1891 peak of 24,068 members and 190 lodges. See Robinson 1920, 21.

[205] American Federation of Labor 1909, 255.

First, consider the 1880s, during which the textile workers denied the benefits of high tariffs while the steel workers supported high tariffs. This cross-case variation cannot be explained by alternative theories, as both unions are identical in terms of skill (high), global-competitiveness (import-competing), region (North), and ideology (craft unionism). Nor can this variation be explained by exogenous temporal factors such as economic depression, as the two unions had opposite policy preferences during each period. However, this cross-case variation is easily explained with attention to profit-sharing institutions. While the unrecognized and blacklisted textile workers reasoned that they would be unable to bargain for a share of the tariff's benefits, the formally recognized steelworkers had established a wage contract that explicitly linked their wages to the profitability of their industry. The textile workers' doubted the benefits of high tariffs because of the absence of profit-sharing institutions during this period, just as the steelworkers supported high tariffs because of the presence of profit-sharing institutions.

Second, consider the 1890s, when both unions reversed their trade policy preferences. The textile workers supported high tariffs while the previously protectionist steelworkers ended their support for high tariffs. Again, this cross-case variation in trade policy preferences is easily explained with attention to profit-sharing institutions. By the 1890s the textile union had been formally recognized by their employers, and their national union negotiated wage increases explicitly based on the profitability of the textile industry. In contrast, the steelworkers' union was decimated by the Homestead strike of 1892 and their employers declared that they would neither recognize nor negotiate with the union. The textile workers supported high tariffs because of the presence of profit-sharing institutions during this period, just as the absence of profit-sharing institutions led the steelworkers to disagree with their employers concerning the benefits of high tariffs.

Immigration and Trade Policy Preferences

As theorized in Chapter 2, immigration increases competition in the labor market and decreases the ability of native workers to capture a share of increased profits in the form of wages. As seen throughout this chapter, American labor unions often pointed to labor market competition from immigrants when explaining why they did not support the same trade policy as their employers. If immigration helped create a wedge between the trade policy preferences of workers and their employers, is it possible

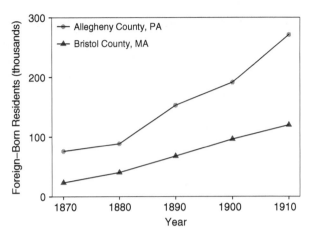

Figure 4.1. Immigration into Bristol County (Fall River) and Allegheny County (Pittsburgh)

that capital-labor agreement was the result of decreased immigration, rather than the presence of profit-sharing institutions? For example, the textile workers first joined their employers in favor of high tariffs in 1894. Was this trade policy agreement caused by a decrease in immigration into the textile hub of Fall River? In contrast, the steel workers first disagreed with their employers in 1892. Was this trade policy disagreement caused by a sudden increase in immigration?

Neither of these alternative hypotheses are supported by data on American immigration during the late nineteenth century. Figure 4.1 displays immigration statistics from the decennial U.S. census for Bristol County, Massachusetts, and Allegheny County, Pennsylvania, the home counties of Fall River and Pittsburgh, respectively. The plot shows that there was not a sudden *decrease* in immigration into the textile hub of Bristol County in the years before textile workers joined their employers in 1894. Immigration steadily increased throughout the period. Similarly, there was no sudden *increase* in immigration into the steel hub of Allegheny County in the years before the steelworkers started to disagree with their employers in 1892. In fact, more immigrants moved to Allegheny County during the 1880s – when the AA agreed with their employers concerning trade policy – than during the 1890s – when the AA disagreed with their employers. While the steady inflow of immigrants into these counties generally raised workers' concerns about their ability to capture a share of increased profits in the form of wages, changes in immigration cannot explain the observed variation in workers' trade policy preferences.

HOMESTEAD AND THE PRESIDENTIAL ELECTION OF 1892

The Homestead strike erupted in June of 1892, only five months before the Presidential election of 1892. Although this chapter focuses on the effect of profit-sharing institutions on workers' trade policy preferences, this section briefly examines the potential effect of workers' changed trade policy preferences on actual political outcomes. Since international trade policy was one of the main partisan issues debated in American politics – Republicans advocated tariff protection, while Democrats advocated downward revision of the tariff – a decrease in worker support for high tariffs would be expected to shift labor support towards the Democratic Party. According to scholars and contemporary observers alike, the Homestead strike had precisely this influence on the Presidential election of 1892, contributing to the victory of the Democratic candidate, Grover Cleveland.

According to Perlman, a prominent labor historian, the strike at Homestead "drove home to the workers that an industry protected by high tariffs will not necessarily be a haven to organized labor."[206] Perlman claims that many votes that would have gone to the Republican candidate, Benjamin Harrison, ended up going to Cleveland, who ran on an anti-protective tariff platform; "it is not unlikely that the latter's victory was materially advanced by the disillusionment brought on by the Homestead defeat."[207]

According to *The Sun*, Republican Representative Alfred Harner of Pennsylvania predicted that the violent labor dispute in the protected steel industry would be disastrous for the party of protection. Upon hearing of the violence at Homestead, Harner proclaimed that, "If this thing goes on much longer Cleveland will carry Pennsylvania."[208] Sure enough, the citizens of Homestead voted for the Democrats by two to one, despite having been a Republican stronghold in 1888. Compared to the past election, the five major steel producing districts of eastern Ohio all reported large gains for the Democrats. Although Harrison went on to win both Pennsylvania and Ohio, he lost the industrial states of Wisconsin, Indiana, Illinois, and New York.[209] According to the *New York Tribune*, the Republican loss was due to the defection of workers in northern cities; "It is clear that many of them have listened to the plea that the improvement in wages has not been due to the tariff and the industrial conditions which protection makes possible."[210]

---

[206] Perlman 1922, 135.
[207] Perlman 1922, 135.
[208] Krooth 2004, 112.
[209] Hogg 1943, 170–171.
[210] Quoted in Hogg 1943, 170.

There were, of course, other factors at play in the presidential election of 1892. For instance, the Republican vice presidential candidate, Whitelaw Reid, had a terrible labor record, which was attacked in the newspapers almost as much as the Homestead strike. In addition, tens of thousands of immigrants, who tended to vote for the Democrats, voted for the first time in 1892. With these complexities in mind, Hogg concluded that "in the face of all this, it would require a hardy soul to assert positively that Homestead was responsible for Harrison's defeat."[211] While Homestead certainly did not single-handedly tip the election in Cleveland's favor, it did change the trade policy preferences of many iron and steel workers, who then contributed to defeating the Republican Party. Moreover, the 1892 election went on to have clear consequences for American trade policy; in 1894, President Cleveland signed the Wilson-Gorman tariff, which lowered American trade barriers for the first time in more than a decade. With this anecdotal evidence in mind, the next chapter systematically examines the effect of workers' trade policy preferences on American trade policy outcomes.

CONCLUSION

This chapter demonstrated that profit-sharing institutions helped determine workers' trade policy preferences during the late nineteenth century. When profit-sharing institutions existed in the American textile and steel industries, labor unions representing these workers joined their employers in favor of high tariffs. When such institutions did not exist, these same unions disagreed with their employers concerning the benefits of high tariffs. The qualitative case studies presented above support the predictions of my theory and also pose a direct challenge to the conventional wisdom regarding American trade politics in the Gilded Age. In contrast to the canonical accounts found in the international political economy and American Political Development literatures, workers did not automatically join their employers in favor of high tariffs. When such cross-class coalitions did emerge, they were built on the foundation of profit-sharing institutions.

In these ways, this chapter demonstrated that profit-sharing institutions helped build cross-class coalitions in favor of trade *protectionism*. According to conventional economic thinking, such protectionist trade policies distort the national economy, producing rents enjoyed by the few, and inefficiencies suffered by the many. Does this mean that profit-sharing institutions only lead to capital-labor cooperation that

[211] Quoted in Hogg 1943, 170.

leaves the rest of society worse off? Do profit-sharing institutions only produce protectionist coalitions, or can they also help to build cross-class coalitions in favor of trade *liberalization*? Unfortunately, it is not possible to examine this question during the late nineteenth century, as America's "infant" industries favored trade protectionism well into the twentieth century. Simply put, Gilded Age America did not contain pro-trade employers with whom workers could join in favor of trade liberalization. To answer these questions – and to demonstrate the potentially broad benefits of profit-sharing institutions – the next chapter therefore skips forward in time to the 1930s, when a growing number of American industries became export-competitive and began to favor free trade. It demonstrates that the creation of profit-sharing institutions led workers to join their employers in favor of free trade, and that capital and labor then successfully pressured U.S. senators to support American trade liberalization.

5

Liberalized by Labor

This chapter explores the influence of profit-sharing institutions on American trade politics in the 1930s and 1940s. It begins by demonstrating the effect of profit-sharing institutions on the trade policy preferences of the American Federation of Labor (AFL) and the Congress of Industrial Organizations (CIO). Throughout this period, the AFL maintained profit-sharing institutions and joined their import-competing employers in favor of high tariffs. In contrast, the CIO did not establish profit-sharing institutions until the early 1940s. Before this, the CIO disagreed with their export-oriented employers concerning trade policy; however, after the creation of profit-sharing institutions, the CIO joined their employers in favor of free trade. The evolution of profit-sharing institutions and the trade policy preferences of the AFL and the CIO are displayed below in Table 5.1.

After demonstrating the effect of profit-sharing institutions on capital-labor trade policy agreement, this chapter uses quantitative methods and an original dataset to demonstrate that these cross-class coalitions influenced the 1945 renewal of the Reciprocal Trade Agreements Act (RTAA). The AFL's cross-class coalition successfully pressured U.S. senators to vote against the RTAA, while the CIO's cross-class coalition successfully pressured them to vote in favor of the RTAA. Most importantly, the CIO's free trade demands convinced protectionist Republicans to support RTAA renewal, therefore helping to establish bipartisan Senate support for free trade. Without this "Republican conversion" to free trade, the RTAA would likely have been dismantled when protectionist Republicans returned to power in 1946. In this way, profit-sharing institutions played a major, but previously unrecognized, role in postwar American trade liberalization.

Table 5.1. *Trade Policy Preferences of the AFL and CIO*

Union	Production Profile	Years	Capital's Trade Policy Preference	Profit-Sharing Institutions		Capital-Labor Agreement
American Federation of Labor	Import-Competing	1930s	Protectionist	Yes	→	Yes
		1940s	Protectionist	Yes	→	Yes
Congress of Industrial Organizations	Export-Oriented	1930s	Free Trade	No	→	No
		1940s	Free Trade	Yes	→	Yes

This chapter will be organized in the following way. The first section follows the same structured-focused approach as the previous chapter. It explores conditions in the labor market during the 1930s, followed by the trade policy preferences of both the AFL and CIO during this period. It then explores the process through which the New Deal led to the creation of profit-sharing institutions and a subsequent change in the CIO's trade policy preferences. The second section begins with a review of the broad literature on the RTAA and the determinants of American trade liberalization following World War II. It then presents my argument that American trade liberalization was sustained by the CIO's endorsement of free trade. Next, it presents a quantitative analysis of Senate voting on the RTAA in 1945, which demonstrates the systematic relationship between CIO trade policy demands and Senate support for free trade.

AMERICAN LABOR MARKETS DURING THE GREAT DEPRESSION

It is impossible to describe, in any great detail, the various labor market conditions that American workers faced during the 1930s. The decade opened with the onset of the Great Depression; by 1933 unemployment reached almost 25 percent as over 11 million Americans looked for work. Responding to the aggressive actions of the early New Deal, the American economy rebounded in 1935, only to slip back into recession in 1937. It was not until American mobilization for World War II, at the end of the decade, that the government provided the increased spending necessary to end the Depression. While economic hardship was surely widespread, the Depression was experienced very differently by the highly skilled, unionized workers in America's craft industries and the unskilled, unorganized workers in America's mass production industries. During the early 1930s, unskilled workers in America's steel and automobile industries were completely unorganized and faced tremendous labor market competition from the unemployed. During the same period, the AFL organized three million workers into craft unions that collectively bargained with their employers on a regular basis.[1] In what Jacoby calls the "pockets of stability scattered throughout the American labor market," AFL unions even managed to maintain the profit-sharing institutions that they had established in previous decades.[2] In order to highlight these differences, this section offers examples of labor market conditions in America's craft and mass-production industries.

Unskilled Workers and Mass Production Industries

Unskilled workers in America's mass-production industries were thoroughly unorganized at the onset of the Great Depression. While there are numerous theories that seek to explain the weakness of American labor unions during the early twentieth century, much scholarship focuses on the effects of what is dubbed "welfare capitalism."[3] Beginning in earnest in the early twentieth century, employers launched a series of industrial relations programs that aimed to increase worker productivity, reduce labor turnover, and deter unionization drives. These efforts included company savings plans, insurance groups, "company unions" through which workers could voice grievances, and wage bonuses such as Ford's famous $5 day. As Slichter explained in 1929, the programs of welfare capitalism, "are one of the most ambitious social experiments of the age, because they aim, among other things, to counteract the effects of modern technique upon the mind of the worker, to prevent him from becoming class conscious and from organizing trade unions."[4] Of course, American industrialists were also infamous for using overt violence to thwart their workers' unionization efforts.[5]

The lack of unionization amongst the unskilled was on clear display in the American steel industry, which had long established a reputation as a "bastion of antiunionism."[6] After years of technological change, declining membership, and a crushing defeat by the United States Steel Corporation

[1] Tomlins 1979.
[2] Jacoby 1998, 11.
[3] For a thorough discussion of the many theories that seek to explain the weaknesses of American labor, see Foner 1984.
[4] Quoted in Brody 1993, 57.
[5] Fink 1988; Orren 1991; Capozzola 2002; Norwood 2002; Archer 2010.
[6] Dennis 2014, 8.

in 1901, the Amalgamated Association of Iron and Steel Workers "eked out a precarious and meager existence."[7] Long gone were the days of collective bargaining and sliding wage scales; according to Brody, "The practice of simply notifying workmen of the conditions of employment became the rule by 1910."[8] As F.N. Hoffstot, President of the Pressed Steel Car Company, boasted, "If a man is dissatisfied, it is his privilege to quit."[9]

The lack of organization amongst steelworkers was so severe that it threatened the ability of workers in related industries to maintain their own unions. The United Mine Workers' (UMW) were particularly worried about their ability to defend their wages and working conditions in the "captive" mines owned by steel companies. As UMW President John Lewis lamented, "certainly the steel companies are going to push us around with a great deal more ferocity if they recognize they are free from organization in their own industry ... unless we carry the fight to the steel companies they are going to carry the fight to the organizations that are hanging on the fringe of the industry."[10]

Whereas the American steel industry violently shed itself of labor unions in the early twentieth century, other mass-production industries were simply born non-union. The automobile industry, for instance, rapidly developed after World War I, a period during which labor unions were shrinking and on the defensive. While the automobile increasingly became a symbol of America's "unfolding saga of invention and industrial development ... a union of auto workers had played no part" in the industry.[11] Employment in the automobile industry often came along with strict and onerous rules that led to high turnover rates. In the late 1920s, the Ford Motor Company maintained a Service Department that was "a private army thinly disguised as a plant protection force [that] strictly enforced an oppressive set of plant rules."[12] Workers were kept under surveillance, forbidden to sit while in the plant, and prohibited from talking. According to Barnard, "a cloud of oppression descended upon the Ford factories that did not lift until the UAW [United Automobile Workers] was established there."[13] However, the 1930s would end before Ford would agree to sign a contract with the UAW. The UAW was not founded until 1935, and at the close of their first annual convention the new union only represented 20,000 workers in an industry that employed

7 Galenson 1960, 75.
8 Brody 1960, 78.
9 Brody 1960, 78.
10 Quoted in Galenson 1960, 77.
11 Barnard 2005, 3.
12 Barnard 2005, 22.
13 Barnard 2005, 22.

as many as 445,000.[14] The UAW did not gain its first major victory until 1937, when a successful sit-down strike wrenched formal union recognition from General Motors. It would take four more years, and successful strikes throughout the automobile industry, before the UAW was finally recognized by Ford in 1941.[15]

In short, America's mass-production industries, such as steel and automobiles, were not unionized during the early years of the Great Depression. Efforts to organize the unskilled did not gain traction until after the Wagner Act, which granted workers' the right to unionize, was upheld as constitutional by the Supreme Court in 1937. It was not until the late 1930s and early 1940s that the CIO used sit-down strikes to first win formal recognition from General Motors, U.S. Steel, Chevrolet, Ford, and other large manufacturing corporations.[16]

Skilled Workers and the American Federation of Labor

In direct contrast to the plight of unskilled workers, highly skilled workers in America's craft industries maintained influential labor unions during the early 1930s. The relative success of AFL craft unions – especially under the auspices of the Great Depression – is well exemplified by the labor unions in the glass and pottery industries. The skilled glass workers were organized by two different craft unions, the American Flint Glass Workers' Union and the Glass Bottle Blowers of the United States and Canada, both of which first established national collective bargaining with their employers during the late nineteenth century. These unions maintained industry-wide wage scales that set price lists and maintained apprenticeships and work rules that limited competition in the labor market.[17] In the face of the highest unemployment rates recorded in American history, the American Flint Glass Workers' wage contract for 1934 maintained a "closed shop" agreement: "The right of the manufacturer to hire and discharge employees is acknowledged, and it is understood that when workmen are hired that members of the A.F.G.W.U. shall have the preference."[18] Similarly, the Glass Bottle Blowers' wage contract for 1935 stated that, "The right of the managers to hire and discharge employees is acknowledged, but it is understood when an operator is to be hired, he shall be a member of the Glass Bottle Blowers' Association."[19] As discussed below, the glass industry also had a long

[14] Galenson 1960, 127.
[15] Bernstein and Piven 1969.
[16] Norwood 2002.
[17] Wolman 1916.
[18] United States Bureau of Labor Statistics 1936, 1206.
[19] United States Bureau of Labor Statistics 1936, 1208.

tradition of increasing workers' wages along with trade policy reforms that benefitted the industry.

The skilled workers in the pottery industry were organized by the National Brotherhood of Operative Potters. This union established collective bargaining with their employers and signed their first "uniform wage scale" in 1900, covering 80 percent of manufacturers in the country.[20] The union maintained strict apprenticeship rules, such as mandating a four-year training period and limiting the number of apprentices to one for every five employed potters.[21] Throughout the early twentieth century, the potters' union cooperated closely with their employers to maintain an industry-wide wage scale.[22] Despite the depths of the Depression, a 1932 study of the pottery industry concluded that "the union has suffered little loss of control of shops in general ware since 1922," when a lost strike destroyed the union in the sanitary ware division.[23] Although the union certainly suffered wage reductions in the early 1930s, by 1933 it was collaborating with employers on a National Recovery Act industrial code that guaranteed collective bargaining in the industry.[24] In December of 1933, the union held a wage conference with their employers at which they successfully negotiated a 12.5 percent wage increase.[25]

These AFL craft unions used their skills and previously established organizations to maintain relatively strong labor market positions during the early 1930s. Workers suffered frequent wage reductions, but they sustained collective bargaining, industry-wide wage scales, and the ability to enforce their employers' promises to increase wages when profitability returned. Surely, it would be foolhardy to claim to have covered the nuances of American labor relations during the Great Depression in just a few pages. However, this rudimentary sketch suggests that skilled and unskilled, unionized and non-unionized workers faced very different labor market conditions in the early 1930s. In short, skilled craft unions organized by the AFL maintained profit-sharing institutions. My theory therefore predicts that these unions would agree with their employers and join them in support of the high tariffs needed to protect their import-competing industries. In contrast, unskilled workers in the mass-production industries were totally unorganized at the start of the Great Depression. Even though the CIO began to organize these industries in the late 1930s, the decade ended without the establishment

---

[20] McCabe 1932.
[21] National Brotherhood of Operative Potters 1915, 95.
[22] Gordon 1994, 114.
[23] McCabe 1932, 49.
[24] Gordon 1994, 114.
[25] Shotliff 1977, 227.

of profit-sharing institutions. My theory therefore predicts that these workers would be more likely to disagree with their employers concerning trade policy, and to question the benefits of the free trade policies favored by their export-oriented employers.

WORKERS' TRADE POLICY PREFERENCES IN THE 1930S

This section reviews the trade policy preferences of the CIO and AFL during the 1930s. As rival labor federations, they focused on organizing different types of workers into different types of unions. The CIO, which was founded in 1938, focused on organizing low-skilled workers in America's mass production industries into what were known as "industrial" unions.[26] The AFL, which was founded in 1881, traditionally organized high-skilled workers in more specialized trades into what were known as "craft" unions.[27] Due to their different organizing goals during this period, the CIO was more likely to represent workers in export-oriented industries, while the AFL was more likely to represent workers in import-competing industries. For example, workers in America's globally competitive automobile and steel industries were members of the CIO's United Automobile Workers and the United Steelworkers. In contrast, workers in America's less competitive glass or footwear industries were members of the AFL's American Flint Glass Workers' Union and the Boot and Shoe Workers' Union.

The different production orientations of the industries organized by the CIO and AFL, combined with the different labor market conditions faced by each union, help set the background for understanding the unions' trade policy preferences. The well-established craft unions of the AFL enjoyed the benefits of profit-sharing institutions and joined their employers in favor of trade protectionism. The fledgling industrial unions of the CIO struggled to gain formal recognition, and disagreed with their employers concerning trade policy. While export-oriented manufacturers lobbied for free trade during this period, the CIO argued that any benefits from free trade would be withheld from workers in these industries.

The CIO's Skepticism Concerning Free Trade

Unfortunately, it is not possible to systematically study the trade policy preferences of unskilled workers before the formation of labor unions in America's mass production industries. Therefore, this section explores

[26] Galenson 1960.
[27] Greene 1998.

the trade policy preferences of the CIO in the years after its creation, and before the creation of profit-sharing institutions. In the years after it was founded in 1938, the CIO consistently argued that American free trade would not benefit workers. Starting with its first annual meeting, the CIO passed a resolution lamenting that,

Corporations such as Bethlehem Steel are unwilling to pay the prevailing wages for employees ... and unwilling to collectively bargain ... and to accomplish such purpose import oil, coal, and iron ore from foreign countries ... Such practices lead to extensive unemployment of workers employed in American industries and subject such American workers to the threat of lowered wage standards and the breakdown of collective bargaining.[28]

Rather than see free trade as an opportunity to increase wages for steel workers, the CIO argued that free trade, in the absence of collective bargaining, actually threatened workers' wages. During this period, the CIO organized nascent unions that were still struggling to receive formal recognition from their employers, let alone power over their industry's profits. As Senator Robert Wagner observed, "technological changes doubled the productive capacity of the average worker between 1919 and 1933 ... But despite reassuring discourse about profit-sharing and employee participation in industry, the increasing size of business brought concentration of wealth in geometric ratio."[29]

In 1939, the CIO warned that increased American exports would lead to increased profits without increasing wages for workers. As CIO President John Lewis explained, "The danger is that while prices soar unchecked except by rhetoric, labor will find itself increasingly restrained in its attempts to adjust wages to the cost of living."[30] According to the traditional Ricardo-Viner approach, the CIO should have supported free trade policies that would simultaneously increase profits and wages for capital and labor, respectively. In direct contrast, Lewis actually argued for policies that would curtail the profitability of American export industries. Lewis called on the federal government to "take appropriate legislative and administrative steps to check and eliminate war time profiteering" and proclaimed that the CIO "favors the passage of effective tax legislation designed to reclaim the excess profits which result from war time conditions."[31] Underlying these preferences, perhaps, was Lewis'

[28] Congress of Industrial Organizations, 1938, 286.
[29] Keyserling 1945, 9.
[30] Congress of Industrial Organizations, 1939, 6.
[31] Congress of Industrial Organizations, 1939, 162.

belief that "working men and women in the US do not receive a fair share of the results of their own labor."[32]

In 1940, Lewis used the logic of relative gains to explain the dangers that labor faced if profits rose while wages remained stagnant. According to Lewis,

Labor must be ever vigilant to guard against any action which, under the pretense of furthering national defense, will seek to deprive the workers of their fair share of these increased earnings or to deny them their fundamental right to organize into unions of their own choice or to strike. The protection of these rights is necessary to assure the workers that they will not be relegated to a position of economic slavery.[33]

That same year, Lewis' concerns were echoed by the CIO's United Automobile Workers and the United Electrical Workers, both of which called on the federal government to control the profits made by their employers.[34]

Although Lewis supported the presidential election of Franklin Delano Roosevelt in 1932 and 1936, Lewis and the CIO withheld support from the Roosevelt administration's RTAA proposal. In contrast, export-oriented manufacturers lobbied in favor of free trade throughout the 1930s. The American Manufacturers Export Association, which included major exporting corporations from the steel, automobile, and electronics industries, began lobbying in favor of the RTAA when it was first proposed in 1934.[35] These manufacturers, however, lobbied alone; not a single labor union lobbied in favor of the RTAA in 1934. When Congress debated the renewal of the RTAA in 1940, the only labor union testimony came from the AFL, which openly opposed the RTAA and further trade liberalization.

In these ways, the CIO clearly disagreed with their employers and openly doubted the benefits that free trade would deliver for workers in America's mass-production industries. Such disagreement is consistent with my theory, which predicts that the absence of profit-sharing institutions would lead the CIO to disagree with their employers concerning trade policy. Although the CIO achieved a major victory when it won formal recognition from General Motors in 1937, the union was unable to establish profit-sharing institutions until further successful strikes and the signing of industry-wide contracts in the early 1940s.

---

32 Congress of Industrial Organizations, 1939, 172.
33 Congress of Industrial Organizations, 1940, 174.
34 Congress of Industrial Organizations, 1940, 218.
35 For a list of corporations active in the American Manufacturers Export Association, see American Manufacturers Export Association 1935.

The AFL's Trade Protectionism

The AFL officially maintained strict neutrality on the tariff starting in 1882. The unions affiliated with the AFL were often bitterly divided over the tariff question, and the Federation found official neutrality its best strategy for not alienating its members. However, the AFL did not bar its constitutive unions from taking a position on the tariff, many of which joined their employers and lobbied the Congress in favor of trade protectionism. As discussed in the previous chapter, the National Mule Spinners' Associations and the Amalgamated Association of Iron and Steel Workers, were both members of the AFL when they lobbied for high tariffs in the late nineteenth century. Although the AFL maintained its official neutrality during the early twentieth century, numerous AFL-affiliated unions consistently lobbied against trade liberalization and the RTAA.

Prominent amongst these protectionist labor unions were the pottery and glass workers' union, both of which maintained profit-sharing institutions during the late nineteenth and early twentieth centuries. The connection between profit-sharing institutions and capital-labor trade policy agreement was concisely explained by James Campbell, ex-President of the Glass Workers of America, who explained that "when there is tariff agitation there has always been a clause inserted in the scale that in case of a reduction of the tariff there will be a rearrangement of the wages. If there is an advance the workmen get an advance."[36] According to Gordon, a similar dynamic marked the pottery industry: "For the union, the National Brotherhood of Operative Potters, high tariffs meant high wages ... union and management cooperated closely in the maintenance of industry standards and shared the chore of presenting the industry's case at congressional tariff hearings."[37]

Following the Great Depression, the AFL's protectionist efforts were coordinated by a group known as America's Wage Earners' Protection Conference (AWEPC). The AWEPC was led by Matthew Woll, the chair of the AFL's Resolutions Committee and a member of the International Photo-Engravers Union. Woll provided AFL-affiliated unions with technical data concerning imports and exports and coordinated the lobbying of 17 separate unions, including the pottery and glass workers' unions discussed above.[38] Although the AWEPC was technically independent from the AFL, Woll's position as a vice-president of the AFL lent authority

---

[36] Quoted in Bensel 2000, 491.
[37] Gordon 1994, 114.
[38] Future research would be required to determine whether or not profit-sharing institutions were established in these other labor unions.

to the AWEPC's activities and led many to believe that the AFL endorsed high tariffs.[39]

Aided by the ambiguous division between the AWEPC and the AFL, Woll led protectionist unions into the logrolling coalition that produced the Smoot-Hawley tariff of 1930. While many decried the "disastrous" tariff schedules that resulted, Woll and the AWEPC lobbied for even greater protectionism just two years later. Testifying before the Senate Finance Committee in 1932, Woll argued that the Treasury Department should adjust import valuations to offset the effects of foreign currency depreciation, which cheapened the price of imported goods.[40] When the original RTAA was debated in 1934, all testimony from AFL-affiliated unions was opposed to the RTAA. According to the AWEPC's M.J. Flynn, an Executive Secretary of the AFL, RTAA passaged would mean that "hundreds of thousands of our industrial workers would necessarily be deprived of employment opportunities."[41] In the lead up to the RTAA renewal of 1940, William Green, the President of the AFL, sent a letter to the House Ways and Means Committee explaining that the Executive Council of the AFL opposed the renewal of the RTAA.[42]

In these ways, the trade policy preferences of the AFL and CIO are broadly consistent with the predictions of my theory. AFL craft unions – most clearly the pottery and glass unions – established profit-sharing institutions and joined their employers in favor of the high tariffs that protected their import-competing industries. CIO unions, still struggling for union recognition and lacking profit-sharing institutions, disagreed with their employers and argued that any benefits from free trade policies would be withheld from unskilled workers in America's export-oriented, mass-production industries.

THE WAGNER ACT AND PROFIT-SHARING INSTITUTIONS

This section explores how the pro-labor legislation associated with the New Deal contributed to the gradual creation of profit-sharing institutions in America's mass-production industries. The National Labor Relations Act of 1935, commonly referred to as the Wagner Act, gave labor unions new legal standing in America and greatly facilitated workers' efforts to organize unions. However, the process set into motion by the Wagner Act was a slow one. Early labor victories were matched by violent and brutal defeats, as the CIO slowly organized unskilled workers

---

39 Donohue 1992, 60–61.
40 Donohue 1992, 67.
41 Ways and Means Committee Tariff Hearing, 1934, 323.
42 Donohue 1992, 58–59.

in America's steel, automobile, and other mass-production industries. CIO-affiliated unions struggled throughout the late 1930s, gradually gaining union recognition, industry-wide contracts, and establishing a credible link between wages and their industry's profits. The AFL also benefited from the pro-labor legislation of the New Deal, organized over three million new union members from 1939 to 1945, and maintained the profit-sharing institutions discussed above. By the early 1940s, labor unions organized by both the AFL and CIO enjoyed the benefits of profit-sharing institutions and joined their employers in support of protection and free trade, respectively.

The process that led to the creation of profit-sharing institutions in America's mass-production industries began with the Wagner Act of 1935. Section 7 of the Act famously declared that,

Employees shall have the right of self-organization, to form, join, or assist labor organization, to bargain collectively through representatives of their own choosing, and to engage in other concerted activities for the purpose of collective bargaining or other mutual aid and protection.

According to Lichtenstein, a generation of unionists would soon declare the Wagner Act to be organized labor's "Magna Carta."[43] By protecting workers' right to unionize, the Wagner Act created a legal framework within which workers could increase their associational power, and thus develop the bargaining power necessary to force their employers to meet their demands. However, the Wagner Act was not an instantaneous shock that established profit-sharing institutions throughout the American economy. When workers first organized unions, appeal to the Wagner Act was crucial; once unions organized members and began to collectively bargain with their employers, unions relied on their own bargaining power without frequent appeal to the Wagner Act. This two-step effect of the Wagner Act on labor's bargaining power was clearly understood by the CIO. For instance, in 1941, CIO President Philip Murray explained that "[m]any of the CIO unions have achieved substantial recognition in their respective industries. This has eliminated any pressing need on the part of such unions to appeal to the Labor Board for protection." However, Murray went on to acknowledge that, "of course, there are still certain industries in which recalcitrant employers are attempting to deny their employees the rights guaranteed them under the Labor Act."[44]

With the aid of the Wagner Act, the CIO enjoyed major organizing victories in the automobile and steel industries during 1937. The CIO's

---

43 Lichtenstein 2003, 19.
44 Congress of Industrial Organizations 1941, 88–89.

United Automobile Workers (UAW) won the famous Flint sit-down strike against General Motors, gaining formal recognition for the union in February 1937. Less than a month later, the CIO's Steel Workers Organizing Committee (SWOC) gained formal recognition from U.S. Steel, America's largest steel producer, without workers even going on strike.[45] The accord with U.S. Steel not only ensured the existence of unionism in the American steel industry, but also provided "inestimable assistance" to the CIO in its efforts to organize other industries.[46]

However, these early victories over GM and U.S. Steel were accompanied by major CIO defeats elsewhere in the automobile and steel industries. Less than three months after General Motors recognized the UAW, the autoworkers' union faced violent opposition from the Ford Motor Company. In what would later be called the "Battle of the Overpass," UAW organizers pamphleting outside Ford's River Rouge complex near Detroit were beaten by private security guards. Just four days later, the steelworkers' union suffered violent repression during the "Little Steel Strike" against some of the industry's largest steel producers, including Bethlehem, Republic, Youngstown, and Inland Steel. It what is known as the "Memorial Day Massacre," ten steelworkers were killed by police officers guarding the Republic Steel Company's factory on the south side of Chicago. According to the federal government's LaFollete Commission, strikers were shot in the back while fleeing from the police.[47] Facing such violent repression, as well as the onset of the 1937 recession, the SWOC would go on to lose the "Little Steel Strike" of 1937. At the end of the year, the CIO's formal recognition in the steel industry was limited to the U.S. Steel Corporation.

The CIO slowly gained ground in 1938. The National Labor Review Board (NLRB) ruled in the CIO's favor in multiple cases related to the steel industry. The NLRB forced Republic Steel to reinstate strikers with back pay, called on Inland Steel to sign a contract with their employees, and demanded that Bethlehem Steel dismantle its company-dominated employee representation plan. With the gradual improvement of business conditions in 1938 and 1939, the SWOC won fifty-nine out of seventy-seven NLRB elections. By November 1940, the SWOC's President reported that the steelworkers' union had 250,000 dues-paying members.[48] Similar gains were made in the automobile industry, where the UAW won strikes at General Motors and Chrysler, thus securing wage increases and formal recognition to bargain on behalf of a growing

---

[45] Lauderbaugh 1976.
[46] Galenson 1960, 93.
[47] Galenson 1960, 102.
[48] Galenson 1960, 113.

number of autoworkers. By July 1940, the UAW reported a dues-paying membership of 294,000.[49]

The CIO then led a strike wave characterized by "great militancy and confidence" in the winter and spring of 1941.[50] In April 1941, the SWOC improved its contract with U.S. Steel and set a new wage pattern that spread throughout the steel industry in the subsequent months. The contract included a 10 cent per hour wage increase, increased vacations, extra pay for holiday work, and additional subsidiary benefits.[51] The CIO also won formal recognition from steel and automobile companies that had previously refused to bargain with the union. The SWOC entered into a written agreement with the "Little Steel" companies that had so badly defeated the union in 1937. As Gallenson explains, "with the important assistance of the federal government, the union had in six years succeeded in forcing the powerful steel industry to revise its labor policy."[52] When the SWOC formally reorganized as the United Steelworkers of America in May 1942, the union reported 660,000 members, 903 steel firms under contract, and 175 "union shop" agreements.[53] Similar triumphs were recorded by the UAW, which finally overcame employer opposition and gained a written contract from the Ford Motor Company in June 1941. The successful strike wave also led to wage increases in other export-oriented companies such as General Motors and General Electric.[54]

With the CIO's victories in the background, American labor relations underwent a major change with the onset of American involvement in World War II. In 1942, the federal government created the National War Labor Board, which sought to increase cooperation between capital and organized labor in order to ensure full industrial production for the war effort. The Labor Board instituted tripartite bargaining, established industry-wide wage contracts, and ordered frequent wage increases to maintain workers' peacetime standard of living, as well as to eliminate what President Roosevelt called "inequalities" and "substandards of living" in American industries. The wage benefits held out to American workers were substantial, and were therefore opposed by many employers. According to an editorial in *The New York Times*, the Labor Board's decision to help workers maintain their real wages as of January 1941, the highest ever achieved, "defies elementary logic and simple

---

[49] Galenson 1960, 177.
[50] Lichtenstein 2003, 46.
[51] Galenson 1960, 177.
[52] Galenson 1960, 118.
[53] Galenson 1960, 119.
[54] Lichtenstein 2003, 47.

arithmetic ... the new formula can only lead to economic disruption and a disastrous inflation."[55]

Concerns about wartime inflation were shared by the federal government. On April 27, 1942, Roosevelt announced that "stabilizing the cost of living will mean that wages in general can and should be kept at existing scales." In turn, the Labor Board decreed that workers' hourly wage rates should not increase by more than 15 percent, the amount that the cost of living had increased between January 1941 and May 1942. Despite these rules, workers' incomes grew rapidly during the war. As Seidman explains, "the board sought to control wage rates, not weekly earnings, so that the great bulk of workers improved their living standards even though some failed to keep pace in straight-time hourly rates with the cost of living."[56] As weekly hours of work increased throughout the war, workers with opportunities for overtime earnings did particularly well, as the Fair Labor Standard Act mandated time-and-a-half pay for such work. The Labor Board also mandated hourly wage rate increases for the "lower wage bracket," including women and minorities, "which might be regarded as inadequate to produce decent standards of living."[57] With the help of the Labor Board, between January 1941 and July 1945 real weekly earnings for manufacturing employees increased by approximately 28 percent.[58]

Even more important than these wage gains, however, was the Labor Board's explicit commitment to establishing powerful and permanent labor unions in America's mass-production industries. In exchange for a "no-strike pledge," the Board bolstered CIO-affiliated unions through two different mechanisms. First, the Board mandated "maintenance of membership" agreements, which stipulated that employees that are members of a union at the time a contract is negotiated, or who subsequently join, must remain members of the union until the contract expires. Although the Board allowed for a fifteen-day window in which workers could withdraw from labor unions, few workers exercised this option, thus amounting to a virtual union shop.[59] In addition, a "dues checkoff" system bound employers to withhold union dues from their workers' paychecks and to pay the membership dues directly to the union. With these new funds, the CIO was able to launch organizing drives throughout the country, including previously non-unionized

---

[55] Quoted in Seidman 1953, 114.
[56] Seidman 1953, 129.
[57] National War Labor Board 1942, 7.
[58] Nominal weekly earnings rose 70 percent while the cost of living increased by roughly one-third, see Seidman 1953, 129.
[59] Lichtenstein 2003, 80 fn. 33.

regions where war production plants were located, such as Texas and Southern California. CIO membership almost doubled during the war years, and overall the unionized sector of the workforce increased from 9.5 to 14.8 million.[60] Looking back on this system, which harbored massive increases in unions' membership and treasuries, the United Steelworkers' accountant described the Labor Board's policy as "manna from heaven."[61]

The Labor Board's commitment to building and maintaining permanent labor unions, or "union security," was on clear display in 1942, when the Board ruled on a case between the United Steelworkers of America and several large steel corporations. It began by recalling the violent history of labor repression in the steel industry,

There is found in this long and bitter struggle ground for the fear of the steel workers concerning the security of their union ... The Corporation became master of the hours, wages and working conditions of the workers as individuals. The unions, decisively beaten, retreated on all the steel fronts. Collective bargaining by steel workers had to wait many years for another day. Meantime scars of past industrial wars remained deep. Workers' memories in the steel towns included terrorism and counter terrorism, mass picketing and mass smear hysteria, jailing of union leaders, injunctions, suppression of meetings of workers and their civil liberties, discriminations against union members, espionage, blacklists, discharges, evictions, muster of company guards, Pinkerton levies, imported strike breakers and the state militia.[62]

Given this bloody record, the Board advocated "more definite provisions for the freedom and security of the union" including "a voluntarily accepted binding maintenance of membership and check-off as definite assurances of good will and mutual cooperation for all-out production to win the war."[63]

With the Labor Board's support, CIO-affiliated unions blossomed during the war and organized roughly one-and-a-half million new industrial workers from 1941 to 1945.[64] At the end of the war, American union density reached an unprecedented peak of 35 percent – a height not reached in any year since. Although the Labor Board's support required the CIO not to launch strikes during the war, the CIO used these years to build up membership and strike funds that it then unleashed in a massive strike wave in 1945–1946. As a result of this new labor power, the

[60] Lichtenstein 2003, 81.
[61] Lichtenstein 2003, 81.
[62] National War Labor Board 1942, 26.
[63] National War Labor Board 1942, 26–27.
[64] Tomlins 1979, 1,023.

postwar period was based on a "treaty" between workers and employers that sought to broadly distribute the gains from growth.[65]

During the late 1930s and early 1940s, the CIO gradually established profit-sharing institutions. CIO-affiliated unions were formally recognized by major steel and automobile firms as early as 1937, and slowly established industry-wide wage contracts after a successful strike wave in 1941. With the creation of the National War Labor Board in 1942, the CIO was assured that the government would systematically pressure manufacturing firms to share the benefits of industrial growth with workers. The average real incomes of manufacturing workers rose and the CIO established previously unheard of fringe benefits, such as paid vacations, for unskilled industrial workers. In addition, CIO unions were granted "union security" agreements that harbored unprecedented increases in membership and union revenue. By the early 1940s, powerful new CIO unions in the steel, automobile, and other mass-production industries had finally established profit-sharing institutions.

WORKERS' TRADE POLICY PREFERENCES IN THE 1940S

As predicted by my theory, the creation of profit-sharing institutions in America's export-oriented, mass-production industries led the CIO to agree with their employers concerning trade policy and to join them in support of free trade. This marked a clear change in the CIO's trade policy preferences. During the late 1930s, the CIO disagreed with their employers and openly expressed skepticism and doubt about the benefits of free trade. After the creation of profit-sharing institutions in the early 1940s, however, it regularly lobbied alongside their employers in favor of American trade liberalization. The AFL, on the other hand, did not experience a change in profit-sharing institutions during this time period and therefore did not change its trade policy preferences. The AFL maintained profit-sharing institutions during the 1930s, and joined their employers in favor of the high tariffs that protected their import-competing industries. Bolstered by the pro-labor legislation of the New Deal, the AFL maintained profit-sharing institutions in the late 1930s and early 1940s, and therefore continued to agree with their employers and support high tariffs.

---

[65] Levy and Temin (2010). For a recent account of how the Taft-Hartley Act rolled back many of these labor gains, see Farhang and Katznelson 2005.

The CIO's New Support for Free Trade

The CIO's skepticism concerning free trade faded in the early 1940s and was soon replaced by consistent support for trade liberalization and renewal of the RTAA. Newly empowered CIO unions achieved formal recognition, negotiated industry-wide contracts, and took part in tripartite wage negotiations with representatives from capital and the state. This creation of profit-sharing institutions was followed by a corresponding change in trade policy preferences. In 1939, the CIO explained its doubts about the RTAA by citing that workers did not receive a "fair share" of their labor. In 1943, the CIO explained its support for the RTAA by proclaiming that free trade is "accompanied by an increase of domestic employment, national income, and general well-being."[66]

The CIO's changing trade policy preferences suggest a fundamental change in how the union viewed their prospects of sharing in their industry's profits. In the late 1930s, the CIO explicitly denied that workers shared in their employers' profits. As noted above, the CIO went as far as to call on the government to expropriate excess profits from their employers. By the mid-1940s, the CIO's profit-sharing institutions made the distinction between the plight of workers and the plight of employers seem to fade away. In 1945, the CIO advocated trade liberalization on the straightforward grounds that it has "direct benefit to the industries which employ our members."[67] The CIO's endorsement of free trade stuck, and by 1951 CIO leader Stanley Ruttenberg explained that, "the CIO has supported the reciprocal trade agreement program for many years. The reasons for this support are, therefore, sufficiently well known to make a detailed restatement at this time unnecessary."[68]

After the CIO's conversion to free trade, the labor federation set out to convince the public, as well as protectionist Republicans, of the benefits of RTAA renewal. As early as 1943, the CIO announced that "without world trade, America's huge production machine will rot, and millions of people will lack jobs and rot with it."[69] Two years later, the CIO testified before the House Ways and Means Committee and aggressively lobbied in favor of the RTAA.[70] For example, in June of 1945, Secretary-Treasurer of the CIO, James B. Carey, "tangled" with Robert Taft (R-Ohio) before

---

[66] J. Raymond Walsh, Director of Research, CIO, Ways and Means Committee, 1943, 1069.

[67] Irving Richter, United Autoworkers, Ways and Means Committee, 1945, 981.

[68] Rupert 1995, 185.

[69] *CIO News*, quoted in Rupert 1995, 45–46.

[70] House Committee on Ways and Means, and Senate Committee on Finance, 1945 Extension of the Reciprocal Trade Agreements Act, 79th Congress, 1st Session.

the Senate Banking Committee. While Taft maintained that the RTAA would damage American industry, Carey argued that it would benefit American workers by contributing to "an expansion to double or triple 1940 exports."[71] Although Taft – the "kingpin of the coalition" against the RTAA – was unpersuaded, the CIO seems to have found a more receptive audience with Taft's Ohio colleague, Senator Harold Burton, who voted in favor of RTAA renewal.[72]

The effectiveness of CIO lobbying can also be gleaned from debates on the Senate floor, where Republican senators explained their new support for the RTAA. According to Howard Smith (R-New Jersey), who voted in favor of the RTAA, he was "encouraged and fortified in the soundness of this position by the actions of many outstanding groups," including "executives of both the American Federation of Labor and the Congress of Industrial Organizations."[73] Although it is difficult to evaluate the national effectiveness of CIO lobbying through such qualitative analysis, it is clear that the CIO actively lobbied in favor of RTAA renewal and that Republican senators were aware of its position.

The AFL's Continued Protectionism

In 1943, an explicit disagreement between the AFL and the AWEPC further complicated the Federation's position on the tariff. In a sudden change of position, President Green of the AFL testified before the House Ways and Means Committee in support of the RTAA and further trade liberalization. Surprised by the AFL's new position, Thomas Jenkins (R-OH) accused Green of misrepresenting the AFL's stance on the RTAA. Jenkins asked, "Mr. Green, I should like to ask you, is this your annual meeting statement? Is this a statement that has been approved by your great organization?"[74] In response, Green acknowledged that he spoke on his own authority as President, but without the official authorization of the AFL. Jenkins then asserted that the National Brotherhood of Potters, as well as other AFL-affiliated unions, had previously testified that the AFL had not endorsed the RTAA. Additionally, Jenkins read into the official record of the hearing a list of AFL-affiliated unions, purported

---

71 *The Spokesman Review*, June 5, 1945.
72 Although Burton joined the CIO in supporting RTAA renewal in 1945, he also co-sponsored the anti-labor Ball-Burton-Hatch Bill which would have abolished the NLRB, see Northrup 1946.
73 *Congressional Record*, June 13, 1945. As noted below, William Green and Daniel Tobin, both executives of the AFL, did testify in favor of the RTAA in 1943 and 1945. However, the bulk of AFL-affiliated unions that testified were opposed to the RTAA.
74 Donohue 1992, 57–58.

to represent 1.5 million workers, that opposed the renewal of the RTAA in 1940. Despite Green's personal policy preferences, the AFL very much remained affiliated with the cause of protectionism. As Peter Donohue explains, the AWEPC's lobbying efforts were effective in "confusing everyone as to whether the views expressed were those of the AFL."[75]

If Green's testimony left doubt concerning where the AFL stood on the RTAA, the union's position was quickly clarified in 1945. In the tariff hearings before the House Ways and Means Committee, as well as the Senate Finance Committee, a group of AFL-affiliated unions testified against the RTAA. Led by Woll and the AWEPC, AFL unions from the watch, glass, lace, and pottery industries all opposed a reduction of tariffs.[76] Walter Cenerazzo, from the AFL's American Watch Workers' Union, explicitly drew attention to the difference of opinion between the protectionist AFL and the pro-trade CIO. Cenerazzo pled with the Ways and Means Committee, "I ask you, gentlemen, to contrast this petition and this plea for economic protection of jobs for American workers against the plea made last Saturday by the CIO representative."[77] For any politician paying attention to the 1945 hearings on RTAA renewal, the message was clear: the CIO endorsed the RTAA while the AFL was dominated by a vociferous faction of highly protectionist unions opposed to the RTAA.

In these ways, the American labor movement was internally divided concerning international trade policy. The AFL joined their employers in favor of high tariffs, while the CIO joined their employers in favor of free trade. However, underlying these harmonious cross-class coalitions was years, if not decades, of violent conflict between capital and labor concerning the distribution of profits. As described above, AFL unions did not join their employers in favor of high tariffs until they were painstakingly able to establish profit-sharing institutions in the late nineteenth and early twentieth centuries. Similarly, the CIO unions did not join their employers in favor of free trade until the pro-labor legislation associated with the New Deal and World War II slowly helped unskilled workers develop the associational power necessary to establish profit-sharing institutions in the early 1940s.

The CIO's change in trade policy preferences is clearly consistent with the predictions of my theory of profit-sharing institutions. However, the CIO's trade policy preferences might have also been influenced by several other factors including changes in union leadership, the onset of American

---

[75] Donohue 1992, 80.
[76] One AFL leader, the Teamsters' Daniel Tobin, testified in favor of the RTAA.
[77] Ways and Means Committee, Tariff Hearing, 1945, 1105.

fighting in World War II, and their strategic decision to embrace partisan politics. In terms of union leadership, the CIO underwent an influential change during this period. Since the CIO's first President, John Lewis, was an outspoken critic of free trade, his replacement by Philip Murray may have played a role in the CIO's endorsement of free trade. In terms of the war effort, CIO leaders often endorsed free trade while also speaking of America's new hegemonic role in the world. Finally, the CIO's support for free trade coincided with its open embrace of partisan politics. The CIO created a political action committee during the mid-1940s and aligned closely with the Democratic party. It is possible that the CIO supported the RTAA – a key piece of Democratic legislation – as a political exchange for the favorable treatment of labor.[78]

Admittedly, it is difficult to discern between these various explanations for the CIO's change in trade policy preferences. Lewis founded the CIO, and held enormous influence over the nascent industrial unions organized in the late 1930s. However, CIO-affiliated unions displayed a clear ability to defy Lewis' political opinions. For example, in 1940, Lewis opposed Roosevelt's decision to seek a third term as President, and backed the Republican candidate, Wendell Wilkie. Lewis's gambit was a complete failure, as most of the major industrial unions endorsed Roosevelt and the overwhelming majority of CIO-organized workers voted for his reelection.[79] Moreover, Lewis resigned from the CIO presidency in 1941, two years before the CIO appears to have first endorsed the RTAA in 1943. If Lewis was singlehandedly stopping the CIO from endorsing free trade, we should expect the CIO to have endorsed the RTAA earlier.

With regard to American involvement in World War II, as well as labor's partisan strategies, it is helpful to compare the CIO to the AFL during the early 1940s. While the AFL and CIO both supported the war, and both formed political alliances with the Democratic party, the AFL did not endorse the RTAA during this period. At the very least, this suggests that labor's commitment to the war effort and the Democratic party were not sufficient conditions for labor to support free trade. While the analysis is unable to control for the myriad factors that influenced American politics during the war, this chapter has presented suggestive evidence that the CIO's change in trade policy preferences resulted from the creation of profit-sharing institutions. Regardless of the exact reasons for the CIO's trade policy shift, however, we are left with the intriguing question of whether or not the union's changed policy

[78] Donohue 1992.
[79] Lichtenstein 2003, 31.

preferences influenced actual trade policy outcomes. It is to this question that this chapter now turns.

AMERICAN TRADE LIBERALIZATION FOLLOWING WORLD WAR II

The CIO disagreed with their employers concerning trade policy during the late 1930s, arguing that the benefits of free trade would be withheld from workers. Starting in 1943, the CIO changed its position and joined their employers in favor of free trade. Did this change in the CIO's trade policy preferences influence American trade policy in the subsequent years? In order to answer this question, this section focuses on the 1945 renewal of the RTAA, a key piece of legislation that facilitated American trade liberalization after World War II.[80] It uses an original dataset on state-level CIO power to demonstrate that the "CIO conversion" to free trade led to an increase in U.S. Senate support for the RTAA.

While American labor unions became major political forces in the 1950s and 1960s, there are numerous reasons to doubt the CIO's ability to influence trade policy outcomes in 1945. The CIO was less than a decade old and had little experience coordinating political activity or lobbying the government. Moreover, the CIO represented a mass of unskilled workers, a body of citizens which seldom influence American government policy. As Gilens explains, "The American government does respond to the public's preferences, but that responsiveness is strongly tilted towards the most affluent citizens."[81] Most importantly, the voluminous literature on American trade liberalization during this period fails to acknowledge the important role that the "CIO conversion" to free trade played in securing bipartisan support for American trade liberalization.[82]

The remainder of this chapter is organized in the following way. First, it reviews the literature on the RTAA and American trade liberalization. Second, it presents a simple argument for why CIO support for free trade would have influenced Senate voting on the RTAA. Third, it describes the quantitative data used in the analysis, including original data on state-level CIO density that I collected from the annual meeting minutes of CIO-affiliated unions. Fourth, it presents the results of quantitative analysis of U.S. Senate voting on the 1945 renewal of the RTAA. Finally,

---

[80] Weingast et al. 1981; Bailey et al. 1997.

[81] Gilens 2012, 1.

[82] Weingast et al. 1981; Goldstein 1993; Shepsle and Weingast 1995; Bailey et al. 1997; Gilligan 1997; Hiscox 1999; Irwin and Kroszner 1999; Destler 2005; Goldstein and Gulotty 2014.

it concludes with a brief summary of the chapter's overall argument concerning profit-sharing institutions and American trade liberalization.

Debating the Causes of American Trade Liberalization

There is broad scholarly agreement that the RTAA was a major cause of American trade liberalization after World War II. The literature points to four ways in which this institutional reform fostered trade liberalization. First, Shepsle argues that the RTAA removed the tariff schedule from the control of Congress, where the tendency to form logrolling coalitions had previously contributed to high tariffs.[83] Second, Weingast argues that the RTAA delegated trade policy making to the President, who, by virtue of representing a national constituency, is expected to pursue a more liberal trade policy that benefits the nation as a whole.[84] Third, Bailey, Goldstein, and Weingast argue that the RTAA decreased the number of Senate votes needed to approve tariff reduction agreements negotiated by the President. Before the RTAA, such agreements required a two-thirds majority, whereas after the RTAA, they could be ratified with only a simple majority of senators in favor of free trade.[85] Fourth, Gilligan argues that the RTAA linked foreign tariff reduction to the lowering of domestic tariff levels and therefore provided new incentives for export-oriented industries to lobby for free trade.[86]

For all four of these reasons, it is reasonable to believe that American trade liberalization would have continued as long as the RTAA remained in place. But what allowed the RTAA to stay in place throughout the postwar decades? As Hiscox and others have argued, the RTAA faced vehement opposition from protectionist Republican senators throughout the 1930s.[87] After decades as the "Party of Protection," few Republicans were prepared to support a bill that would facilitate the lowering of American tariffs. In fact, only 8 percent of Republicans in the House and Senate voted in favor of the original RTAA in 1934. Two years later, the GOP's election platform of 1936 promised to "repeal the present reciprocal trade agreement law."[88] In 1937 and 1940, the percentage of Republican representatives supporting RTAA extension dropped to only 3 percent. In 1943 not a single Republican Senator voted in favor of the RTAA.[89] At that point in American history, it would have seemed obvious

[83] Shepsle and Weingast 1995.
[84] Weingast et al. 1981.
[85] Bailey et al. 1997.
[86] Gilligan 1997.
[87] Hiscox 1999; Irwin and Kroszner 1999.
[88] Quoted in Irwin and Kroszner 1999, 650.
[89] Hiscox 1999, 676.

Table 5.2. *Senate Votes on the RTAA, 1934 and 1945*

	RTAA Passage, June 4, 1934			RTAA Renewal, June 20, 1945		
	Yea	Nay	Total	Yea	Nay	Total
Democrats	53 (91%)	5 (9%)	58 (62%)	45 (87%)	7 (13%)	52 (59%)
Republicans	6 (17%)	30 (83%)	36 (38%)	15 (42%)	21 (58%)	36 (41%)
Total	59 (63%)	35 (37%)	94 (100%)	60 (68%)	36 (32%)	96 (100%)

Sources – 3d Cong., 2d Sess., 78, pt. 10 Cong. Rec. 10,395 (June 4, 1934); and 79th Cong., 1st Sess., 91, pt. 5 Cong. Rec. 6364 (June 20, 1945), presented in Irwin and Kroszner 1999, 650.

that the RTAA would die as soon as Republicans achieved a majority in the House or Senate.

However, after decades of opposition to free trade, Republicans rapidly came to support free trade in the mid-1940s. In the 1945 vote to renew the RTAA, nearly half of all Republican senators voted in favor of the RTAA. Three years later, the Republican party's election platform of 1948 stated that "[W]e shall support the system of reciprocal trade."[90] During the 1940s and 1950s, Republicans joined Democrats to establish bipartisan support that sustained further trade liberalization. For this reason, scholars have argued that the real puzzle of American trade liberalization is why the Republican party came to support the RTAA starting in 1945. As Irwin and Kroszner explain, "The conversion of the Republicans, who could have abolished the RTAA when they returned to power, was crucial to the stability and durability of this institutional change."[91] The "Republican conversion," and general bipartisan support for the RTAA renewal of 1945, is displayed in Table 5.2. In 1934, only 17 percent of Republicans voted for the RTAA. By 1945, 42 percent of Republicans voted in favor of RTAA renewal.

For Irwin and Kroszner, the key to explaining this "Republican conversion" to free trade lies in the rapid growth of export-oriented industries. The basic argument is that World War II destroyed the foreign competition that American industry had previously faced and thus gave them the ability to compete in international markets. A

[90] Quoted in Irwin and Kroszner 1999, 645.
[91] Irwin and Kroszner 1999, 645.

similar argument is made by Hiscox who explains that, "these changes reflected the dramatic, *exogenous* effects of World War II on U.S. export and import-competing industries as well as longer-term shifts in U.S. comparative advantage and in party constituencies."[92] In short, these scholars argue that the rise of American export industries led to growing constituent demands for free trade, and that previously protectionist Republicans eventually capitulated. The key turning point was the RTAA renewal of 1945, when a large percentage of Republican senators first voted in favor of the RTAA.[93] In this way, the long debate over American trade liberalization has progressively narrowed to a debate over why Republicans began to support free trade during the RTAA renewal vote of 1945.

Undeniably, the shock of World War II and the rise of American export-oriented industries was a crucial part of the Republican conversion and the survival of the RTAA. However, I argue that previous work on the topic suffers from key theoretical and methodological errors that obscure the important role played by profit-sharing institutions and the CIO's conversion to free trade. Theoretically, work by Hiscox, as well as Irwin and Kroszner, incorrectly assumes that workers automatically join their employers in favor of the same trade policy. As seen throughout this book, this assumption is unwarranted when workers lack profit-sharing institutions. It is, therefore, a theoretical mistake to assume that all workers in export-oriented industries joined their employers in favor of free trade in 1945. We know that the CIO established profit-sharing institutions in major mass-production industries during the early 1940s, but the CIO's coverage varied widely across the United States.

For example, the CIO was incredibly strong in states such as Pennsylvania and Michigan, where it organized 37 and 51 percent of all manufacturing workers, respectively. It is therefore reasonable to assume that CIO union members in export-oriented industries in these states joined their employers in favor of free trade. In contrast, the CIO was exceedingly weak in states such as California and Texas, where it organized an average of 6 percent of all manufacturing workers. In states where the CIO was so weak, workers in export-oriented industries likely lacked profit-sharing institutions and therefore should be presumed to have disagreed with their employers concerning the benefits of free trade. In other words, in states where export-oriented industries were strong, but the CIO was weak, capital would have lobbied the government for free trade without assistance from their workers. For

---

[92] Hiscox 1999. Italics in original.
[93] Hiscox 1999; Irwin and Kroszner 1999.

these reasons, the importance of the CIO's endorsement of free trade can only be appreciated once we acknowledge that workers in export-oriented industries do not automatically support free trade.

Methodologically, past work has mistakenly used measures of industrial activity as a proxy measure for the trade policy demands of both capital and labor. For instance, Irwin and Kroszner use a state-level measure of exports as a proxy for the free trade demands of capital and labor in that state. Clearly, this measure mistakenly assumes that workers join their employers in favor of the same trade policy regardless of the labor market conditions that they face. When these scholars find that the size of a state's exports is a significant predictor of U.S. Senate support for the RTAA, there is no way of discerning whether or not this influence was due to successful lobbying by capital, labor, or a cross-class coalition of both. In short, previous scholars overlook the CIO's role in the RTAA renewal because of the mistaken neoclassical assumption that workers automatically join their employers in favor of the same trade policy.

At the heart of my argument is a simple theory of senators' voting behavior. Senators seek reelection by satisfying the demands of their constituents. Satisfying capital can attract helpful campaign donations and information, while satisfying organized labor can attract much-needed votes. All else being equal, senators are more likely to vote for policies that are supported by broad coalitions of both capital and labor.[94] In this straightforward way, labor's conversion to free trade in the early 1940s added political weight to their employers' ongoing demands for free trade. Where export-oriented manufacturers were joined by pro-trade labor unions, senators were more likely to vote for free trade. Where export-manufacturers continued to lobby without the assistance of pro-trade unions, senators were less likely to vote for free trade.

QUANTITATIVE ANALYSIS

This section uses quantitative methods to test my argument that the CIO's support for free trade increased Senate support for the RTAA and American trade liberalization. The main empirical contribution stems from the use of an original dataset on state-level CIO union density. Importantly, this new data permits me to differentiate between the trade policy demands of capital, on the one hand, and the trade policy demands of a cross-class coalition of capital and labor, on the other. The analysis ultimately demonstrates that the "CIO conversion" to free trade led

---

[94] Hansen 1991.

to a cross-class coalition of capital and labor that successfully lobbied Republican senators in favor of the RTAA renewal of 1945.

As discussed above, the AFL and CIO both lobbied the government during debates over the 1945 renewal of the RTAA. Some senators explicitly mentioned such labor union lobbying when explaining the position they took on the 1945 vote. While such qualitative evidence suggests that senators were aware of AFL and CIO demands, it remains unclear whether or not labor's trade policy demands actually influenced these senators. This section, therefore, uses quantitative methods to systematically evaluate the relationship between labor's trade policy preferences and RTAA voting in the U.S. Senate.

The analysis tests two related hypotheses. First, since the CIO favored free trade and the renewal of the RTAA, CIO union density should have a positive effect on Senate support for renewal of the RTAA. This leads to the following hypothesis:

Hypotheses 1. *CIO union density is positively associated with the probability of a Senator voting in favor of RTAA renewal in 1945.*

Second, in 1945 the AFL contained protectionist unions that adamantly opposed free trade and the RTAA. Although some national AFL leaders may have personally favored the RTAA, I expect that the protectionist demands of the AFL's constitutive unions would have had a more important effect on the voting behavior of senators. This leads to the following hypothesis:

Hypotheses 2. *AFL union density is negatively associated with the probability of a Senator voting in favor of RTAA renewal in 1945.*

In order to test these hypotheses, I developed a dataset that includes original data on state-level CIO union density, as well as existing data on the industrial characteristics of each state.

Dependent and Independent Variables

The main focus of this analysis is to explain Senate voting on the 1945 renewal of the RTAA. The dependent variable therefore takes the value of one for a vote in favor of the RTAA and zero otherwise.[95] The main independent variable is the state-level density of CIO unions. In order to compile original data on state-level CIO membership, I culled through the annual meeting minutes of the CIO's five largest unions: United Electrical

---

[95] Senators who abstained from voting are coded as 0. However, the results reported below are also robust to dropping all abstaining senators.

Workers (UE), United Steelworkers (USW), United Autoworkers (UAW), Textile Workers' Union of America (TWUA), and the American Clothing Workers' Union (ACWA). Prior to this data collection, the only existing statistics on American state-level union density were limited to the years 1939 and 1953.[96]

Although the CIO meeting minutes do not report actual union membership at the state level, they do include the information necessary to construct such an estimate. First, each union reports its national membership. Second, each union reports a voting procedure and the number of delegates allotted to each local union, based on their number of dues-paying members. The number of delegates can then be aggregated to the state level in order to calculate the percentage of union members affiliated with each state. For example, if the local UAW lodges from Michigan were collectively allotted 300 out of 1,000 national delegates, then Michigan is estimated to have 30 percent of the UAW's national union membership. The total number of union members from each of the five largest CIO unions are then added together to create an estimate of CIO union members at the state level. The total number of CIO union members is then divided by the number of manufacturing workers employed in the state in order to calculate CIO union density at the state level, or *CIO*. In total, I gathered data on 1,057 local union delegations.

Where the CIO was strong in 1945, workers enjoyed profit-sharing institutions and joined their export-oriented employers in favor of free trade. The result was a large cross-class coalition of capital and labor in favor of free trade. Where the CIO was weak, workers lacked profit-sharing institutions and were less likely to join their export-oriented employers in favor of free trade. The result was a group of export-oriented employers lobbying for free trade without assistance from their workers. For these reasons, I argue that *CIO* serves as a proxy measure for the size of the cross-class coalition of capital and labor in favor of free trade in each state.

The regression models presented below also include *Imports* and *Exports*, both of which measure the relative importance of exports and imports for each state.[97] States with high values of *Exports* have economies that contain relatively large export-oriented industries and therefore large groups of employers favoring free trade. For example, Michigan was a relatively large industrial exporter in 1945, and is therefore assumed to have had an influential group of manufacturers

---

[96] Data on AFL and CIO union density in these two years is available from Troy 1957.
[97] Both variables were constructed by Irwin and Kroszner using data from the Bureau of Economic Analysis and the *Census of Manufacturers*.

that favored free trade. Including *Exports* and *CIO* in the same model therefore enables us to differentiate between the trade policy demands of capital and labor. Holding *CIO* constant, *Exports* represents the effect of capital lobbying for free trade. In contrast, holding *Exports* constant, *CIO* represents the effect of joint capital-labor lobbying in favor of free trade.

The new data on CIO density therefore allows for major methodological improvements over previous work. For instance, Irwin and Kroszner use state-level measures of imports and exports as proxy measures for the joint trade policy demands of capital and labor. An increase in exports is interpreted as an increase in the free trade demands of both capital and labor; an increase in imports is interpreted as an increase in the protectionist demands of both capital and labor. This line of reasoning is based on the neoclassical assumption that the benefits of trade policy are automatically shared between capital and labor, and that workers and employers automatically form a harmonious cross-class coalition in favor of the same trade policy. In contrast, my new measure of CIO density provides a far superior measure of capital and labor demands in favor of free trade. Rather than assuming that labor automatically joins capital, my measure merely assumes that once workers support the trade policy that benefits their industry, capital will join workers in favor of the same trade policy.[98]

To clarify this important difference, consider trade politics in the American automobile industry. In 1947, Michigan and California were the United States' two largest producers and exporters of automobiles and transportation equipment. It is reasonable to assume that both states contained large groups of automobile manufacturers in favor of free trade. However, the strength of the CIO, and therefore the prevalence of profit-sharing institutions, varied enormously between these two states. In Michigan, the United Automobile Workers (UAW) organized roughly 600,000 autoworkers; overall, the CIO organized 51 percent of the state's manufacturing workers. In contrast, the CIO had the smallest of footholds in California in 1945. The UAW organized 20,000 autoworkers and, overall, the CIO only organized 5 percent of the state's manufacturing workers. If we use *Exports* to measure joint capital-labor demands for free trade then we ignore the enormous difference in labor market institutions between Michigan and California. Irwin and Kroszner implicitly assume that California's workers (without

---

[98] Even if *CIO* only captures the strength of the CIO in each state, without capturing the joint strength of a capital-labor coalition, the analysis still clearly demonstrates that labor's trade policy preferences have an important impact on trade policy outcomes.

profit-sharing institutions) were just as likely as Michigan's workers (with profit-sharing institutions) to join their employers in favor of free trade. In contrast, the *CIO* variable enables us to predict that capital and labor were more likely to form a cross-class coalition in favor of free trade in CIO-dominated Michigan than in CIO-weak California.

The stark difference between export-oriented industries and the strength of the CIO is displayed below in Figure 5.1.[99] These maps help demonstrate that many of the states that contained large export-oriented industries often lacked strong CIO unions. For example, Wyoming, Oklahoma, Texas, California, and Kansas were amongst the most export-oriented states, but contained almost no CIO presence. Seven out of the ten senators representing these five states voted against the RTAA in 1945, despite the free trade interests of employers in these states.[100]

Control Variables

The model includes various control variables to address alternative explanations of Senate voting on the RTAA. First, the model includes the *Imports* and *Exports* variables constructed by Irwin and Kroszner. As discussed above, once measures of union density are included in the model, *Imports* and *Exports* represent the trade policy demands of capital without assistance from workers. Second, the model includes *Ideology* in order to control for the past voting behavior of each senator. I use Poole and Rosenthal's D-Nominate spatial mapping of legislators onto a left-right spectrum ranging from -1 to 1. This allows me to control for the possibility that senators' trade policy voting was influenced by a general ideological shift towards free trade after the Great Depression.[101] Third, to control for the possibility that voting was determined by a senator's affiliation with the Democrat or Republican parties, the model also includes *Party*. Fourth, the model includes *Manufacturing* which measures each state's total manufacturing employment. The inclusion of this variable helps ensure that CIO union density is not simply a proxy measure for the size of each state's industrial output. This data is available from the *Handbook of Labor Statistics*.[102]

---

99 The Pearson correlation between *Export* and *CIO* is only 0.12.

100 As can be seen in Figures 5.1(a), the state of Utah had a surprisingly high density of CIO unions in 1945. This estimate resulted from Utah having a large number of delegates at the United Steelworkers annual meeting of 1945, and a small number of total manufacturing workers in the state. The regression results are unchanged by dropping the two observations from Utah.

101 Pastor 1983.

102 United States Bureau of Labor Statistics 1979.

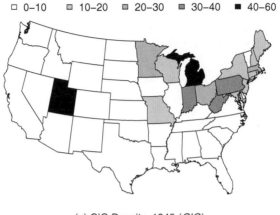

(a) CIO Density, 1945 (*CIO*)

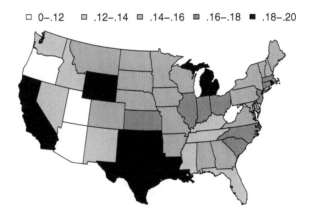

(b) Export Shares, 1947 (*Export*)

Figure 5.1. CIO Density and Export Shares

Additional Measures of Union Density

In addition to the original measure of CIO density, the analysis below includes data on the strength of the AFL and other unions. Unfortunately, data on state-level union density is almost non-existent during this period; the only available measures are for the years 1939 and 1953, respectively. This limited data was collected by Leo Troy in 1957, and contains information on the AFL, the CIO, unaffiliated unions, and total union density. To calculate estimates of union density for 1945, I have simply taken the mean of each measure from 1939 and 1953.[103] The resulting

[103] Troy 1957.

variables – *AFL.Troy*, *CIO.Troy*, *Unaffiliated.Troy*, and *Total.Troy* – are included in the models reported below in Table 5.4.

This alternative measure has two important limitations. First, union growth across the United States did not follow a perfectly linear trend between 1939 and 1953. Therefore the mean of these two measures may not accurately represent union density in 1945. Second, there were significant changes in union affiliations between 1939 and 1953. For example, in 1939, one of the largest labor unions in the country, the United Mine Workers (UMW), was affiliated with the CIO. By 1953, the UMW was independent – that is, not affiliated with the CIO or the AFL. In this way, Troy's estimates of unaffiliated union members in 1939 and 1953 likely represent workers in different sets of unions. Therefore, the mean density of unaffiliated unions in 1939 and 1953 may not accurately represent the density of unaffiliated union in 1945.

There is currently no way to address the first limitation, regarding the lack of state-level union data for the AFL and unaffiliated unions in 1945. However, the second limitation, regarding the measure of unaffiliated unions, can be partially addressed econometrically. Since Troy collected data on total union membership, this can be used alongside my new measure of CIO density to indirectly measure the effect of AFL density on Senate voting. The key insight is that the AFL and CIO, respectively, organized the vast majority of American labor union members during this period.[104] Therefore, an increase in total union density, while keeping CIO union density constant, likely represents an increase in AFL union density. By including both *Total.Troy* and *CIO* in the model, the coefficient on *Total.Troy* therefore estimates the effect of AFL union density on Senate voting.

Main Results

In order to systematically examine the determinants of Senate voting, I employ a probit voting model of the 1945 Senate vote on the renewal of the RTAA. Table 5.3 reports the estimated coefficients from various model specifications in which the dependent variable is one for a vote in favor of the RTAA and zero otherwise.[105] Model 1 starts by only including the measure of a senator's ideological disposition. The negative and statistically significant coefficient on *Ideology* means that more "liberal" senators were more likely to vote in favor of the RTAA.

---

[104] In 1939, the AFL and CIO organized 87 percent on all unionized workers. By 1953, the AFL and CIO organized 90 percent.

[105] The votes are taken from 79th Congress, 1st Session, 91, pt. 5 Congressional Record 6364 (June 20, 1945) and includes all votes of yea, nay, and abstain.

Model 2 introduces our main variable of interest, *CIO*. As predicted, the coefficient is positive and statistically significant, suggesting that an increase in CIO union density was associated with senators voting in favor of the RTAA.[106] Model 3 then adds *Import* and *Export* to help differentiate between the trade policy demands of capital and labor. Importantly, the coefficient on *Export* is statistically insignificant, while the coefficient on *CIO* remains positive and statistically significant. This means that an increase in a state's export-oriented industry, holding CIO density constant, did not have an independent effect on Senate support for the RTAA. However, holding export shares constant, an increase in CIO density made senators more likely to support the RTAA. As discussed above, this suggests that when capital lobbied alone, it was unable to pressure senators to support free trade. In contrast, when workers in export-oriented industries joined their employers in favor of free trade, this cross-class coalition of capital and labor successfully pressured senators to vote in favor of the RTAA.

Model 4 further test the robustness of these findings by introducing an additional control variable for the number of manufacturing employees in each state. The coefficient on *CIO* is not affected, and remains positive and statistically significant. Model 5 introduces an interaction term between CIO and Party in order to investigate whether the influence of the CIO's cross-class coalition varied between Democratic and Republican senators.[107] As discussed above, the Democrats supported the RTAA from its birth in 1934, whereas Republicans first began to "convert" to free trade in the pivotal RTAA renewal vote of 1945. Did the "CIO conversion" in the early 1940s help cause the "Republican conversion" in 1945? The results from Model 6 suggest yes. Since *Party* takes the value of 1 for Democrats and 0 for Republicans, the coefficient on *CIO* now represents the effect of CIO density on Republican senators only. This coefficient is positive and statistically significant, which suggests that a cross-class coalition of the CIO and their employers successfully lobbied Republican senators in favor of the RTAA in 1945. Although the coefficient on the interaction term is statistically insignificant, this merely suggests that the effect of this coalition on Democrats was not significantly different.[108] In an effort to demonstrate the focused influence

---

[106] According to the AIC, Model 2 offers the best model fit for the data. The introduction of additional control variables only increases the AIC, suggesting worse fit.

[107] Party and ideology are highly correlated, but the reported findings are not significantly affected by excluding one or the other of these variables.

[108] The absence of a significant interaction effect may be due to the relative lack of variation amongst Democrats. As displayed above, 87 percent of Democrats voted in favor of the RTAA in 1945.

Table 5.3. *Probit Model. DV = Vote in Favor of RTAA 1945*

	Model 1	Model 2	Model 3	Model 4	Model 5	Model 6
(Intercept)	0.432**	0.491**	0.512**	0.513**	0.638	0.529
	(0.152)	(0.163)	(0.166)	(0.166)	(0.391)	(0.545)
Ideology	−0.865***	−1.066***	−1.068***	−1.066***	−1.167***	−1.220*
	(0.170)	(0.214)	(0.218)	(0.219)	(0.354)	(0.535)
CIO		0.498*	0.561*	0.551*	0.563*	0.562†
		(0.202)	(0.234)	(0.259)	(0.268)	(0.305)
Import			0.011	0.012	0.029	−0.230
			(0.160)	(0.161)	(0.178)	(0.421)
Export			−0.130	−0.135	−0.130	0.187
			(0.179)	(0.188)	(0.191)	(0.291)
Manufacturing				0.021	0.019	−0.324
				(0.255)	(0.256)	(0.357)
Party					−0.234	
					(0.567)	
CIO:Party					−0.072	
					(0.535)	
N	96	96	96	96	96	40
AIC	98.711	93.402	96.835	98.829	102.649	52.935
BIC	119.226	124.174	148.122	160.373	184.708	93.468
log L	−41.355	−34.701	−28.418	−25.414	−19.325	−2.467

Standard errors in parentheses
† significant at $p < 0.10$; *$p < 0.05$; **$p < 0.01$; ***$p < 0.001$

of the CIO's coalition on Republicans, Model 6 estimates the regression model on the subset of Republican senators. The coefficient on *CIO* remains unchanged, but due to the extremely small sample size (40 Republican senators) drops just below the traditional level of statistical significance ($p = 0.065$).[109]

The regression results reported in Table 5.4 introduce alternative measures of labor union density. Model 1 is identical to Model 4 from Table 5.3 and is included for reference only. Model 2 introduces *AFL.Troy*, which estimates the state-level density of unions affiliated with the AFL. The coefficient on *AFL.Troy* is negative and almost statistically significant at the 90 percent level ($p = 0.104$). This negative relationship is consistent with Hypothesis 2, which predicted that AFL density would lead senators to vote against free trade and the RTAA. With the addition

---

[109] The results are similar when estimated with robust standard errors clustered at the state level. This alternative specification assumes that the errors are independent across states but not between senators from the same state.

Table 5.4. *Probit Model. DV = Vote in Favor of RTAA 1945*
Alternative Union Density Measures

	Model 1	Model 2	Model 3	Model 4	Model 5
(Intercept)	0.513**	0.542**	0.578**	0.491**	0.611***
	(0.166)	(0.170)	(0.184)	(0.171)	(0.181)
CIO	0.551*	0.513†	1.054***		0.843**
	(0.259)	(0.267)	(0.320)		(0.291)
Ideology	−1.066***	−1.101***	−1.232***	−1.075***	−1.188***
	(0.219)	(0.222)	(0.252)	(0.217)	(0.242)
Import	0.012	−0.041	0.314	0.131	−0.012
	(0.161)	(0.170)	(0.234)	(0.192)	(0.177)
Export	−0.135	−0.215	−0.605*	−0.395†	−0.396†
	(0.188)	(0.201)	(0.247)	(0.213)	(0.219)
Manufacturing	0.021	0.159	−0.125	0.031	0.247
	(0.255)	(0.285)	(0.294)	(0.294)	(0.294)
AFL.Troy		−0.284	−0.098	−0.138	
		(0.175)	(0.213)	(0.203)	
Unaffiliated.Troy			−1.019***	−0.877**	
			(0.293)	(0.272)	
CIO.Troy				0.524*	
				(0.255)	
Total.Troy					−0.607**
					(0.209)
N	96	96	96	96	96
AIC	98.829	98.261	84.228	92.506	91.861
BIC	160.373	170.063	166.287	174.565	163.663
log L	−25.414	−21.131	−10.114	−14.253	−17.930

Standard errors in parentheses
† significant at $p < 0.10$; $^{*}p < 0.05$; $^{**}p < 0.01$; $^{***}p < 0.001$

of *AFL.Troy*, the coefficient on *CIO* decreases slightly and drops just below the standard cut-off for statistical significance (p = 0.054).

Model 3 introduces *Unaffiliated.Troy*, which measures the state-level density of labor unions that were not affiliated with the AFL or CIO. The coefficient on *Unaffiliated.Troy* is negative and highly statistically significant, suggesting that unaffiliated labor unions were an important source of protectionist pressure on U.S. senators. With the inclusion of this variable, the coefficient on *CIO* nearly doubles and becomes highly statistically significant (p < 0.001). However, the inclusion of *Unaffiliated.Troy* also results in the coefficient on *AFL.Troy* becoming highly statistically insignificant.

Models 2 and 3 use my new measure of CIO density – *CIO* – along with less reliable measures of AFL and unaffiliated union density gathered by Troy. As a robustness test, Model 4 drops *CIO* and replaces it with *CIO.Troy*, a measure of CIO union density compiled from Troy's data. The results from Model 4 are very similar to Model 3, which suggests that Troy's measures of CIO density, despite the limitations discussed above, may be relatively accurate for 1945. However, the negative and statistically significant effect of unaffiliated labor unions on Senate voting for the RTAA is puzzling, especially considering that unaffiliated unions only represented 1 in 10 unionized workers during this period.

In order to address these concerns, Model 5 presents an alternative specification that may better estimate the effects of different labor unions on Senate voting. Model 5 introduces *Total.Troy*, which measures total union density at the state level in 1945. This measure includes members of the AFL, the CIO, and unaffiliated labor unions. Since Model 5 also includes my new measure of CIO density, *CIO*, the coefficient on *Total.Troy* represents the influence of non-CIO unions on Senate voting. Since the overwhelming majority of non-CIO union members were organized by the AFL, the coefficient on *Total.Troy* can be interpreted as the effect of the AFL on Senate voting. Consistent with Hypothesis 2, the negative and statistically significant coefficient on *Total.Troy* suggests that the AFL joined with their employers and successfully pressured senators to vote against the RTAA.

The effect of CIO and AFL trade policy demands were not only statistically significant, but were substantively important as well.[110] First, consider the effect of CIO density on Senate voting for the RTAA. Holding all other variables at their mean values, we can examine the effect of increasing CIO density from 4.5 (0.5 standard deviations below the mean) to 18.6 percent (0.5 standard deviations above the mean). When CIO density is 4.5, the probability of a Senator voting for free trade is estimated at 0.57. When CIO density increases to 18.6, the probability increases to 0.85. The effect of AFL density on Senate voting was of a similar magnitude, albeit in the opposite direction. When AFL density was .5 standard deviations below the mean, the probability of a Senator voting for the RTAA was 0.82. When AFL density increases to 0.5 standard deviations above the mean, the probability drops to 0.62. These marginal effects are displayed below in Figure 5.2.

In general, the results from the probit models provide strong support for Hypothesis 1 and Hypothesis 2. An increase in CIO union density

---

[110] The estimated effects discussed in this paragraph are based on the regression results reported in Model 5 of Table 5.4.

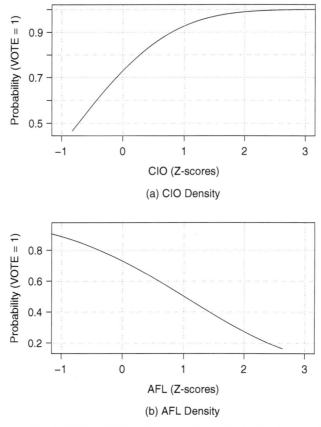

Figure 5.2. Marginal Effect of Union Density on Senate Voting for the 1945 RTAA

had a positive and statistically significant effect on the probability of a U.S. Senator voting in favor of free trade and the renewal of the RTAA in 1945. The CIO joined their employers in favor of free trade in 1945, and senators – especially from the Republican party – appear to have bent to the pressure of these cross-class constituent demands. In contrast, an increase in AFL union density had a negative and statistically significant effect on the probability of a U.S. Senator voting in favor of renewal. The AFL contained a well-organized group of unions who joined their protectionist employers and consistently opposed free trade during the period. Senators from states with cross-class coalitions of AFL unions and protectionist employers represented these constituent demands by not voting for the renewal of the RTAA. Finally, it should be noted that export share, on its own, was not a significant predictor of Senate voting on the RTAA. In contrast to previous work, which argues that American trade liberalization can be explained by the growth of export industry, this analysis demonstrates that profit-sharing institutions and the CIO conversion also played an important role in this pivotal trade policy reform.

CONCLUSION

This chapter began by demonstrating that profit-sharing institutions can bring workers and their employers together in favor of trade *liberalization*, as well as trade *protectionism*. In order to do so, it examined the trade policy preferences of two labor union federations, the Congress of Industrial Organizations and the American Federation of Labor. The CIO lacked profit-sharing institutions in the 1930s, and therefore disagreed with their export-oriented employers concerning the benefits of free trade. After establishing profit-sharing institutions in the early 1940s, the CIO changed its trade policy preferences and joined their employers in favor of free trade and the renewal of the RTAA. In contrast, AFL unions established profit-sharing institutions by the early twentieth century and maintained them throughout the 1930s and 1940s. AFL unions therefore agreed with their import-competing employers concerning trade policy and joined them in support of trade protectionism.

This chapter then examined whether or not workers' trade policy preferences influenced American trade policy outcomes. It used quantitative analysis and original data on CIO power to demonstrate that workers' trade policy demands had an important effect on U.S. Senate voting on the 1945 renewal of the RTAA. More specifically, it showed that in states where export-oriented employers lobbied without assistance from workers, senators were not influenced. In contrast, in states where export-oriented employers were joined by CIO union members, senators were successfully pressured into voting in favor of the RTAA. In this way, the creation of profit-sharing institutions in America's mass production industries aligned the trade policy preferences of the CIO and their employers in favor of free trade. This cross-class coalition of capital and labor then successfully pressured the Republican party to support the renewal of RTAA in 1945 and set the stage for bipartisan support for American trade liberalization after World War II. In this way, profit-sharing institutions played a previously unrecognized role in one of the most influential, and celebrated, trade policy reforms in modern history.

6

Trade Politics in Britain and Argentina

As the previous chapters on American trade politics demonstrated, capital and labor are unlikely to share the same trade policy preferences in the absence of profit-sharing institutions. Building off these findings, this chapter seeks to demonstrate that the effect of profit-sharing institutions on workers' trade policy preferences is generalizable across space and time. This chapter presents two case studies of the political economy of trade from the past two centuries. First, Britain during the 1840s and the political economy of the repeal of the Corn Laws. Second, Argentina during the interwar years and the political economy of import-substitution industrialization.

In both cases, the neoclassical approach makes clear predictions about the trade policy preferences of workers. In Britain, workers are predicted to join capital in favor of free trade and the repeal of the Corn Laws. In Argentina, workers are predicted to join capital in favor of trade protection and the implementation of import-substitution industrialization. Rogowski makes these precise predictions and goes on to claim that the historical record supports such claims.[1] While Hiscox does not discuss Argentine trade politics, his predictions and historical account of the British case are both in complete agreement with Rogowski.[2] In direct contrast, I will show that British workers were skeptical of the benefits of free trade, and argued that industrial profits would increase without an increase in wages. Argentine workers, whether organized as labor unions or political parties, actually opposed import-substitution industrialization throughout the 1930s. It was not until Juan Perón's pro-labor reforms in the early 1940s that Argentine workers obtained

---

[1] Rogowski 1989, 34, 47, 75.
[2] Hiscox 2002, 73.

profit-sharing institutions and then joined their employers in favor of protection.

The British and Argentine cases were carefully selected to accomplish two important methodological goals. First, both offer additional crucial cases for comparing my theory to extant political economy theories; my predictions and findings directly contradict the field's conventional wisdom in both cases. In this sense, the well-studied British case is particularly powerful in demonstrating the theoretical and empirical shortcomings of previous research, as well as the contributions of my own. Second, these cases allow me to test the generalizability of my theory using a "most different, similar outcome approach." Despite the tremendous differences between the British, Argentine, and American cases, each displays the same timeless dynamic: workers disagree with their employers concerning international trade unless profit-sharing institutions establish a credible connection between an industry's profits and workers' wages. Combined, these case studies cover over one hundred years, protectionist and liberalizing trade policy reforms, three different continents, economies with four different types of factor endowments, and various political regimes.

The two case studies in this chapter are each structured in the same way. First, I present a brief background on the trade policy reform in question, as well as the neoclassical prediction concerning workers' trade policy preferences. Second, I present information on domestic labor market conditions and note the general absence of profit-sharing institutions in each case. Third, I present evidence that workers disagreed with their employers and expressed skepticism and doubt about the trade policy that benefited their industry of employment. The only deviation from this general structure is in the Argentine case, which includes additional sections on the development of profit-sharing institutions and the subsequent change in workers' trade policy preferences.

BRITAIN AND THE REPEAL OF THE CORN LAWS

This section examines British trade politics in the years leading up to the repeal of the Corn Laws in 1846. The protectionist Corn Laws stretched back to 1815, when Britain raised import restrictions following the end of the Napoleonic Wars. Rather than embrace the return of international trade, Britain chose to protect domestic grain producers from import competition. The Corn Laws increased rents for Britain's landed elite but generated balance of payment problems that limited the export of Britain's new manufactured goods. The 1846 repeal of the Corn Laws therefore marked a radical turning point in both British and

European history. For Britain, repeal marked the triumph of ascendant, middle-class manufacturers over the declining, landed aristocracy. For European history, it marked the beginning of a liberal trading system that spread from England to Belgium, France, Holland, and the Scandinavian countries during the late nineteenth century.[3]

Given its clear historical import, the repeal of Britain's Corn Laws is perhaps the most studied case of trade politics in modern history. As Kindleberger claimed, "rivers of ink have been spilled on the repeal of the Corn Laws."[4] For nearly two centuries, scholars have fiercely debated the causes of Britain's pioneering turn towards free trade, weighing the independent effects of interests, institutions, and ideas.[5] Revisiting this famous period of reform, IPE scholars argue that the repeal of the Corn Laws is well explained by the class-based politics predicted by the Heckscher-Ohlin model. According to the canonical wisdom in the field, repeal was won by a cross-class coalition of capital and labor that opposed the protectionist policies of Britain's landed aristocracy.

As Rogowski writes, "Most clearly in Britain, expanding trade was associated with the triumph of a liberalism that united capital and labor, guaranteed free trade, and curtailed landed power ... By the early 1840s, the Anti-Corn Law League had attracted a mass following among urban and, to some extent, rural workers."[6] Hiscox also writes of a cross-class coalition of capital and labor in favor of repealing the protectionist Corn Laws; "the push for reform soon drew a mass following among both the urban middle and working classes and attracted support from the working-class Chartist reform movement."[7] According to both Rogowski and Hiscox, then, Britain's working class actively joined manufacturers in support of free trade and the repeal of the Corn Laws.

In direct contrast, this chapter argues that the lack of profit-sharing institutions left the British working class skeptical over the benefits of repeal. Workers therefore disagreed with their manufacturing employers and did not support the repeal of the Corn Laws during the trade policy debates of the 1840s. The trade policy disagreement between labor and capital is most clearly seen in the antagonism between their two representative organizations: the Chartists and the Anti-Corn Law League, respectively. Far from the harmonious coalition portrayed by Rogowski and Hiscox, the Chartists explicitly challenged the Anti-Corn

---

3 Eichengreen 1991, 9.
4 Quoted in Anderson and Tollison 1985, 197.
5 Schonhardt-Bailey 2006.
6 Rogowski 1989, 34.
7 Hiscox 2002, 73.

Law League's mission to repeal the Corn Laws. While the League blanketed Britain with its campaign of pamphlets and pro-trade propaganda, the Chartists sought to act as a counterweight, fiercely debating League representatives in public meetings concerning the consequences of repeal. In language that would echo throughout trade policy debates for the next two centuries, British workers argued that repeal would increase profits for manufacturers without increasing wages for workers. As one Chartist explained at a public meeting in Leicester in 1840, "repeal, unaccompanied by other financial and social measures of reform, would be productive of no benefit to the wealth-producing millions."[8] According to the Chartists' *Northern Star*, working men "were deaf to the voice of the charmer" who promised "good wages and cheap bread."[9]

Repression and Labor Market Institutions

The Chartists' skepticism regarding the repeal of the Corn Laws was structured by conditions in the British labor market. In the 1840s, the British working class struggled against labor laws that severely restricted their rights to act collectively. The British Parliament's Combination Act of 1825 declared trade unions to be, at best, "non-lawful societies," and opened striking workers to prosecution for conspiracy.[10] Such repressive labor laws severely limited the ability of workers to organize and negotiate higher wages. For example, consider the following 1842 report from the *Manchester Guardian*,

About half-past nine o'clock this morning, about 500 persons assembled in Tinker's Gardens, Saint George's Road. Information having reached the B division of police, Superintendent Stephenson proceeded with 60 policemen to disperse the mob. When he arrived at the gardens, a chartist, name Dixon, was addressing the meeting on the subject of wages. Mr. Stephenson interrupted the speaker, and informed him that the meeting was illegal, and must disperse. Dixon inquired who Mr. Stephenson was; and being informed that he was a superintendent of police, and that the meeting must disperse in five minutes, Dixon advised the meeting never to return to their work till they got what wages they required. The meeting was then informed, that force would be employed if they did not immediately separate.[11]

Under the Combination Act of 1825, it was not meeting in public that was illegal, but rather the discussion of striking for higher wages. Such actions could conceivably interfere with the individual freedom of contract on the part of an individual worker or with the right of a master

---

[8] *Northern Star*, December 5, 1840.
[9] *Northern Star*, April 3, 1841.
[10] Dicey 1904, 522.
[11] *Manchester Guardian*, August 27, 1842.

to manage his business in the way he thought fit.[12] As the Chartists explained at a Manchester debate with the League, the "working classes have been robbed of the rights of labour" and therefore, "no good could be done for the working classes until they were protected by the law; until the labour of the artisan was protected equally with the capital of the rich man."[13]

The repressive nature of British labor law was matched by similarly strict restrictions on the franchise. Despite the Reform Act of 1832, which extended the franchise to a segment of Britain's middle-class manufacturers, by the 1840s, still only one in every six British men held the right to vote.[14] The limited extension of the franchise following the Reform Act of 1832 proved to be a major source of tension between the working-class Chartists and the middle-class Anti-Corn Law League. James Leach, a Chartist from Manchester, asserted that "the laborers had been duped by the middle class over the Reform Bill and might be again over repeal" and that "laborers would not profit by the increase in trade which the League promised would result from repeal."[15] According to McCord, "most of the Chartists scarcely bothered to conceal their contempt and derision for the new move [League], which they decried as yet another middle-class trick to hoodwink the worker and distract them from Chartism."[16]

The Anti-Corn Law League repeatedly failed to convince workers that they would share in the benefits of repeal. First, the League was caught contradicting itself concerning how repeal would affect workers' wages. As poignantly captured in an 1843 Chartist pamphlet, League lecturers promised manufacturers that repeal would *decrease* wages at the same time that they promised workers that it would *increase* wages.[17] Second, the League openly opposed the factory legislation supported by the Chartists, including the Ten Hours Bill, which many workers believed were prerequisites for labor to benefit from repeal or any other policy that benefited British industry.[18] When workers demanded that pro-labor reform come before repeal, the Anti-Corn Law League condescendingly suggested that repealing the Corn Laws would cure all problems. For example, when the Chartists sought League support for universal male

---

[12] Dicey 1904, 521; Orren 1991.

[13] *Northern Star*, March 27, 1841.

[14] The Reform Act increased the electorate from around 366,000 to 650,000, about 18 percent of the total adult-male population in England and Wales. See Barnes 2005, 269.

[15] Barnes 2005, 247, fn. 27.

[16] McCord 2005, 78.

[17] Barnes 2005, 255.

[18] Anderson and Tollison 1985.

suffrage, the League responded that the repeal of the Corn Laws, once accomplished, would usher in worker suffrage. As John Bright, a founder of the League, explained to workers, "Your first step to entire freedom must be *commercial* freedom – freedom of industry."[19]

Chartism and Repeal of the Corn Laws

Due to the highly repressive nature of Britain's labor market and the clear lack of profit-sharing institutions, my theory predicts that British workers would disagree with their employers concerning the repeal of the Corn Laws. While manufacturers organized the Anti-Corn Law League and actively lobbied the government in favor of repeal, we should expect the Chartists to express skepticism and doubt concerning this proposed trade policy reform. Although Rogowski and Hiscox claim that the Chartists supported repeal, there is ample evidence that they disagreed with their employers and doubted the benefits of repealing the Corn Laws. This section presents such evidence from primary documents left behind by the Chartists, including pamphlets and articles in the Chartist's newspaper, *The Northern Star.*

As expected, concerns about labor market competition were at the heart of the Chartists' trade policy preferences. Such concerns were pointedly presented in an 1841 pamphlet by John Campbell, the Secretary of the National Chartist Association. According to Campbell,

What would be the effects of their repeal, without accompanying measures? And the answer to that must be, wide-spreading ruin, making us far more miserable than we are; bringing scores of thousands of individuals from the pursuits of agriculture to the unhealthy occupations afforded in the pestilential cotton and woolen mills, to give birth to a pale, miserable, stunted, decrepit, unhealthy race of human beings.[20]

According to Barnes, a historian of the Corn Laws, such concerns were widespread; "Most of the Chartists strongly believed in protection for agriculture, because they believed that free trade in grain would throw out of cultivation a great deal of land and drive thousands of agricultural laborers to the factories to compete and to reduce wages."[21] As Lusztig explains, "the principal working class movement of the day, the Chartists, advocated agricultural protectionism because they believed that agricultural free trade would take too much land out of production,

[19] Quoted in Schonhardt-Bailey 2006, 101.
[20] Campbell 1840, 70.
[21] Barnes 2005, 247.

thereby forcing agricultural laborers to the cities and driving down wages."[22]

The Chartists were not shy about their disagreement with the Anti-Corn Law League. In fact, they systematically organized public lectures throughout Britain at which they debated speakers from the Anti-Corn Law League. In debate after debate, Anti-Corn Law League speakers extolled the virtues of free trade while Chartist debaters and audience members explicitly disagreed and sought to "expose the fallacies of the Corn Law repealers."[23] My analysis of the Chartists' newspaper, *The Northern Star*, identified approximately 300 such events between 1838 and 1846, the year in which the Corn Laws were repealed. The debates occurred all across the country, from the metropolitan hubs of London, Glasgow, and Leeds, to the tiny hamlets and towns of rural Britain.

These lectures contain a wealth of information regarding the trade policy preferences of the Chartists, only a small portion of which can be presented here. The following discussion is based on a random sample of fifteen of these articles, all of which contain explicit disagreement between the Chartists and the Anti-Corn Laws League.[24] As described below, the Chartists' consistently disagreed with the Anti-Corn law League and argued that the repeal of the Corn Laws would not benefit workers.

On November 23, 1840, an audience gathered in a "spacious amphitheatre" in Leicester, England in order to listen to a debate between a Chartist named Mr. Bairstow and an Anti-Corn Law League lecturer named Mr. Pinnigan. These two speakers were invited to discuss "the benefits likely to result to the working class from a repeal of the Corn Laws."[25] During a speech that elicited cheers from the crowd, Bairstow argued that "the real object of the manufacturers and millocracy of the country in their outcry for repeal was merely to reduce the wages of their workmen with the view of enabling them the better to compete with foreign manufacturers." The meeting concluded with a public resolution that without "other remedial measures" the repeal of the Corn Laws

---

[22] Lusztig 1995, 405, fn 23.
[23] *Northern Star*, June 5, 1841.
[24] Five of these articles were randomly selected when I first began reading *The Northern Star*. The newspaper is digitized and searchable by word, and these first articles were identified by searching for the term "Corn Laws." With the help of research assistants, I then compiled a dataset of 300 such debates. In order to ensure that the original five articles were representative of the broader set of lectures, I then randomly selected an additional ten articles from the dataset. Specifically, I sorted the debates alphabetically by location and then selected every thirtieth debate.
[25] *Northern Star*, December 5, 1840.

"would confer no benefit on the working class." According to *The Northern Star*, this resolution was "carried by a majority of ten to one."[26]

Three months later, an illustrative debate took place in a pub in central London called the Crown and Anchor. A secretary of the Anti-Corn Law League read a report that began by acknowledging that the League "had enormous difficulties to encounter ... arising first from the apathy of the middle class; and secondly, from the hostility of the political portion of the working classes."[27] When the Secretary then announced that both of these problems "were fast disappearing" he was interrupted by Chartist cries of "No, no, never." When he claimed that Anti-Corn Law League lecturers "had been well received in every part of the kingdom," *The Northern Star* reports that "this was rather too barefaced for even those who were not Chartists, and, therefore this veracious statement was received with great laughter from all parts of the room." After this report, a Chartist stood upon a table to speak and was "received with uproarious shouts of applause." The speaker went on to deliver the common Chartist argument that "the sole reason why the manufacturers had come forward was because they knew that owing to high wages they were not able to compete with the foreign manufacturers – and hence it was that they were desirous of reducing the wages of the labouring class by a repeal of the Corn Laws."[28]

Weeks later, a crowd in Manchester heard from a Chartist named Robert Buchanan, who argued that "the repeal of the corn-laws [sic] would not be a benefit unless they could guarantee that ... the orders from abroad for manufacturers, so increases, as to keep the demand for laborers above the supply" – a condition that many Chartists, concerned with rural-urban migration, did not believe would hold.[29] In explaining their position on repeal, the Chartists also occasionally presented arguments based on the logic of relative gains. In April 1841, the Chartists' newspaper declared that, "The fact is clear to the people that if the Corn Laws were repealed, the masters would require, aye and would soon acquire, a despotic House of masters, with a *National Gendarmerie*, to confine the whole benefit to capitalists."[30] Expressing a similar split between the interests of capital and labor regarding trade policy, another Chartist lecturer lamented that workers "were told the Corn Laws were injurious to manufacturing interests; but they must

[26] *Northern Star*, December 5, 1840.
[27] *Northern Star*, March 6, 1841.
[28] *Northern Star*, March 6, 1841.
[29] *Manchester Guardian*, March 20, 1841.
[30] *Northern Star*, April 3, 1841.

always understand that to mean the interests of the masters, not the workmen."[31]

A year-and-a-half later, Chartists expressed similar concerns during a debate in the English town of Hull. As a Chartist speaker named Mr. Jones explained, "in my opinion a repeal of the Corn Laws will not benefit the working classes under existing circumstances. Amidst cheers of "hear, hear, hear" Jones went on to argue that, "By repeal we should destroy the strong hold of the aristocrat, and only be opening a way for the manufacturer and merchant to oppress us farther by entering into the citadel of corruption – they are equally as bad. It would only be a change of masters ... If I am to be a slave, I care not who is to be my master."[32] It is with these Chartist debates in mind that Barnes concludes that in the early 1840s "the League failed not only to secure definite results in Parliament, but also to get the united support of the laboring classes."[33]

It is worth emphasizing the Chartists' specific focus on how competition in the labor market broke the connection between trade policy, profits, and wages. In explaining workers' opposition to repeal in 1843, Chartist leader Feargus O'Connor explained that the "manufacturing market was overloaded with labourers. Many of his poor countrymen were compelled by dire necessity to come to the land of the stranger for that sustenance denied to them in the land of their birth, and thereby constituted a reserve for the employers to fall back upon."[34] Another Chartist lecturer accused the Anti-Corn Law League of ignoring the economic consequences of the fact that "hundreds of thousands are wandering the streets for want of employment."[35] Rather than address such concerns about labor market competition, the Anti-Corn Law League debaters "content themselves with uttering forth an experience-exploded 'principle' of Political Economy: Extended trade causes extended employment. Extended employment causes extended wages: therefore extended trade is beneficial to the worker."[36] The similarity between this "experience-exploded 'principle' of Political Economy" and the current conventional wisdom in international political economy is, of course, startling.

How far can we generalize from such Chartist speeches, pamphlets, and newspapers? Did the British working class doubt the benefits of repeal, or was such skepticism limited to a handful of outspoken Chartists? Rogowski and Hiscox acknowledge instances of Chartist

---

[31] *Northern Star*, May 22, 1841.
[32] *Northern Star*, March 19, 1841.
[33] Barnes 2005, 246.
[34] *Northern Star*, May 23, 1843.
[35] *Northern Star*, January 28, 1843.
[36] *Northern Star*, January 28, 1843.

opposition to Repeal, but both authors claim that such opposition was limited to a small, radical group of Chartist leaders. For example, Rogowski admits that "Some leaders of the largely working-class Chartist movement, however, supported the Corn Laws."[37] As Hiscox concedes, "The more radical elements of the Chartist movement were deeply distrustful of the manufacturers."[38]

Without public opinion data from this period, it is admittedly difficult to gauge the trade policy preferences of the British working class. Perhaps radical, Chartist leaders opposed the repeal of the Corn Laws, while the rest of the working-class flocked to the Anti-Corn Law League and added their voices to the demands for free trade. Since British workers were disenfranchised until the Reform Act of 1867, even general election results from the 1840s offer few hints of working-class policy preferences. Despite the lack of such data, we can find additional clues of working-class opinion by studying the Anti-Corn Law League, which made careful efforts to attract labor to its cause in the early 1840s. According to Richard Cobden, the founder and leader of the Anti-Corn Law League, the Chartist opposition to repeal had forced the League to rely on support from the middle-class. As Cobden explained at a League meeting in 1842,

I have no objection in admitting here, as I have admitted frankly before, that these artifices and maneuvers have, to a considerable extent, compelled us to make our agitation a middle-class agitation ... we have carried it on by those means by which the middle class usually carries on its movements. We have had our meetings of dissenting ministers; we have obtained the co-operation of the ladies; we have resorted to tea parties, and taken those pacific means for carrying out our views, which mark us rather as a middle class set of agitators.[39]

The League's decision to maintain a "middle-class agitation" was no doubt influenced by more than just the opposition of a few Chartist radicals. In fact, throughout the early 1840s, the League often found itself in direct violent conflict with large gatherings of Chartists. As Cobden described one public meeting, "The Chartist leaders attacked us on the platform at the head of their deluded followers. We were nearly the victims of physical force; I lost my hat, and all but had by head split open with the leg of a stool."[40] Of course, the level of violence, and who was seen as the perpetrator, depended crucially on the eye of the beholder. While the League often complained of violent Chartist mobs, the League's opponents often focused on the violence perpetrated by

37 Rogowski 1989, 34, fn. 43
38 Hiscox 2002, 73, fn. 2.
39 Morley 1883, 249.
40 McCord 2005, 103.

the League itself. According to the Tory *Standard*, the League could be quite hostile to Chartists who attended public meetings and voiced their opposition to repeal; in 1842 the newspaper lamented "the wanton and cowardly brutality exercised by the Leaguers upon the persons of the working men who opposed the resolutions" in favor of repeal.[41]

The Chartists' skepticism about the repeal of the Corn Laws has been empirically ignored in the international political economy literature and cannot be theoretically explained by the neoclassical models traditionally used by political economists.[42] In contrast, my theory of profit-sharing institutions predicts exactly this type of conflict; workers concerned about labor surpluses and their lack of bargaining power disagreed with their employers and expressed skepticism and doubt about the trade policies that would benefit their industry of employment. Far from credibly committing to share profits with workers, the Anti-Corn Law League was caught promising manufacturers that the repeal of the Corn Laws would actually decrease workers' wages and thus lower overall labor costs.[43] In the end, it was not possible for the Anti-Corn Law League to convince workers that they were fighting for higher wages, while simultaneously working to defeat factory laws that would have protected workers from long hours and dangerous working conditions.[44]

ARGENTINA AND IMPORT-SUBSTITUTION INDUSTRIALIZATION

The case of Argentina in the 1930s and 1940s also clearly demonstrates the shortcomings of the neoclassical approach to the political economy of trade. Like other "frontier" countries, Argentina had an abundant supply of land and a scarce supply of capital and labor throughout the late nineteenth and early twentieth centuries. According to Rogowski's prediction, "expanding trade [from 1840 to 1914] should have augmented the political demands of landowners, who will have embraced free trade; capitalists and workers ... will have united in support of protection."[45] In support of this prediction, Rogowski claims that landowners' demands

---

[41] Quoted in McCord 2005, 103. See pp. 100–101 for a story in which League members in Manchester accosted Chartists at a public meeting, tore down the banner they were carrying, broke the banner shafts into sticks, and barely escaped without being beaten with an "iron bar" or stabbed with a "short stave."

[42] As noted above, historians have repeatedly noted Chartist opposition to the repeal of the Corn Laws. Interestingly, when economists have acknowledged Chartist opposition to repeal, they cite it as an example of "willful ignorance" on behalf of workers, see Krueger 2004.

[43] Barnes 2005, 255.

[44] Anderson and Tollison 1985, 209.

[45] Rogowski 1989, 32.

for free trade triumphed over the protectionist demands of "notoriously weak capitalists" and "inarticulate and, often racially oppressed workers" until the depression and early phases of World War II.[46] At this historical juncture Argentina "intensified an 'import-substituting industrialization' that inevitably augmented the numbers and the strength of domestic workers and capitalists ... There can be little doubt of the accuracy of the theoretical prediction for this region in the 1930s: labor and capital gained strength, united and often prevailed, against landowners."[47] In short, Rogowski argues that Argentine workers supported trade protection through the late nineteenth and early twentieth centuries.

In direct contrast to Rogowski's predictions and historical claims, the Argentine working class doubted the benefits of trade protection throughout much of this period. Plagued by concerted employer and state repression and declining real wages, Argentine workers argued that the potential benefits of trade protection would not be shared with them. Whether we look to the policy platform of the worker-backed Socialist Party, or to Argentina's labor unions, workers consistently argued that high tariffs increased the cost of living, and enlarged profits without increasing workers' wages.[48] For example, when industrialists attempted to enroll workers in their fight for high tariffs in the early 1930s, Argentina's largest labor confederation denied that workers would benefit from protection and engaged in an ongoing public debate about the distributional consequences of high tariffs.[49]

However, Argentine workers slowly shifted their policy preferences towards trade protection, as institutional changes in the labor market increased their chances of capturing a share of increased profits. Following a wave of strikes in the mid-1930s, the Argentine state began to selectively intervene into capital-labor relations and promoted the signing of collective employment contracts between labor unions and their employers. Such pro-labor state intervention enhanced the bargaining power of workers and facilitated the occasional creation of profit-sharing institutions. For instance, the Argentine textile workers' union established profit-sharing institutions in 1936 and subsequently joined their employers in support of high tariffs.

The Argentine working class did not fully embrace trade protectionism, however, until the rise of Juan Perón and institutional reforms that revolutionized workers' bargaining power in the labor market. The

[46] Rogowski 1989, 47.
[47] Rogowski 1989, 75.
[48] Solberg 1973; Walter 1977; Tamarin 1985; Bergquist 1986.
[49] Tamarin 1985, 101.

"golden age" of labor legislation instituted by Perón after 1943 increased state involvement in industrial relations and ensured the rights of workers to collectively bargain and to strike.[50] Perón's reforms helped workers to gain formal union recognition, establish industry-wide wage contracts, and create a clear link between profits and wages. With such profit-sharing institutions in place, Argentine workers joined their employers in support of high tariffs. According to James, it was Perón's ability to premise "the very notion of national development on the full participation of the working class" that drew workers to support Perón's economic nationalism and import-substituting industrialization: "Industrialization within his discourse was no longer conceivable, as it had been prior to 1943, at the expense of the extreme exploitation of the working class."[51]

Labor Repression in Argentina

The working class did not share in the benefits produced by the expansion of Argentine industry in the early twentieth century. The interruption of international trade during World War I led to the rapid expansion of light industries, such as textiles, paper products, and shoes in the subsequent decade.[52] When unions organized and led a wave of strikes throughout 1918, employers and other elites formed their own organizations to try to counter workers' demands and break unions. The tension exploded in bloody repression during an infamous "Tragic Week" of January 1919. Afterwards, elites formed the Patriot League, a far-right pressure group that espoused love of country while mobilizing to break strikes.[53] Police began to issue certificates of good conduct to unemployed workers in order to help employers identify union organizers and other "troublemakers."[54]

Despite a doubling of industrial output from the early 1930s to the late 1940s, real wages declined throughout the 1930s and salaries lagged behind inflation. As James explains, "faced with concerted employer and state repression, workers could do little to successfully improve wages and work conditions."[55] Under the Neo-Conservative, military rule of the early 1930s, "political repression permitted employers to fire workers,

---

[50] Collier and Collier 1991, 336–339.
[51] James 1993, 20.
[52] Solberg 1973, 262.
[53] For an interesting example of rightwing nationalist groups breaking labor unions in the United States during the same year, see Cohen 2007.
[54] Horowitz 1990, 28, 128–133.
[55] James 1993, 8.

cut wages, and cripple unions. At best unions could survive."[56] In such conditions, import-substitution industrialization promoted industrial expansion without benefiting workers; according to Miguel Teubal, "The ISI process of the 1930s had not been redistributive or reformist in any sense ... as the new trade union movement ... [was] relatively excluded from reaping the fruits of industrial development."[57]

Labor Skepticism Regarding High Tariffs

In Argentina, the tariff first became a controversial issue during World War I and the decade immediately following.[58] Before World War I, Argentina's tariff policy was traditionally formulated by export interests and was constructed to raise government revenue, rather than to protect industries from imports. However, the curtailment of international trade during World War I raised the price of imports and thus stimulated the growth of Argentine industries such as textiles, shoes, and paper products. With the end of World War I and the looming return of international trade, Argentine manufacturers turned to the government for increased tariff protection.

In 1918, the tariff debate centered on a proposal from President Horatio Yrigoyen and his Radical Party to double the tariff on shoes. Unsurprisingly, support for the new shoe tariff came predominately from shoe manufacturers seeking to protect their growing industry, which had doubled in size from 1914 to 1918.[59] Perhaps more surprising, however, was that the shoe manufacturers were joined by Argentina's most powerful interest group, the *Sociedad Rural*, which was composed of large landowners and cattle fatteners. Although the *Sociedad* traditionally supported free trade, in the years after World War I it came to support tariff protection for Argentina's "natural industries" that could increase domestic demand for cattle products. Increased demand for Argentine shoes meant increased demand for Argentine leather, which meant increased demand for Argentine cattle.[60]

However, the increase in the shoe tariff was denounced by workers, and was not supported by the shoe workers' union, *Sindicato Obreros de la Industria del Calzado*. Throughout the early twentieth century

---

[56] Horowitz 1990, 68.
[57] Teubal 2001, 33.
[58] Solberg 1973.
[59] Solberg 1973.
[60] Solberg 1973. The *Sociedad Rural* would reverse its trade policy position in 1927 following an English threat of tariff retaliation. Fearing the loss of its main export market for beef, the *Sociedad* turned against tariff protection and changed its official slogan to "Buy From Those Who Buy From Us!"

the Socialist Party, which drew its support from skilled blue-collar workers, "consistently advocated free trade and opposed the creation of 'artificial' domestic industry." According to Carl Solberg, the Socialist Party "vigorously opposed protective tariffs" for shoes and the Party's newspaper, *La Vanguardia*, attacked the shoe tariff as "absurd and scandalous."[61] Such protectionism was also denounced by numerous syndicalist labor unions, who had declared themselves in favor of free trade as early as 1915.[62]

In fact, tariff policy was a principal area of contention between the Socialist Party, representing workers, and the *Unión Industrial Argentina* (UIA), representing owners and employers.[63] While the UIA argued that trade protection would lead to more industrial jobs and higher wages, the Socialist Party argued that high custom duties would increase the cost of living, contribute to the creation of monopolies, and lead to high profits that would not be shared with workers.[64]

Such concerns were on clear display during debates over tariff protection for the Argentine sugar industry. Based in the northwest province of Tucuman, the Argentine sugar industry provided the livelihood for more than half of the northwest's 550,000 inhabitants. Despite its large size, the sugar industry suffered from poor climatic and soil conditions that made it dependent on tariff protection. However, while tariff protection made the Argentine sugar industry profitable, the Socialist Party argued that the tariff generated a sugar monopoly that increased sugar prices without passing the benefits on to sugar plantation workers.

In 1913, the Socialist Party made an appeal to the Argentine Parliament to pass labor legislation that would protect sugar workers. The proposed legislation provided for the eight-hour day normally, a ten-hour day during harvest time, twenty-four hours continuous rest a week, overtime pay, and regulation of child and female workers.[65] The principal speech in support of this proposal was delivered by Mario Bravo, the Socialist Chamber Deputy. At the heart of his argument was the accusation that tariff protection for the sugar industry only protected the industry's owners, without extending any protection to workers in the labor market. As Bravo explained, "I aspire with the presentation of this project to extend the blue and white banner of industrial protection [the colors of the Argentine flag], which only waves over the chimneys of the sugar mills, out to the fields of cultivation, to the poor dwellings, so that one

---

[61] Solberg 1973, 265.
[62] Tamarin 1985.
[63] Walter 1977.
[64] Walter 1977, 110; Tamarin 1985, 100.
[65] Walter 1977, 109–110.

hundred thousand Argentines can share in this way in the defensive legal action that only pertains today exclusively to the caudillos [overlords] of the industry."[66] That is, this Socialist member of parliament proposed legislation that would ensure that the benefits of trade protection would be extended to workers in protected industries.

Continued labor opposition to tariff protection created political problems for the ruling Radical Party, which sought to attract working-class support away from the Socialist Party.[67] When, in 1922, President Alvear proposed an 80 percent increase in all tariffs to help close a budget deficit, the Radical Party divided over the tariff question.[68] By October 1923, Alvear had decided to scrap the tariff increase and formed an alliance with the Socialist Party in favor of tariff reduction. Despite Alvear's shift on tariff policy, there was sufficient political support from both the Radical and Conservative Parties to increase tariffs "despite violent Socialist objections."[69] According to the Argentine Socialist Party, "free trade and socialism march forever united."[70]

The deep trade policy disagreement between organized labor and capital was on clear display in 1933, when Argentina negotiated a free trade agreement with Britain. The final Roca-Runciman Treaty guaranteed Argentine beef exports to Britain, but committed Argentina to lower its tariffs on industrial goods imported from Britain.[71] Argentine industrialists, organized in the UIA, were deeply opposed to the agreement, arguing that free trade with Britain would destroy Argentina's infant industries. However, the UIA was keenly aware that Argentine workers did not share their fervent support for trade protection. Seeking allies in their fight against free trade, the UIA launched an advertising campaign to convince workers of the benefits of high tariffs.

The details of this protectionist advertising campaign are carefully recorded in the *Anales de la Unión Industrial Argentina*, the UIA's monthly newsletter. In February 1933, the UIA announced its plans "to convince the public that defending and protecting national industries was the best means of avoiding unemployment and improving the economic situation faced by the country."[72] As the UIA explained, "we want the worker to understand that his interest lies in the progress of industry."[73]

---

[66] Walter 1977, 110.
[67] Horowitz 2010.
[68] Solberg 1973, 285.
[69] Walter 1977, 188.
[70] Tamarin 1985, 100.
[71] Camargo 2007, 44.
[72] *Anales de la Unión Industrial Argentina*, February, 1933, 39.
[73] *Anales de la Unión Industrial Argentina*, February, 1933, 39.

In order to spread their message, the UIA handed out 500,000 brochures that explained the benefits of trade protection. They also distributed 1 million free paper bags, printed with pro-tariff messages, to every store in Buenos Aires. The UIA hoped that workers would receive these bags when shopping, and then unfold them and hang them as posters in their local clubs. To reach workers who did not shop or read brochures, the UIA launched a series of short radio lectures that it boasted would "bring to the heart of every home the wholesome thought that inspires our defense of the country's workers."[74]

The UIA also printed up protectionist posters that it hung up throughout working-class neighborhoods in Buenos Aires. The *Anales* contain the slogans from twelve of these posters, which proclaimed the unity of capital and labor, that tariff decreases would lower wages, and that free trade would increase unemployment. According to one poster, "What must be finally understood is that capital and labor are not enemies and when factories close, the employer is harmed just as much as the worker."[75] Another poster explained that tariff reductions would mean, "1) Increased unemployment, 2) Lower salaries, 3) The closing of factories, which cannot compete with foreign industries."[76] Still other posters addressed workers' concerns about the cost of living, arguing that, "The enemies of industrial protection say that tariffs make life more expensive. This is a serious mistake, because, on the contrary, encouraging the growth and creation of factories facilitates internal competition and lowers consumer prices."[77]

The UIA's advertising campaign culminated in a pro-protection rally in Luna Park, a stadium in central Buenos Aires, on June 12, 1933. In the days leading up the rally, the neighborhood surrounding the stadium was covered in yet more posters, this time proclaiming that, "Every peso spent on foreign products means a peso taken away from the Argentine workman."[78] According to the UIA, 70,000 people filled the stadium and the surrounding streets "with the sole purpose of demonstrating their unanimous support for measures that defend their jobs."[79] Those in attendance listened while Luis Colombo, President of the UIA, proclaimed that the huge rally, "demonstrates that the differences between capital and labor, that fantastic cloud that darkens even the most simple social

---

74 *Anales de la Unión Industrial Argentina*, February, 1933, 39.
75 *Anales de la Unión Industrial Argentina*, February, 1933, 39.
76 *Anales de la Unión Industrial Argentina*, February, 1933, 40.
77 *Anales de la Unión Industrial Argentina*, February, 1933, 42.
78 "Protectionists and Roca Treaty," *Buenos Aires Herald*, June 13, 1933.
79 *Anales de la Unión Industrial Argentina*, June, 1933, 22.

problems, disappears when the common good necessitates unity and joint defensive action."[80]

Was the UIA's advertising campaign a complete success? Did Argentine workers unanimously join their employers in favor of high tariffs? While no one denies that the rally in Luna Park took place, the days after the demonstration produced various re-interpretations that sought to minimize worker support for trade protection. The *Buenos Aires Herald*, an English-language newspaper that served the pro-British, export-oriented agricultural community, suggested that the rally's attendance may have been as low as 30,000. Moreover, the paper insisted that, "It is probable that not more than one per [thousand] understood anything of the subjects being dealt with, but it was an afternoon's holiday, and no loss of pay. No wonder all were enthusiastic."[81] While it may not be surprising that the pro-trade *Herald* sought to discredit the UIA rally, what did organized labor think about the demonstration?

The answer can be found in the *Boletín*, the weekly newspaper of the *Confederación General del Trabajo de la República Argentina* (CGT), a central labor federation founded in 1930. The week after the Luna Park demonstration, the *Boletín* published an article titled, "Protection and Free Trade," which explicitly denied worker support for high tariffs. According to the CGT, the demonstration was organized by the UIA to defend capital's "sacred interests," and protective tariffs were only "artificial measures designed to maintain class privilege."[82] Moreover, the CGT asserted that the UIA attracted a crowd to the rally by paying workers generously for their attendance, and threatening to fire them if they were absent. The CGT argued that free trade and a reduction in the hours of the workday were the best measures to relieve unemployment and maintain workers' salaries. Intent on leaving no ambiguity, the CGT stated that their stance on international trade was "in direct contrast to the theory supported by the UIA."[83]

The CGT continuously pointed to the fact that the two areas of the Argentine economy that enjoyed high protection, the sugar and yerba mate industries, also had the worst working conditions in the republic.[84] The CGT accused the UIA of hypocritically seeking tariffs that provided protection for capital, while simultaneously opposing labor laws that would protect workers. As David Tamarin explains, organized labor asked,

---

[80] *Anales de la Unión Industrial Argentina*, June, 1933, 22–23.
[81] "Protectionists and Roca Treaty," *Buenos Aires Herald*, June 13, 1933.
[82] "Protection and Free Trade," *Boletín de la CGT*, June 25, 1993, 2.
[83] "Protection and Free Trade," *Boletín de la CGT*, June 25, 1993, 2.
[84] Tamarin 1985, 101.

[why] does industry demand protective tariff legislation yet oppose protective labor legislation on the basis that only the latter constitutes intolerable artificial intervention in the free-market mechanism?[85]

In these ways, and in contrast to Rogowski's claims, the Argentine working class did not support high tariffs during the early decades of the twentieth century. Under the auspices of employer and state repression, and with real wages declining in the face of expanding industrial output and profits, workers argued that trade protection would benefit industrialists without increasing their wages. To put the organized tariff opposition of Argentina's working class into perspective, recall that Rogowski claims that free trade was imposed by the landed elite, over the "inarticulate" demands of the Argentine working class. In direct contrast, Argentine workers were far from advocates of trade protection. In fact, they often articulately questioned and challenged the high tariffs that protected Argentine industry.

Government Support and the Origins of Labor Protectionism

The plight of Argentine labor unions began to change in the mid-1930s, following a wave of successful strikes orchestrated by new industrial unions. Throughout Argentina, striking workers demanded higher wages, union recognition, and "closed shop" agreements that would reduce competition in the labor market.[86] The first large strike, in 1935, was led by the construction workers' union and craft unions of painters, stonemasons, pasturers, and electricians. The strike lasted over three months and was supported by 95 percent of workers.[87] The industrial dispute quickly expanded, as a confederation of twenty-four labor organizations called a general strike in solidarity with the 60,000 construction workers. With workers controlling the streets in many working-class neighborhoods of Buenos Aires, violent clashes between strikers and police left at least six people dead and dozens injured and arrested. *La Prensa*, the Argentine daily newspaper, explained that "its dimensions allow us to assign it the same magnitude as that reached by the events in this capital in January 1919."[88]

Following the violence and disruption of the general strike, state authorities granted new power to the national labor department to mediate conflicts between workers and their employers. According to

---

[85] Tamarin 1985, 101.
[86] Korzeniewicz 1989, 12. Such demands were made by both agricultural and manufacturing workers.
[87] Korzeniewicz 1989, 18.
[88] *La Prensa*, January 8, 1936, p. 10, quoted in Korzeniewicz 1989, 19.

the director of the labor department in the province of Buenos Aires, mediation of disputes was a more promising avenue for state intervention than merely relying on the police to control strikes. As he explained, "through all the efforts carried out to build union organizations and in their struggle for improvement, the police have always appeared as a repressive institution, with little capacity for reaching satisfactory solutions."[89] State mediation not only pushed employers to increase wages and to cease retaliating against striking workers, but it also led to the creation of tripartite commissions between workers, employers, and representative of the labor department, which regulated wages, hours, and working conditions.[90]

Such state mediation was a boon for struggling Argentine labor unions, which thereby received official recognition from both the state and their employers. According to Joel Horowitz, "in 1936 the labor movement was healthier than it had been at any time since the onset of the depression," and "workers struck with a growing hope of victory."[91] However, the state was most likely to offer such mediation in industries where conflict was both economically and politically costly. The state's cost–benefit analysis of where to intervene therefore required labor unions that could actually provide labor peace and a cessation of strikes. As one labor department official explained, "the intervention of the state to increase wages can only be effective when it can count on the support of professional organizations capable of maintaining certain principles of discipline, order, and legal concurrence among the workers."[92]

Such improved capital-labor relations were on clear display in the Argentine textile industry. In April 1936, the textile workers' union, the *Unión Obrera Textil* (UOT), pressured their employers to sign a collective contract with clauses related to salaries, freedom of association, abolition of favoritism, the rotation of workers instead of dismissals, the reinstatement of workers dismissed because of union activism, and the creation of a joint committee between workers and employers to discuss problems. In addition, the contract required that capital-labor relations would be supervised by the national labor department and the provincial labor department in Buenos Aires.[93] According to Horowitz, this first successful negotiation of an industry-wide contract in the textile industry was a "stunning victory" for the union. In an effort to avoid future strikes, the textile industry's manufacturing association, *Asociación Textil*

---

[89] Quoted in Korzeniewicz 1989, 24.
[90] Korzeniewicz 1989, 26.
[91] Horowitz 1990, 96–97.
[92] Korzeniewicz 1989, 32; Horowitz 1990, 146.
[93] van Voss et al. 2010, 31.

Argentina, called on the Congress to regulate the minimum wage and establish a tripartite commission to negotiate an industry-wide wage scale.[94]

By 1937, the Argentine textile union had been formally recognized by their employers, signed an industry-wide wage scale, and enjoyed government oversight that would help ensure that workers' wages would rise along with profits. After the creation of such profit-sharing institutions, the UOT "supported formal ties with the textile employers' association to work out common positions aimed to protect and stimulate the industry."[95] During the recession of 1937–1938, which interrupted Argentina's recovery from depression, the UOT petitioned the government for "immediate and energetic" state intervention and anti-dumping legislation. According to the union, such tariff protection would "facilitate the further development of national industry as an important factor in the country's economy."[96] In a letter to President Ortiz dated July 14, 1938, the union called for the "defense of national industry [which is] the source of popular welfare and of economic liberty, because it means the daily bread of modest Argentine homes and because it leads to the elevation of the standard of living for the country's workers."[97]

The textile union, however, also made clear that its support for tariff protection was conditional on its newly improved labor market position. The UOT argued that workers only benefit from trade protection when such trade policies are accompanied by government regulations that provide workers with the bargaining power necessary to capture a share of increased profits. According to the union,

Unless the establishment of measures against 'dumping' [trade protection] is accompanied by the regulation of labor, registers, and remunerative salaries for workers ... the magnates of the industry will turn it into a monopoly, leaving the workers in the same precarious situation in which they find themselves today, if not worse, to the detriment of the development of the industry, turning consumers over to monopolist avarice.[98]

Moreover, the textile industry's cross-class coalitions of capital and labor in favor of protection was rare in the late 1930s. Despite the potential appeal of economic nationalism, many labor unions maintained an implacable hostility towards industrialist organizations and continued to disagree with their employers concerning trade policy. In 1940,

[94] Korzeniewicz 1989, 29.
[95] Collier and Handlin 2009, 23.
[96] Quoted in Tamarin 1985, 165.
[97] Quoted in Tamarin 1985, 165.
[98] Quoted in Korzeniewicz 1989, 34.

organized labor continued to characterize the UIA as "evidently ... having been born and of living in order to oppose labor laws. It is not an organization of conciliation between bosses and workers."[99] According to David Tamarin, "labor never failed to differentiate its economic nationalism from that of the industrialists. It consistently linked the issue of industrial protection to the demand for the expansion and enforcement of protective social and labor legislation."[100]

In these ways, most Argentine workers continued to disagree with their employers concerning trade policy during the 1930s. In small pockets, such as the textile industry, labor unions established profit-sharing institutions and joined their employers in favor of high tariff. However, the union was careful to qualify its support, demanding that trade protection be accompanied by union recognition and expanded state regulation of capital-labor relations. Although this instance of capital-labor agreement is consistent with Rogowski's prediction, it was only made possible by the creation of profit-sharing institutions that helped to reassure workers that they would share in the benefits of trade protection.

Perón's Reforms and Worker Support for Trade Protection

The rise of Juan Perón revolutionized what industrialization meant for Argentina's working class. Whereas industrial growth in the 1930s was accompanied by a decline in real wages, Perón's reforms of the 1940s led to the growth of unions and a 60 percent increase in real wages from 1946 to 1949.[101] Coming to power in the military coup of 1943, Perón held a series of government positions that enabled him to build strong relationships with union leaders. As the head of the National Labor Department, and then the cabinet-level Secretary of Labor, Perón worked for the passage of pro-labor legislation and "set about addressing some of the basic concerns of the emerging industrial labor force."[102]

In 1945, the Law of Professional Associations granted formal state recognition to labor unions, obliged employers to collectively bargain with unions, and protected union leaders from victimization. Following these reforms, industrialization was translated into material benefits for

---

[99] Tamarin 1985, 167.

[100] Tamarin 1985, 167; *Acta del Segundo Congreso* 1943, 144. The CGT supported national industrialization but was still far from openly supporting high tariffs. In December 1942, the CGT called on its central committee to study the possibilities for the development of national industry, and for affiliated unions to support all efforts to promote the development of Argentine industry. However, the CGT made no mention of tariff protection.

[101] Collier and Collier 1991, 337.

[102] James 1993, 9.

workers; as James explains, "concrete economic gains for the working class were clear and immediate. As Argentine industry expanded, impelled by state incentives and a favorable international economic situation, workers benefited."[103] According to Tulio Halperin Donghi, "all these innovations were presented as a reparation that the nation presented to its working classes, they were therefore invited to look upon themselves as a legitimate part of the nation."[104]

Perón's pro-labor reforms drastically increased the associational power of Argentine workers. From 1945 to 1947 the CGT grew from roughly 500,000 union members to 1.5 million. Over the next four years, the CGT doubled its membership to 3 million. With increased membership came a new-found ability to launch successful strikes. In 1942, only 10 percent of Argentine strikers won their demands, while in 1945, roughly 95 percent of strikers were victorious.[105] The increase in Argentine workers' bargaining power was unprecedented; as Brennan explains, "Perón took a nascent working class, one that was largely apolitical and unorganized, and within a few years made it a formidable factor of power in the country."[106] According to Buchanan, "Perón gave the workers in months what they previously had been unable to achieve in years."[107]

Argentine labor unions then translated this power into a national system of industry-wide wage contracts. From 1946 to 1948, unions signed contracts throughout Argentine industry that regulated wage scales and mandated sick leave, maternity leave, and vacations. According to James, "Employers were obliged by law to bargain with the recognised union, and conditions and wages established in such bargaining were applicable to all workers in that industry regardless of whether they were unionised or not."[108] The wage gains for workers were massive, as "Perón greatly expanded the scope of organized labor and brought collective bargaining into fields where it had never been before."[109]

Perón not only helped workers develop the bargaining power necessary to collectively bargain with their employers, but also had the government directly intervene in negotiations. By the late 1940s, wage negotiations were regularly negotiated in the headquarters of the Ministry of Labor in Buenos Aires, where the government could "keep a sharp eye on what was going on."[110] Under the auspices of such pro-labor tripartite bargaining,

[103] James 1993, 11.
[104] Quoted in Teubal 2001, 36.
[105] Kappner 1985, 201.
[106] Brennan 2009, 10.
[107] Buchanan 1985, 64.
[108] James 1993, 10.
[109] Alexander 1962, 210.
[110] Alexander 1962, 193.

"government officials stepped in quickly if there were a deadlock. Usually, Ministry of Labor officials took the workers' side in such instances."[111] According to Buchanan, "The operative rule was the worker was always correct, and the Secretaría [Minister of Labor] always sided with the workers."[112] Through such tactics, Perón "taught workers that what they were denied by their employers they could regain through the efforts of their friends in the Casa Rosada."[113]

Perón's empowerment of labor was accompanied by an explicit commitment to guarantee Argentine workers a share of industrial profits. Perón described his initial reforms as "necessary to balance out past inequities. Social justice was needed as an antidote to prior policies which always sided with business and deprived workers of the just rewards for their labor."[114] The 1930s were viewed as a period during which the benefits of industrialization were not shared with workers – "a period when industrial output and employment were on the rise while labor's share of the national income declined."[115] Perón encouraged workers to use their new bargaining power to "refuse to abide by market forces" and to "politicize income distribution."[116] Workers eagerly took Perón's advice; from 1945 to 1950 workers' share of national income rose from 46.7 to 60.9 percent.[117]

According to Alexander, a typical wage contract from this period was to be seen in the Argentine glass industry.[118] The agreement was made between the glassworkers' *Sindicato Obrero de la Industria del Vidrio y Afines* and a federation of glass manufacturers. The contract was fifty-one pages long and included thirty-six pages detailing the proper wage rates to be paid to workers. Similar to wage contracts signed by the CIO during World War II, this agreement also included a checkoff clause that required employers to deliver workers' union dues directly to their labor union. Like all Argentine industries during this period, the glass industry agreement also included a powerful steward committee, the factory *comisiones interna*, which provided workers with effective advocates on the shop floor regarding all aspects of the agreement and the enforcement of Perón's new labor legislation.[119]

A similar industry-wide contract was established in Argentina's metalworking industry. The agreement granted workers a closed-shop rule,

[111] Alexander 1962, 193.
[112] Buchanan 1985, 63.
[113] Turner and Miguens 1983, 33.
[114] Kappner 1985, 195.
[115] Kappner 1985, 198–199.
[116] Kappner 1985, 198–199.
[117] Kappner 1985, 186.
[118] Alexander 1962, 193.
[119] Brennan 2009, 12.

which prohibited employers from hiring non-union workers, ostensibly limiting the supply of labor, and helping the workers to increase their wages along with profits. Metal workers also benefited from the uniform wage scales established throughout Argentine industries, which equalized wages in Buenos Aires with those in other Argentine provinces.[120] As discussed above, such contracts take wages out of competition and make it easier for unionized employers to increase wages. With increased bargaining power and the labor market institutions discussed above, the metalworkers were consistently able to capture a share of their industry's profits. In fact, workers were so successful that the metal industry's main employer association, the *Cámara Argentina de Industrias Metalúrgicas*, "frequently complained about what it considered to be excessive wage increases granted to workers in collective bargaining negotiations."[121] By the late 1940s, the *Cámara* pleaded with the government that "wage increases be commensurate with increases in productivity."[122] In these ways, wages in the metal industry may have risen even faster than profits.

In short, Perón's pro-labor reforms fostered the development of profit-sharing institutions throughout Argentine industry. Workers' labor unions were formally recognized by their employers, they established industry-wide wage scales, and tripartite collective bargaining helped establish a credible link between profits and workers' wages. Under Perón, workers did not simply share in their industry's new profits, they appear to have captured a share of the profits that had eluded them during the previous decade.

The creation of such profit-sharing institutions fundamentally altered the distributional consequences of high tariffs, import-substitution industrialization, and Argentine industrialization. According to James,

> the working class recognized in Perón's espousal of industrial development a vital role for itself ... Indeed Perón consistently premised the very notion of national development on the full participation of the working class ... Industrialization within his discourse was no longer conceivable, as it had been prior to 1943, at the expense of the extreme exploitation of the working class.[123]

According to Murmis and Potantiero, working-class support for Perón and import-substitution industrialization was thus a rational response, as the alliance "served as a solution to an industrialization process that had been carried out under the control of a traditional elite, without any working-class participation or social interventionism of any

---

[120] Alexander 1962, 191.
[121] Brennan 1998, 86.
[122] Brennan 1998, 86.
[123] James 1993, 20.

sort."[124] Labor support for Perón and import-substitution industrialization became ubiquitous. When Perón was jailed by the military in 1945, the CGT organized a massive protest in Buenos Aires on October 17 that ensured his release.[125] After this, the trade union movement was one of the main supporters of the developing *peronista* movement. When Perón was elected President in 1946, "ISI policies were continued along with pro-labor and social welfare measures unknown up to then."[126]

Perón's institutional reforms offered a "different potential meaning of industrialism" that led to a close alliance between Perón and the CGT.[127] As Horowitz explains, "The state shifted the balance between labor and capital in favor of the former. Perón tapped long-standing union desire for better relations with the government and a growing dissatisfaction with the old norms and existing political parties."[128] While the labor movement opposed ISI and trade protectionism throughout the early twentieth century, Perón's reforms guaranteed workers that they would share in the benefits of industrialization.

The evolution of Argentine workers' trade policy preferences provides further evidence for my theory of profit-sharing institutions. During the 1920s and early 1930s, Argentine workers faced fierce labor repression that weakened labor unions and resulted in the stagnation of real wages. Given the lack of profit-sharing institutions during this period, it should be unsurprising that Argentine workers expressed skepticism and doubt concerning the potential benefits of tariff protection for Argentine industry. Workers' trade policy preferences did not begin to align with their protectionist employers until government intervention in the late 1930s began to tilt the balance of bargaining power towards labor in specific industries. Such institutional change inspired cross-class support for high tariffs in the textile industry but did not spread to the rest of the economy until Juan Perón's sweeping labor market reforms of the early 1940s. These reforms led to the creation of profit-sharing institutions that assured workers that they would share in the benefits of ISI and therefore led them to finally support high tariffs.

CONCLUSION

Trade politics in both of these cases provide further evidence for my theory of profit-sharing institutions. The British case demonstrates that, in

---

[124] Murmis and Portantiero 2004, 124, quoted in Teubal 2001, 33.
[125] James 1993, 19.
[126] Teubal 2001, 34.
[127] James 1993, 20.
[128] Horowitz 1990, 180.

the absence of profit-sharing institutions, workers express skepticism and doubt about the trade policies that benefit their industries of employment. The Argentine case supports the same argument, and additionally demonstrates that workers tend to share the same trade policy preferences as their employers once profit-sharing institutions are in place. Together, these cases demonstrate the generalizability of my theory well beyond the American cases examined in the previous two chapters. The presence or absence of profit-sharing institutions helps to explain workers' trade policy preferences across various levels of economic development, types of political regimes, and directions of trade policy reform, as well as at least two centuries, and three continents.

7

Power Over Profits

Scholars have long recognized that international trade policy has important domestic distributional consequences. Free trade policies can contribute to soaring profits for export-oriented firms, just as protectionist policies can increase returns for industries shielded from the global market. As explained in Chapter 2, the neoclassical trade models suggest that trade policy influences wages through its effects on the marginal revenue product of labor. For example, a tariff that protects an import-competing steel industry increases the domestic price of steel, which increases the marginal revenue product of labor in the steel industry, which increases labor demand, which automatically increases steel workers' wages. In contrast to the canonical wisdom in the field, this book argues that the benefits of such trade policies are not automatically shared with workers in these favored industries. Instead, workers' ability to capture a share of increased profits depends on the balance of bargaining power between capital and labor.

In this way, the link between the marginal revenue product of labor and workers' wages – what I call the "profit-sharing rate" – is a key causal mechanism of my theory. This chapter therefore tests this crucial aspect of my theory by analyzing quantitative data from 28 manufacturing industries, in 117 countries, from 1986 to 2002. Since it is difficult to observe workers' bargaining power independent from its effect, the analysis uses a country's level of respect for labor rights as a proxy measure for workers' bargaining power. When a state respects labor rights, it provides a permissive context in which workers can act collectively and therefore increase their bargaining power vis-à-vis their employers. Most importantly, the analysis demonstrates that when respect for labor rights is very low, the profit-sharing rate is statistically indistinguishable from zero. Put simply, when workers lack bargaining power they are right to believe that they will not share in the benefits of favorable trade policy reform.

Beyond testing the causal logic of my theory, this chapter's large-N analysis has four methodological advantages. First, examining the determinants of profit-sharing in over one hundred developed and developing countries helps to avoid the selection bias that may influence the qualitative case studies presented earlier in the book. Second, quantitative analysis easily controls for alternative explanations and avoids the inferential difficulties faced when studying a small number of cases. Third, the analysis produces precise estimates of the relationship between different variables, thus permitting us to examine the relationship between profits and wages at various levels of respect for labor rights. Last, since the analysis focuses on relatively recent data, it helps demonstrate my theory's relevance for the study of contemporary political economy.

CROSS-NATIONAL QUANTITATIVE ANALYSIS

The quantitative analysis presented below focuses on the theoretical relationship between the marginal revenue product of labor and workers' wages, or what I call the profit-sharing rate. Unfortunately, the marginal revenue product of labor (i.e. the contribution to the value of output of the last worker hired) cannot be readily measured, especially across more than one hundred countries. This chapter therefore follows the standard approach in labor economics and relies on a measure of average labor productivity.[1] For the sake of clarity and consistency, the remainder of this chapter therefore simply refers to the marginal revenue product of labor as "productivity." For instance, when discussing the profit-sharing rate this chapter will refer to it as the relationship between worker productivity and workers' wages.

It is also important to note that the analysis focuses on the profit-sharing rate, not on actual trade policy changes. There are two main advantages to this focus on the determinants of the profit-sharing rate. First, it allows for a simultaneous test of how policy reforms in opposite directions might influence wages. For example, consider how international trade policies are predicted to affect wages. According to the Ricardo-Viner model, free trade policies increase productivity and wages in export-oriented industries, while protectionist trade policies do the same in import-competing industries. Focusing on the profit-sharing rate therefore has implications for how liberalization, as well as protectionism, affects wages. Second, it allows for a parsimonious test of the causal

[1] Wakeford 2004.

logic of a broad range of political economy theories. If an increase in productivity does not generally lead to an increase in wages, then it is unclear why a specific policy – whether related to international trade, foreign exchange rates, or foreign direct investment – that increases productivity, should be expected to increase wages. Although this book focuses on the political economy of trade, this chapter's results speak to a much broader set of issue areas in international and comparative political economy.

Since the Ricardo-Viner and Heckscher-Ohlin models make different assumptions about inter-industry factor mobility, each model makes different predictions about the level at which productivity and wages will be related. The Ricardo-Viner model predicts that wage growth and productivity growth will be related at the industry-level because of the assumption of zero inter-industry factor mobility. In contrast, the Heckscher-Ohlin model predicts that wage growth and productivity growth are related at the country-level because of the assumption of perfect inter-industry factor mobility.

The first hypothesis tests the relationship between the profit-sharing rate and labor rights at the industry-level. Therefore, this hypothesis tests the causal logic of the Ricardo-Viner model as well as the causal logic of IR theories that are based on the Ricardo-Viner model.

Hypotheses 1. *The protection of labor rights has a positive effect on the profit-sharing rate at the industry-level. That is, the effect of productivity growth on wage growth, at the industry-level, is larger when the protection of labor rights is high.*

The second hypothesis tests the relationship between the profit-sharing rate and labor rights at the country-level. Therefore, this hypothesis tests the causal logic of the Heckscher-Ohlin model as well as the causal logic of IR theories that are based on the Heckscher-Ohlin model.

Hypotheses 2. *The protection of labor rights has a positive effect on the profit-sharing rate at the country-level. That is, the effect of productivity growth on wage growth, at the country-level, is larger when the protection of labor rights is high.*

The third hypothesis tests the claim that in the absence of labor rights, workers' wages do not rise along with profits. When a state does not protect labor rights, workers are unable to act collectively and tend to lack the bargaining power necessary to capture a share of increased profits in the form of wages.

Hypotheses 3. *In the absence of the protection of labor rights, the profit-sharing rate is zero.*

Data Sources

In order to test these hypotheses, this chapter uses data from 28 manufacturing industries, in 117 developed and developing countries, from 1986 to 2002. The 28 industries cover all manufacturing sectors, and the dataset includes countries from every region of the world. Although data is not available for the complete universe of countries, the 117 countries included in the dataset accounted for approximately 96 percent of global GDP in 2000.[2] Testing these hypotheses on such a large and diverse set of countries is ideal, as the relationship between labor rights and the profit-sharing rate is theorized to be generalizable across all countries.[3] The range of years covered by the data are recent and thus any conclusions drawn from the analysis should be applicable to contemporary political economy. This data is available from the United Nations Industrial Development Organization (UNIDO),[4] the World Bank, the Penn World Tables, and Polity IV. The data on the protection of labor rights was collected by Mosley (2011).

Dependent and Independent Variables

The main focus of this chapter is to examine the degree to which an increase in productivity is associated with an increase in wages, or what we have called the profit-sharing rate. Following the standard approach in the labor economics literature, this elasticity of wages with respect to productivity can be calculated by regressing the wage growth rate onto the productivity growth rate.[5] Thus, the dependent variable in this analysis is the real wage growth rate, measured at the industry-country-year level. This variable is calculated by taking the first difference in the natural logarithm of real average wages in the following way:[6]

$$Wage^*_{ijt} = log(Real\,Average\,Wage_{ijt}) - log(Real\,Average\,Wage_{ijt-1}) \qquad (7.1)$$

Where i represents industry, j represents country, and t represents year. A similar calculation is also used to calculate the real productivity growth

---

[2] The percent of global GDP represented by the countries included in the dataset were calculated using data from the World Bank's World Development Indicators. For a list of the 117 countries, see Table 7.13 in the Appendix.

[3] This chapter focuses on data from manufacturing industries, therefore further research is required to extend the findings to agricultural and service sectors of the economy.

[4] The data used in this chapter is available on the INDTAT-3 CD-ROM.

[5] Hall 1986; Alexander 1993; Strauss and Wohar 2004; Wakeford 2004, Klein 2012.

[6] Real wages are calculated using the consumer price index, while real productivity is calculated using the producer price index. See, Bosworth et al. 1994; Strauss and Wohar 2004; Wakeford 2004; Klein 2012.

rate at the industry-country-year level:

$$Productivity^*_{ijt} = log\left(\frac{Real\ Output_{ijt}}{Employment_{ijt}}\right) - log\left(\frac{Real\ Output_{ijt-1}}{Employment_{ijt-1}}\right) \quad (7.2)$$

While the primary reason for this data transformation is to focus the analysis on the elasticity of wages with respect to productivity, it also reduces autocorrelation and the non-normal distributions that characterize wages and productivity in their level form.[7] Following this transformation, the coefficient on *Productivity** represents the degree to which an increase in average worker productivity is associated with an increase in average wages.

Unfortunately, the data available does not include worker benefits, and therefore represents less than total worker compensation. However, estimating the model on workers' wages, rather than total compensation, likely biases the results against my hypothesis by underestimating the effect of labor rights on the profit-sharing rate. This is because workers regularly use their bargaining power to increase benefits, and not just wages. As Freeman and Medoff explain, "The conclusion is inescapable: unionization is a major determinant of fringe-benefit programs and expenditures."[8] Therefore, it should be more difficult to find a positive relationship between labor rights and the profit-sharing rate, which only captures the degree to which productivity gains are translated into wage gains.[9]

The main independent variable of interest in this analysis is the interaction between *Productivity** and *LaborRights*, where *LaborRights* measures the protection of labor rights at the country-year level. The coefficient on this interaction term represents the effect of a one point increase in *LaborRights* on the profit-sharing rate. We therefore expect the coefficient on the interaction term to be positive because the more a country protects labor rights, the more an increase in productivity is expected to lead to an increase in wages.

The cross-sectional time-series data on labor rights measures the legal rights of workers to organize, associate freely, bargain collectively and strike, as well as the observation of these rights in practice.[10]

[7] Harvey 1980.
[8] Freeman and Medoff 1984, 68. For recent work that finds the same positive impact of unionization on worker benefits, see Rosenfeld 2014.
[9] Future research using individual-level data is required to examine if labor rights are more likely to increase the profit-sharing rate for workers with different skill levels or employed in different types of firms.
[10] Mosley 2010.

The *LaborRights* index is based on recorded violations of thirty-seven specific labor rights in six broad categories: freedom of association and collective bargaining-related liberties; the right to establish and join worker and union organizations; other union activities; the right to bargain collectively; the right to strike; and rights in Export Processing Zones. These thirty-seven violations are based on "core" labor rights as promulgated by the International Labour Organization and encompass the *absence* of legal rights, the *limitation* of legal rights, and the *violation* of legal rights by the government or employers. After documenting labor rights violations, the scale is reversed so that higher values now represent fewer violations of labor rights, or greater protection of labor rights.

The dual focus on labor rights in law, as well as practice, ensures that a country cannot receive a high *LaborRights* score by simply withholding legal protections for workers, and then not having any domestic labor laws to violate.[11] In these ways, *LaborRights* measures the degree to which domestic institutions provide the antecedent conditions for worker collective action and bargaining power. Importantly, *LaborRights* varies across time within countries, thus allowing us to estimate its effect on the profit-sharing rate while also including country fixed effects that control for omitted, time-invariant variables.[12] The hypothesized relationship between labor rights and profit sharing is asymmetrical, depending on whether productivity growth is positive or negative. When productivity growth is positive, the protection of labor rights is expected to increase the ability of workers to raise their wages along with productivity. In contrast, when productivity growth is negative, the protection of labor rights is expected to increase the ability of workers to decouple their wages from productivity. Such "sticky wages," which result from workers' ability to increase their wages during good times, but then resist wage cuts during bad times, are a well-documented phenomenon.[13] Failure to control for this asymmetrical effect would result in sample bias that would skew the estimated effect of *LaborRights* downward.

This asymmetry can be addressed through two methodologically equivalent techniques. First, the model can be estimated on the subset of the data for which *Productivity** is positive.[14] Second, the asymmetry

---

[11] For regression results based on disaggregated measures of labor rights (law vs. practice), see Table 7.10 in the Appendix.

[12] Beck 2011.

[13] Harris and Todaro 1970.

[14] The results reported below are also robust to estimating the two-way interaction model on the full dataset. As expected, the estimated effect of *LaborRights* on

can be addressed by constructing a dummy variable that distinguishes between positive and negative productivity growth and interacting it to the interaction term between *Productivity** and *LaborRights*, as well as to each control variable and the fixed effects at the industry, country, and year levels. The coefficient on this three-way interaction term then estimates the effect of *LaborRights* on profit sharing, conditional on productivity growth being positive. Both of these approaches produce identical coefficient estimates and standard errors. For presentation purposely only, the regression results reported below are based on the former approach and the relatively easy to interpret two-way interaction term between *Productivity** and *LaborRights*.

Control Variables

In addition to these independent variables of interest, I include several control variables that address alternative explanations. First, the model includes controls for a country's level of democracy (*Polity*) and economic development (*GDPpc*), both of which likely influence a country's protection of labor rights. Second, the model includes two measures of the tightness of the labor market; *Unemployment* measures economy-wide unemployment at the country-year level and *Employment* measures the number of people employed at the industry-country-year level.[15] To control for additional labor market dynamics, the model includes industry-country-year controls for the percentage of the population employed (*PopEmployed*), the capital-labor ratio (*Capital/Labor*), as well as fixed effects at the industry-level.

Third, the model controls for a country's exposure to the global economy by including measures of trade openness (*Openness*), and foreign direct investment (*FDI*).[16] Last, the profit-sharing rate may be influenced by other labor market institutions and variables associated with labor power. As robustness checks, the model includes *Union*, which measures the percentage of the labor force that belongs to a labor union, *Bargain*, which measures the level of wage bargaining centralization, and *Left*, which measures the percentage of cabinet seats held by left-wing

---

profit-sharing is smaller, though still statistically significant, when using data on both positive and negative productivity growth.

[15] High unemployment reduces the possibility of finding jobs elsewhere and therefore leads workers to accept lower real wages in their current job, see Blanchflower and Oswald 1995.

[16] While some scholars argue that openness may increase respect for workers' rights, others see international integration as a potential threat. See, Cameron 1978; Katzenstein 1985; Adsera et al. 2002; Kohli 2004.

political parties.[17] For descriptive statistics and Pearson correlations for all variables, please refer to Tables 7.3 to 7.5 in the Appendix.[18]

Model and Method

In order to address all of these alternative explanations, the full regression model includes the control variables discussed above. The baseline model can be specified in the following way:

$$Wage^*_{ijt} = \beta_1 Productivity^*_{ijt} + \beta_2 LaborRights_{jt} + \beta_3 (Productivity^*_{ijt} * LaborRights_{jt})$$

$$+ \sum_k \beta_k Controls_{jt} + \sum_n \beta_n Controls_{ijt} + \gamma_i + \eta_j + \mu_t + \epsilon_{ijt} \tag{7.3}$$

Where i identifies industry, j identifies country, t identifies year. The γ_i, η_j, and μ_t therefore represent fixed effects at the industry, country, and year levels, respectively.[19] The ϵ_{ijt} are independent and identically distributed errors with variance σ^2. As described above, *Wage** and *Productivity** represent the growth rates of wages and productivity, respectively.

The country fixed effects control for all time-invariant characteristics of each country, such as colonial legacy, religion, geography, and unchanging policymaking institutions.[20] The inclusion of country fixed effects also focuses the analysis on variation within each country, rather than pooling observations across countries at vastly different levels of economic development. The industry fixed effects control for any global economic shocks that equally affect the same industry in different countries, such as a sudden change in commodity prices. Last, the year fixed effects control for trends that simply occur over time. The inclusion of these fixed effects helps to control for omitted variables that may be endogenously associated with both the dependent and independent variables, thus leading to a spurious correlation between labor rights and the profit-sharing rate.[21]

Wages and productivity vary from year to year within each industry and therefore the industry-country-year is the basic unit of analysis.

---

[17] The data on union density was compiled by Rama and Artecona of the World Bank. The data on wage bargaining centralization was compiled by Golden, Wallerstein, and Lange, and the data on Left-wing cabinet seats was compiled by Swank.

[18] For histograms of *LaborRights*, *Wage**, and *Productivity**, see Figure 7.4 in the Appendix.

[19] A Breusch and Pagan Lagrangian multiplier test rejects the null hypothesis of no country-specific variance and a Hausman test confirms that estimating the model with fixed effects is preferable to random effects.

[20] In addition to the theoretical reasons to include fixed effects at the country and year levels, F-tests using ANOVA suggest that the inclusion of these variables adds significantly to the explanatory power of the model.

[21] Green et al. 2001.

Although labor rights only vary at the country-year level, the hypotheses above suggest that such variation should be associated with variation in the profit-sharing rate in each industry within the respective country. The dataset in this analysis has 2,734 units (industry-countries), from 117 countries, and a maximum of 17 time periods (years). Due to missing observations for some industry-countries, the dataset is an unbalanced panel.[22] In order to control for the cross-sectional heteroskedasticity and correlation associated with panel data, all models are estimated using OLS with fixed effects and panel-corrected standard errors.[23]

MAIN RESULTS

The regression results presented below provide strong evidence that the protection of labor rights is positively associated with the profit-sharing rate. The findings are not only statistically significant, but also suggest that the effect is large and substantively important. When labor rights are in the top 10 percent of the global distribution, the profit-sharing rate is predicted to be 71 percent higher than when labor rights are in the bottom 10 percent. The substantive importance of labor rights can be seen clearly in Figure 7.1, where the slope of each line represents the profit-sharing rate at different levels of *LaborRights*.[24]

Table 7.1 presents the results of five regression models that establish this chapter's baseline results. Model 1 starts by including the main effects of *Productivity** and *LaborRights*, without the interaction between the two terms. According to this model, *LaborRights* is positively correlated with wage growth, even when controlling for *Productivity**. Although the relationship just misses the standard cut-off for statistical significance (p = .078), these initial results suggest that labor rights may permit workers to bid up their wages beyond the level "justified" by their productivity. However, this preliminary conclusion is quickly overturned by the introduction of the interaction term between *Productivity** and *LaborRights* in the next model. Model 2 establishes that labor rights

---

[22] Due to missing data on some variables, the full regression model in Model 4 of Table 7.2 is estimated on only 1,559 industry-countries from 71 countries. However, these 71 countries still represented 89 percent of global GDP in 2000.

[23] As shown in Table 7.8 of the Appendix, the results are also robust to the estimation of standard errors clustered by country. PCSE are reported in the main results tables in accordance with Beck and Katz 1995; Beck and Katz 1996.

[24] This plot represents the bivariate relationship between *Wage** and *Productivity** for two different subsets of the data, and includes 95 percent confidence intervals. The solid, blue line represents all observation for which the *LaborRights* score was a perfect 37; the dashed, red line represents all observations for which the *LaborRights* score was less than 9. The estimates do not include controls or fixed effects, as do the regression results and marginal effects plots presented below.

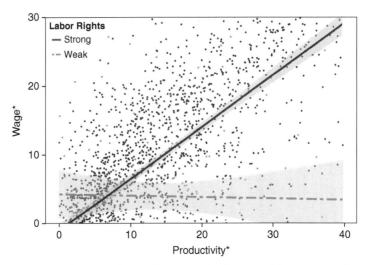

Figure 7.1. The Effect of Labor Rights on Profit Sharing. With *Wage** on the *y*-axis and *Productivity** on the *x*-axis, the *slope* of these two regression lines represent the profit-sharing rates at extreme ends of the global *LaborRights* spectrum

merely permit workers to capture a share of their increased productivity in the form of wages. In other words, in the absence of productivity growth, an increase in labor rights does not increase workers' wages.[25]

The positive association between labor rights and the profit-sharing rate can be seen in the positive coefficient of the interaction term between *Productivity** and *LaborRights*. The positive (0.009) and statistically significant ($p < 0.01$) interaction term means that an increase in productivity is associated with a larger increase in wages when *LaborRights* is high, compared to when *LaborRights* is low. Specifically, the coefficient on the interaction term represents the effect of a one point increase in *LaborRights* on the profit-sharing rate, holding *Productivity** constant.[26] Importantly, the coefficient on *LaborRights* is neither positive nor anywhere near statistical significance. This suggests that, holding productivity growth constant at zero, an increase in labor rights does not have a direct effect on workers' wages. In order to increase the robustness

[25] This finding is robust to estimating the model on the full dataset, including all cases of negative productivity growth.

[26] A joint significance test suggests that the interaction term must remain in the model. The value of the *F* statistic was 56.94 with 14,132 degrees of freedom and a *P* value of < 0.01.

Table 7.1. *Baseline OLS Regression Results. DV = Wage**

	Model 1	Model 2	Model 3	Model 4	Model 5
(Intercept)	−1.332	2.806	−2.567	4.349	5.104
	(1.691)	(1.792)	(3.655)	(3.670)	(3.678)
Productivity*	0.404***	0.156*	0.145*	0.177*	0.184**
	(0.040)	(0.079)	(0.073)	(0.069)	(0.068)
LaborRights	0.113†	−0.041	−0.001	−0.127	−0.125
	(0.066)	(0.074)	(0.092)	(0.100)	(0.099)
Productivity*:LaborRights		0.009**	0.009**	0.007**	0.007**
		(0.003)	(0.003)	(0.003)	(0.003)
Country Fixed Effects	no	no	yes	yes	yes
Year Fixed Effects	no	no	no	yes	yes
Industry Fixed Effects	no	no	no	no	yes
N	14136	14136	14136	14136	14136
R^2	0.102	0.105	0.175	0.195	0.197
adj. R^2	0.102	0.105	0.168	0.187	0.188
Resid. sd	15.262	15.231	14.691	14.519	14.512

Panel-corrected standard errors in parentheses
† significant at $p < 0.10$; *$p < 0.05$; **$p < 0.01$; ***$p < 0.001$

of the analysis, Models 3 through 5 successively add fixed effects at the country, year, and industry levels.

The regression models reported in Table 7.2 further increase the robustness of the analysis by including additional control variables. Model 1 replicates the baseline model (Model 5 of Table 7.1) by only including the *Productivity*:LaborRights* interaction term, its main effects, and fixed effects at the country, year, and industry levels. Model 2 starts with the baseline model and adds control variables that vary at the industry-country-year level. These include *Employment*, which measures total employment in the industry; *Capital/Labor*, which measures the relative capital or labor-intensiveness of the industry; and *PopEmployed*, which measures the percentage of the total population employed in the industry. The coefficient on the interaction between *Productivity** and *LaborRights* increases slightly (from 0.007 to 0.009) and remains statistically significant ($p < 0.05$). Model 3 starts with the baseline model and adds control variables that vary at the country-year level. These include *FDI*, which measures a country's net flow of foreign direct investment; *Polity*, which measures a country's level of democracy; *Openness*, which measures a country's openness to international trade; *GDPpc*, which measures a country's GDP per capita;

Table 7.2. *OLS Regression Results with Controls. DV = Wage**

	Model 1	Model 2	Model 3	Model 4	Model 5
(Intercept)	5.104	−32.911***	−10.886	5.639	63.129
	(3.678)	(4.881)	(61.255)	(69.145)	(117.280)
Productivity*	0.184**	0.124	0.122	0.109	−0.806[†]
	(0.068)	(0.089)	(0.113)	(0.110)	(0.446)
LaborRights	−0.125	−0.159	−0.094	−0.093	0.004
	(0.099)	(0.127)	(0.148)	(0.164)	(0.225)
Productivity*:LaborRights	0.007**	0.009*	0.009*	0.009*	0.041*
	(0.003)	(0.004)	(0.004)	(0.004)	(0.018)
Employment		0.453[†]		0.361	
		(0.275)		(0.300)	
Capital/Labor		−0.237		−0.116	−2.332
		(0.184)		(0.251)	(1.828)
PopEmployed		−0.630		−1.221	
		(0.592)		(0.759)	
FDI			0.408	−0.594	−0.458
			(1.310)	(1.963)	(3.409)
Polity			0.769***	0.852***	1.270*
			(0.197)	(0.234)	(0.593)
Openness			−1.935	1.360	2.274
			(5.527)	(4.859)	(8.037)
GDPpc			0.165	−0.262	−8.136
			(5.494)	(6.257)	(10.331)
Unemployment			−0.640*	−0.866**	−0.825
			(0.258)	(0.273)	(0.502)
Country Fixed Effects	yes	yes	yes	yes	yes
Year Fixed Effects	yes	yes	yes	yes	yes
Industry Fixed Effects	yes	yes	yes	yes	*no*
N	14136	10406	9853	7755	303
R^2	0.197	0.208	0.248	0.266	0.439
adj. R^2	0.188	0.198	0.238	0.254	0.237
Resid. sd	14.512	13.913	13.385	12.942	10.934

Panel-corrected standard errors in parentheses
[†] significant at $p < 0.10$; *$p < 0.05$; **$p < 0.01$; ***$p < 0.001$

and *Unemployment*, which measures a country's economy-wide unemployment rate. The coefficient on the interaction between *Productivity** and *LaborRights* does not change and remains statistically significant ($p < 0.05$).

Model 4 starts with the baseline model and then adds both sets of control variables – the controls that vary at the industry-country-year, as well as the controls that vary at the country-year levels. When all control variables, as well as the fixed effects at the country, industry, and year levels are included, the coefficient on the interaction between

*Productivity** and *LaborRights* does not change and remains statistically significant (p < 0.05), thus providing support for Hypothesis 1.[27]

To substantively interpret this interaction coefficient, consider how the United States' secular decrease in the protection of labor rights is predicted to have influenced the profit-sharing rate for American workers. From a perfect *LaborRights* score of 37 in 1986, the United States' protection of labor rights dropped to a low of 23.75 in 1997. The 0.009 coefficient on the interaction terms tells us how much the profit-sharing rate increases for every one point increase in *LaborRights*. According to the regression results, in 1986 the United States had a predicted profit-sharing rate of .442.[28] Holding all other variables constant, this 13.25 point decrease in *LaborRights* is associated with a profit-sharing rate of .323, a drop of 27 percent. Of course, the substantive impact of *LaborRights* is significantly larger if we examine countries that have had more volatile respect for labor rights. For example, consider the positive experience of Chilean workers emerging from the repressive Pinochet dictatorship in the early 1990s. From a 1985 *LaborRights* score of only 10.25, Chile rapidly increased its respect for labor rights to a *LaborRights* score of 33.25 in 1996. Starting from a predicted profit-sharing rate of 0.207 in 1985, and holding all other variables constant, by 1996 Chilean workers are predicted to have enjoyed a profit-sharing rate of 0.408, an astonishing increase of 103 percent.

As mentioned above, testing the profit-sharing implications of the Heckscher-Ohlin model and Hypothesis 2 requires us to examine the relationship between worker productivity and wages at the country-level.

[27] Due to relatively limited data for many of the controls, the inclusion of these variables decreases the number of observations from 14,136 to 7,755. Including these variables reduces the number of countries from 117 to 71. For a list of the 46 countries missing data on these variables, Table 7.14. In order to check for bias introduced by this missing data, I estimated the baseline model, with no controls, using the subset of countries that have data on all control variables (71 countries) and compared the results to those reported in Model 4, Table 7.1 (117 countries). The coefficient estimate for the interaction between *Productivity** and *LaborRights* is nearly identical in both models, which suggests that the restricted sample is unbiased.

[28] According to the marginal productivity theory of wages, the elasticity of wages with respect to productivity should be 1, or unit elastic. My regression results suggest that even when labor rights are perfectly protected, the profit-sharing rate is only 0.442. For other studies that also find that wage growth lags behind worker productivity growth, see Strauss and Wohar 2004; Wakeford 2004; Klein 2012. For a review of the statistical obstacles to obtaining a unit elasticity between wages and productivity, see, Bosworth et al. 1994. The estimated elasticities reported below are nearly identical whether worker productivity is deflated using the consumer price index or the producer price index.

Therefore, Model 5 in Table 7.2 examines the effect of average productivity growth on average wage growth throughout the manufacturing sector. Estimating the model on such average values changes the unit of analysis from the industry-country-year to the country-year and decreases the number of observations from 7,755 to only 303. Despite this much-reduced sample size, the coefficient on the interaction between *Productivity** and *LaborRights* is still positive and statistically significant (p < 0.05). The magnitude of the coefficient (0.041) is larger than the estimates from previous models, but the overall interpretation is substantively similar. According to this estimate, starting with the protection of labor rights at its mean, a one standard deviation increase in labor rights is associated with a 100 percent increase in the profit-sharing rate. Alternatively, according to the previous estimate in Model 4, the same one standard deviation increase in the protection of labor rights is associated with a 20 percent increase in the profit-sharing rate. This finding provides support for Hypothesis 2 and is robust to the same controls and fixed effects used in the previous models.

Hypotheses 1 and 2 predict that the profit-sharing rate will increase along with the protection of labor rights, but Hypothesis 3 focuses specifically on the profit-sharing rate in the absence of labor rights. Hypothesis 3 can therefore be tested by examining the coefficient on *Productivity**. This coefficient represents the effect of productivity growth on wage growth when *LaborRights* is zero. According to Model 4 in Table 7.2, which examines the profit-sharing rate at the industry-level, the coefficient on *Productivity** is positive, but very small (0.109) and statistically indistinguishable from zero (p = 0.32). According to Model 5, which examines the profit-sharing rate at the country-level, the coefficient on *Productivity** is actually negative (−0.806) and nearly statistically significant (p = 0.07). Together, these models provide strong support for Hypothesis 3 and the claim that in the absence of labor rights, workers are unable to capture any share of increased profits. In fact, throughout the various robustness tests and alternative model specifications explored in the Appendix to this chapter, the coefficient on *Productivity** is never statistically distinguishable from zero.

Figure 7.2 in the Appendix graphs the marginal effect of productivity growth on wage growth, or the profit-sharing rate, as a function of the protection of labor rights. When *LaborRights* is at zero, the profit-sharing rate is indistinguishable from zero. At increasingly high levels of labor rights, productivity growth has an *increasingly positive* effect on wage growth. These findings suggest that when labor rights are not well protected, the neoclassical trade models systematically exaggerate the wage increases that workers' receive from trade policy reforms. Caution is needed in interpreting the coefficient on *LaborRights*, which represents the effect of an increase in labor rights on wage growth when productivity growth is zero. Figure 7.3 of the Appendix shows that *LaborRights* has a positive and statistically significant effect on wage growth only when *Productivity** takes much higher values.

The regression results also contain two additional statistically significant findings. First, holding productivity growth and all other variables constant, *Unemployment* is negatively associated with wage growth. This finding is consistent with the theoretical discussion above, which argued that unemployment and labor surpluses dampen wage growth. Second, *Polity* is positively associated with wage growth, which is consistent with the common argument that democracy is positively correlated with economic growth.[29]

In summary, the fixed-effect regression results demonstrate that the protection of labor rights is positively associated with the profit-sharing rate, and therefore support all three hypotheses presented above. These findings are robust to the inclusion of controls for economic development, globalization, democratization, various industry characteristics, fixed effects at the industry, country, and year levels, and panel-corrected standard errors. These controls should give us confidence that the results are not due to an omitted variable that causes both labor rights and profit-sharing. Any time-invariant, idiosyncratic characteristic of countries that might be associated with labor rights and profit sharing is controlled for by the inclusion of country-level fixed effects.

Endogeneity of Labor Rights and Productivity

Does the protection of labor rights increase profit-sharing, or does profit-sharing increase the protection of labor rights? Although the empirical analysis presented above is unable to identify the direction of causality, there are reasons to believe that an increase in labor rights causes an increase in the profit-sharing rate. First, this chapter presents a direct causal mechanism through which we expect the protection of labor rights to increase the bargaining power of workers and thereby increase the profit-sharing rate. As discussed above, a basic tenet of labor economics holds that an increase in labor rights and worker

---

[29] Haggard and Tiede 2011. However, neither variable appears to directly moderate the relationship between productivity growth and wage growth. This is tested by including additional interaction terms between *Productivity** and *Polity* and *Unemployment*, respectively. Although neither interaction term is statistically significant, the association between *LaborRights* and the profit-sharing rate is robust to the inclusion of these additional interaction terms. For further discussion and regression results, see Table 7.11 in the Appendix.

bargaining power directly increases wages.[30] Second, the *sign* of the reverse causal mechanism is not clear, *a priori*. On one hand, an increase in profit-sharing increases the resources available to workers and may facilitate their ability to organize and lobby the government for better legal protections for workers. If this were the case, the estimated effect of labor rights on profit-sharing would be biased upwards. On the other hand, a decrease in profit sharing may frustrate workers, thus leading to increased organization and demands for legal protections. If this were the case, the estimated effect of labor rights on profit sharing would be biased downwards. In these ways, the biases introduced by the possibility of reverse causality may partially cancel each other out.

There is also potential endogeneity in the wage-productivity relationship. According to the efficiency wage literature, above-market wages may increase productivity by deterring workers from shirking, decreasing turnover, and attracting more efficient workers.[31] Importantly, this does not create serious problems for this chapter's findings concerning labor rights and the profit-sharing rate. There is no theoretical reason to expect the *efficacy* of efficiency wages – the degree to which an increase in wages spurs workers on to higher levels of productivity – to increase along with respect for labor rights. Therefore, the positive relationship between the profit-sharing rate and labor rights should be interpreted in the following way: respect for labor rights increases workers' ability to capture a share of productivity growth in the form of wages.

Methodologically, this chapter addresses possible endogeneity by carefully controlling for variables that may simultaneously influence productivity, wages, and labor rights. Trade liberalization, for instance, may dynamically spur innovation and efficiency over time, thus increasing productivity, but also potentially undercuts workers' bargaining power and wages. Alternatively, economic policy changes may affect resource allocation that alter productivity levels, as well as the labor-intensiveness of production. These concerns are addressed by the inclusion of numerous control variables. *Openness* and *FDI* control for relevant policy changes related to trade and investment, fixed effects at the industry-year level control for technological change and innovation, and *Capital/Labor* controls for changes in resource allocation and level of capital investment. Future research could further address these concerns by controlling for additional variables, especially at the level of individual firms. However, this chapter's broad scope – covering twenty-eight industries in over

---

[30] MaCurdy and Pencavel 1986; Bentolila and Saint-Paul 2003; Borjas 2005; Layard et al. 2005.

[31] Stiglitz 1974; Shapiro and Stiglitz 1984; Yellen 1984; Krueger and Summers 1988.

one hundred countries – unfortunately does not allow for more detailed controls.

Even without completely solving the complicated relationship between labor rights and the profit-sharing rate, this chapter has important implications for comparative and international political economy. Regardless of the direction of causality, attention to labor rights helps identify countries in which the distributional predictions of the neoclassical models may be less accurate. In countries with low protection for labor rights and low profit-sharing rates, these models appear to overstate the benefits that workers receive from economic policy reforms. Although future research should focus on identifying the direction of causality, this chapter nonetheless identifies domestic labor market institutions as an important omitted variable in the political economy literature.

Robustness Checks

The results reported above are robust to a number of additional model specifications and controls. First, the results are robust to the inclusion of additional variables that are traditionally used to proxy for labor power, such as union density, left government, and the level of wage bargaining. Second, the results are robust to dropping rarely changing variables, such as *GDPpc* and *Openness*, which may be collinear with the country-level fixed effects.[32] Third, the results are robust to estimation of cluster-robust standard errors, rather than the PCSE reported above. Fourth, the results are robust to the inclusion of fixed effects at the industry-year and industry-country levels, which control for the possibility that technological change systematically affects the profit-sharing rate in different industries or countries. Fifth, the results are robust to disaggregating the measure of labor rights into its component parts based on labor rights in law and labor rights in practice. Sixth, the results are robust to the inclusion of additional interaction terms between each independent variable and *Productivity**, so as to control the relationship between each variable and the profit-sharing rate. Finally, the results are robust to estimating the model separately for OECD and non-OECD countries.

These robustness checks, as well as the inclusion of various control variables and fixed effects at the country, year, and industry levels, should increase our confidence that labor rights are positively associated with the profit-sharing rate. In all of these alternative specifications, the interaction term between *Productivity** and *LaborRights* remains positive

32 Plümper and Troeger 2007.

and statistically significant. This means that when labor rights are not well protected, an increase in productivity does not automatically lead to the equal wage increase predicted by the neoclassical trade models. Additional information on these robustness checks is available in the Appendix.

CONCLUSION

How does international trade policy influence workers' wages? According to the neoclassical trade models, favorable trade policy reform increases the marginal revenue product of labor, which automatically increases wages. In contrast, this chapter argued that the connection between trade policy and workers' wages depends on conditions in the domestic labor market. Specifically, it argued that workers without bargaining power are unlikely to capture a share of the benefits from trade policy reforms. This chapter tested this argument by examining the "profit-sharing rate" across twenty-eight manufacturing industries, in 117 countries, from 1986 to 2002. The analysis demonstrated that when labor rights are not protected, the profit-sharing rate is statistically indistinguishable from zero. Moreover, as the protection of labor rights increases, so too does the ability of workers to capture a share of increased profits in the form of wages. In short, workers are correct when they assert that market forces do not establish an automatic connection between trade policy and wages.

APPENDIX

This Appendix presents additional information concerning the robustness of the main finding that the protection of labor rights is positively associated with the profit-sharing rate.

Labor Rights and Labor Power

How does the protection of labor rights compare to other variables associated with labor bargaining power? In order to examine the independent effect of labor rights on the profit-sharing rate, I introduce variables often used to measure labor power: union density, the electoral strength of left-wing political parties, and the level of wage bargaining. Unfortunately, data on these variables is relatively limited, and their inclusion greatly reduces, and biases the data. While data on union density, *Union*, is available for fifty-four developed and developing countries, data on left-wing parties is only available for twenty OECD countries, and data on wage bargaining centralization is only available for fifteen OECD countries. Due to correlation between *LaborRights* and these various measures of labor power, only one new control can be added to the model at a time.[33] However, as can be seen in Table 7.6 of the Appendix, the association between *LaborRights* and the profit-sharing rate is robust to the inclusion of each of these different measures of labor power. Although not displayed below, the results are also robust to the inclusion of interaction terms between *Productivity** and each of the labor power variables, respectively.

Fixed-Effect Regression and Rarely Changing Variables

Next, I check to make sure that the results are not driven by the inclusion of country-level fixed effects and variables that are rarely changing at the country level.[34] I use the Variance Inflator Factor (VIF) to test for multicollinearity between *LaborRights* and the country fixed effects. The test yields a VIF of only 2.83 for *LaborRights*, which is well below the traditional threshold of 5.[35] The full model includes *Openness* and *GDPpc*, both of which do not vary much within countries from year to year, and therefore may be collinear with the country-level fixed effects. The variance inflator factor (VIF) suggests that *GDPpc* contains little information not contained by the other independent variables (VIF of 12.4). This high VIF value means that GDP per capita is being controlled for in the model even without the inclusion of this variable. Similarly, *Openness* has a VIF of 6.3 and therefore is also likely collinear with the country-level fixed effects. However, as can be seen in Table 7.7 of the Appendix, the coefficient on the interaction term between *Productivity** and *LaborRights* is of a nearly identical magnitude and statistical significance whether or not these variables are included. Model 1 replicates the full model, while Models 2 and 3 alternatively drop *GDPpc* and *Openness*. Last, Model 4 drops both *GDPpc* and *Openness*. We should therefore have high confidence that the main results reported earlier are not due to multicollinearity among the regressors.

Standard Errors: PCSE vs. Cluster-Robust Standard Errors

I also re-estimate the main findings using cluster-robust standard errors instead of the panel-correct standard errors reported previously. Table 7.8 of the Appendix replicates the full model tests of Hypotheses 1 and 2

---

33 For correlations between *LaborRights*, *Union*, *Left*, and *Bargain*, see Table 7.5 in the Appendix.
34 Plümper and Troeger 2007.
35 For a discussion of identifying multicollinearity using VIF, see O'Brien 2007. The results reported below are robust to dropping Sweden and France, the two countries with the least *LaborRights* variation over time.

(Model 4 and Model 5 in Table 7.2, respectively) using robust standard errors, clustered at the country-level. The coefficient on the interaction between *Productivity** and *LaborRights* remains statistically significant in both Model 1 and Model 2. The cluster-robust standard errors are slightly larger than the panel-corrected standard errors reported above, but do not undermine the main finding that the protection of labor rights is positively associated with the profit-sharing rate.[36]

Technological Change and Fixed Effects

Might the results be driven by technological change that alters the profit-sharing rate in different industries or countries? To address this concern, I re-estimate the model with additional fixed effects at the industry-year and industry-country levels. Including these extra fixed effects helps to control for additional omitted variables that may be related to technological changes. For instance, if a new technology suddenly diffused through a specific industry in every country, the effect would be control for by the inclusion of industry-year fixed effects. Similarly, if a new industry-specific technology was developed in one country, and then not allowed to diffuse to other countries, the effect of such innovation would be controlled for by the inclusion of industry-country fixed effects. As can be seen in Table 7.9 of the Appendix, including these fixed effects barely alters the coefficient on the interaction terms between *Productivity** and *LaborRights*, and the coefficient remains highly statistically significant ($p < 0.001$). Model 1 adds industry-year fixed effects only, while Model 2 adds industry-country fixed effects only. Finally, Model 3 adds both industry-year and industry-country fixed effects. By including these two extra types of fixed effects, in addition to the full model specification with control variables and fixed effects at the country, year, and industry levels, we are able to further ensure the robustness of this chapter's findings.

Disaggregating Labor Rights

Which is more important for the profit-sharing rate, the legal protection of labor rights or the actual protection of labor rights in practice? In order to answer this question, I disaggregate *LaborRights* into its two component parts based on the protection of labor rights in law and

---

[36] Although not presented below, the findings are also robust to clustering the standard errors at the industry-country level.

the protection of labor rights in practice. By estimating the model with each of these two labor rights measures we can see if the results are driven by variation in only one part of the *LaborRights* index. As can be seen in Table 7.10 of the Appendix, the results are robust to estimating the model with both *LRLaw* and *LRPractice*, the two disaggregated measures of *LaborRights*. Model 1 estimates the model using the measure based on labor rights in law and therefore includes an interaction term between *Productivity** and *LRLaw*. The coefficient on this interaction term is positive, and of a similar magnitude (0.011) as the interaction term when estimated with *LaborRights* in Model 4 of Table 7.2, but is only statistically significant at the p < .10 level. Model 2 estimates the model using the measure based on labor rights in practice and therefore includes an interaction term between *Productivity** and *LRPractice*. The coefficient on this interaction term is positive (0.017) and statistically significant (p < 0.05). Since the coefficients on the labor rights interaction terms in both models are of similar signs, magnitudes, and levels of statistical significance, this robustness check suggests that the findings are not being driven overwhelmingly by only one type of labor rights violation.

Determinants of the Profit-Sharing Rate

The regression results presented above include many variables that are expected to influence wage growth or to be associated with the protection of labor rights. While this approach controls for alternative explanations, it does not directly estimate the relationship between the control variables and the profit-sharing rate. In order to do so, the model presented in Table 7.11 of the Appendix adds additional interaction terms between *Productivity** and each independent variable.[37] These additional interaction coefficients estimate whether or not the relationship between productivity growth and wage growth is moderated by any of the control variables.[38] As can be seen in Table 7.11, the only additional variable that has a statistically significant association with the profit-sharing rate is *FDI*.[39] According to these results, an increase in FDI is associated

---

[37] All variables have been centered at their mean in order to reduce multicollinearity and ease the interpretation of the interaction terms. See, Robinson and Schumacker 2009.

[38] Model 1 does not include *GDPpc* or *Openness*. As explained above, the inclusion of these rarely changing variables leads to multicollinearity with the country-level fixed effects.

[39] The relationship between *Employment* and the profit-sharing rate just misses the traditional threshold for statistical significance.

with wages that lag behind productivity growth. Most importantly, the main findings are robust to the inclusion of these additional interaction terms. The coefficient on the interaction term between *Productivity** and *LaborRights* is statistically significant and nearly identical to the estimates in other models.

Labor Rights in OECD and Developing Countries

The results presented above assume that the effect of labor rights on profit-sharing is similar across countries. However, is it possible that the effect of labor rights varies across levels of economic development? In order to address this concern, I disaggregate the data and estimate the model separately for OECD and non-OECD countries. The results are presented in Table 7.12 of the Appendix. Model 1 estimates the full model using data on all available countries. Model 2 estimates the model using data only from countries that are members of the OECD. Model 3 estimates the model using data only from non-OECD countries. Due to missing data on unemployment in developing countries, Model 3 drops *Unemployment* and instead uses Rudra's measure of potential labor power, *PLP*. This variable provides an alternative measure of labor market conditions and has the benefit of wider coverage in developing countries.[40] The coefficient on the interaction term between *Productivity** and *LaborRights* is positive and statistically significant when estimating the model on either subset of countries. This robustness check suggests that labor rights have a positive effect on profit-sharing in both developed and developing countries.

These robustness checks, as well as the inclusion of various control variables and fixed effects at the country, year, and industry levels, should increase our confidence that labor rights are positively associated with the profit-sharing rate. The results are robust to adding alternative measures of labor power, dropping rarely changing variables, cluster-robust standard errors, fixed effects at the industry-year and industry-country levels, as well as disaggregated measures of labor rights. In all of these alternative specifications, the interaction term between *Productivity** and *LaborRights* remains positive and statistically significant. This means that when labor rights are not well protected, an increase in productivity does not automatically lead to the equal wage increase predicted by the neoclassical trade models.

---

[40] For more information concerning "potential labor power," see Rudra 2002.

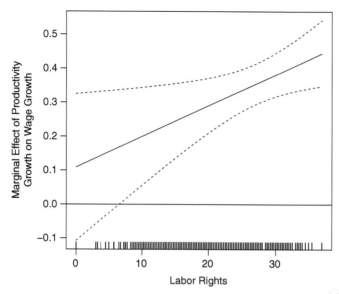

Figure 7.2. Marginal Effect of Productivity Growth on Wage Growth

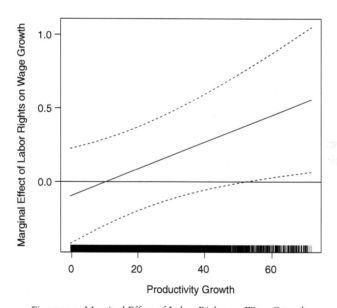

Figure 7.3. Marginal Effect of Labor Rights on Wage Growth

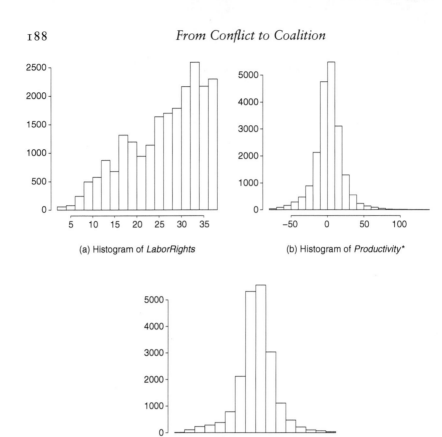

(a) Histogram of *LaborRights*

(b) Histogram of *Productivity**

(c) Histogram of *Wage**

Figure 7.4. Distribution of Variables

Table 7.3. *Descriptive Statistics*

	Obs.	Mean	Standard Deviation	Min.	Max.
Productivity*	16,047	14.41	12.75	0.00	69.24
Wage*	16,047	8.25	16.08	−69.28	69.11
LaborRights	14,136	27.37	7.98	0.00	37.00
Employment (thousands)	16,047	58.20	165.00	1.00	2,620.00
Capital/Labor	11,799	5.46	166.43	0.00	11,900.00
PopEmployed	14,703	0.19	0.34	0.00	7.47
FDI (billions)	14,352	4.96	18.70	−4.55	321.00
Polity	13,894	4.96	6.39	−10.00	10.00
Openness	14,686	73.83	52.64	0.62	371.82
GDPpc (thousands)	14,703	13.30	11.00	0.19	72.70
Unemploy-ment	10,842	8.36	4.82	0.50	36.40
Union	9,336	27.85	22.05	0.00	95.50
Left	4,157	39.82	41.36	0.00	100.00
Bargain	3,124	2.81	1.30	1.00	5.00

Table 7.4. *Correlation Table – Industry-Country-Year Variables*

	Wage*	Productivity*	Capital/Labor	PopEmployed	Employment
Wage*	1.00	0.52	−0.00	0.02	0.01
Productivity*	0.52	1.00	−0.02	0.01	0.01
Capital/Labor	−0.00	−0.02	1.00	−0.01	−0.01
PopEmployed	0.02	0.01	−0.01	1.00	0.41
Employment	0.01	0.01	−0.01	0.41	1.00

Table 7.5. *Correlation Table – Country-Year Variables*

	LaborRights	GDPpc	Openness	Polity	Unemployment	FDI	Union	Left	Bargain
LaborRights	1.00	0.36	0.07	0.32	0.12	0.09	0.52	0.38	0.55
GDPpc	0.36	1.00	0.15	0.34	-0.26	0.34	0.41	-0.08	0.03
Openness	0.07	0.15	1.00	-0.13	-0.07	-0.07	0.09	0.01	0.25
Polity	0.32	0.34	-0.13	1.00	0.02	0.18	0.39	-0.15	0.15
Unemployment	0.12	-0.26	-0.07	0.02	1.00	-0.07	-0.01	0.03	-0.19
FDI	0.09	0.34	-0.07	0.18	-0.07	1.00	-0.04	-0.06	-0.38
Union	0.52	0.41	0.09	0.39	-0.01	-0.04	1.00	0.04	0.63
Left	0.38	-0.08	0.01	-0.15	0.03	-0.06	0.04	1.00	0.30
Bargain	0.55	0.03	0.25	0.15	-0.19	-0.38	0.63	0.30	1.00

Table 7.6. *Robustness Check: Labor Rights and Labor Power Variables*

	Model 1	Model 2	Model 3	Model 4
Productivity*	0.109	0.044	−0.908*	−0.504
	(0.110)	(0.132)	(0.364)	(0.506)
LaborRights	−0.093	0.213	−0.496[†]	−0.525[†]
	(0.164)	(0.227)	(0.270)	(0.288)
Productivity*:LaborRights	0.009*	0.011*	0.039***	0.028[†]
	(0.004)	(0.005)	(0.011)	(0.015)
Employment	0.361	0.383	−0.457	−0.930[†]
	(0.300)	(0.365)	(0.326)	(0.562)
FDI	−0.594	2.410	2.812	2.813
	(1.963)	(2.212)	(2.292)	(3.043)
Capital/Labor	−0.116	−0.084	−0.660	−1.542*
	(0.251)	(0.320)	(0.477)	(0.649)
PopEmployed	−1.221	−1.179	−1.112	1.228
	(0.759)	(0.798)	(1.092)	(1.488)
Polity	0.852***	0.847*		
	(0.234)	(0.371)		
Openness	1.360	6.759	0.080	−5.146
	(4.859)	(7.463)	(10.611)	(13.670)
GDPpc	−0.262	3.022	−21.366	−28.955
	(6.257)	(8.450)	(18.716)	(31.410)
Unemployment	−0.866**	−1.145**	−0.219	−0.131
	(0.273)	(0.367)	(0.550)	(0.640)
Union		0.360***		
		(0.089)		
Left			0.022	
			(0.021)	
Bargain				−0.922
				(1.453)
Country Fixed Effects	yes	yes	yes	yes
Year Fixed Effects	yes	yes	yes	yes
Industry Fixed Effects	yes	yes	yes	yes
N	7755	5599	3227	2372
R^2	0.266	0.344	0.514	0.520
adj. R^2	0.254	0.332	0.503	0.507
Resid. sd	12.942	12.084	8.658	8.957

OLS Regression Results. DV = *Wage**.
Panel-corrected standard errors in parentheses
[†] significant at $p < 0.10$; *$p < 0.05$; **$p < 0.01$; ***$p < 0.001$

Table 7.7. *Robustness Check: Fixed-Effect Regression and Rarely Changing Variables*

	Model 1	Model 2	Model 3	Model 4
(Intercept)	4.878	4.520	10.798	9.175
	(69.284)	(48.757)	(67.215)	(45.270)
Productivity*	0.110	0.110	0.110	0.111
	(0.111)	(0.112)	(0.111)	(0.113)
LaborRights	−0.093	−0.093	−0.100	−0.100
	(0.164)	(0.164)	(0.156)	(0.156)
Productivity*:LaborRights	0.009*	0.009*	0.009*	0.009*
	(0.004)	(0.004)	(0.004)	(0.004)
Employment	0.359	0.359	0.367	0.367
	(0.297)	(0.295)	(0.292)	(0.289)
FDI	−0.609	−0.611	−0.559	−0.567
	(1.952)	(1.938)	(1.951)	(1.934)
Capital/Labor	−0.377	−0.376	−0.374	−0.373
	(0.796)	(0.801)	(0.793)	(0.798)
PopEmployed	−1.197	−1.197	−1.184	−1.186
	(0.748)	(0.738)	(0.760)	(0.749)
Polity	0.852***	0.851***	0.858***	0.856***
	(0.235)	(0.235)	(0.232)	(0.232)
Openness	1.377	1.380		
	(4.862)	(4.894)		
GDPpc	−0.045		−0.213	
	(6.193)		(6.233)	
Unemployment	−0.867**	−0.866***	−0.879**	−0.876***
	(0.273)	(0.235)	(0.275)	(0.236)
Country Fixed Effects	yes	yes	yes	yes
Year Fixed Effects	yes	yes	yes	yes
Industry Fixed Effects	yes	yes	yes	yes
N	7755	7755	7755	7755
R^2	0.266	0.266	0.266	0.266
adj. R^2	0.254	0.254	0.254	0.254
Resid. sd	12.943	12.942	12.942	12.942

OLS Regression Results. DV = *Wage**.
Panel-corrected standard errors in parentheses
[†] significant at $p < 0.10$; *$p < 0.05$; **$p < 0.01$; ***$p < 0.001$

Table 7.8. *Robustness Check: Standard Errors Clustered by Country*

	Model 1	Model 2
(Intercept)	5.639	63.129
	(89.147)	(153.124)
Productivity*	0.109	−0.806
	(0.102)	(0.639)
LaborRights	−0.093	0.004
	(0.151)	(0.328)
Productivity*:LaborRights	0.009*	0.041[†]
	(0.004)	(0.024)
Employment	0.361	
	(0.325)	
FDI	−0.594	−0.458
	(1.828)	(3.242)
Capital/Labor	−0.116	−2.332[†]
	(0.253)	(1.306)
PopEmployed	−1.221	
	(0.646)	
Polity	0.852**	1.270*
	(0.284)	(0.541)
Openness	1.360	2.274
	(5.713)	(9.719)
GDPpc	−0.262	−8.136
	(7.728)	(10.393)
Unemployment	−0.866*	−0.825
	(0.340)	(0.731)
Country Fixed Effects	yes	yes
Year Fixed Effects	yes	yes
Industry Fixed-Effects	yes	no
N	7755	303
R^2	0.266	0.439
adj. R^2	0.254	0.237
Resid. sd	12.942	10.934

OLS Regression Results. DV = Wage*.
Cluster-robust standard errors in parentheses
[†] significant at $p < 0.10$; *$p < 0.05$; **$p < 0.01$; ***$p < 0.001$

Table 7.9. *Robustness Check: Technology, Industry-Country and*
Industry-Year Fixed Effects

	Model 1	Model 2	Model 3
(Intercept)	0.489	−1.988	−16.173
	(89.265)	(104.153)	(32.846)
Productivity*	0.119	0.053	0.052
	(0.107)	(0.133)	(0.144)
LaborRights	−0.087	−0.090	−0.086
	(0.159)	(0.171)	(0.171)
Productivity*:LaborRights	0.010*	0.012**	0.013**
	(0.004)	(0.004)	(0.005)
Employment	0.450	1.280	1.224
	(0.325)	(1.273)	(1.302)
FDI	−0.829	−0.359	−0.450
	(1.868)	(2.099)	(2.093)
Capital/Labor	−0.670[†]	0.352	0.152
	(0.386)	(0.724)	(0.802)
PopEmployed	−1.261*	−3.180	−3.997
	(0.622)	(3.463)	(3.373)
Polity	0.815**	0.811**	0.782**
	(0.279)	(0.311)	(0.299)
Openness	1.590	1.123	1.836
	(5.77)	(6.68)	(6.660)
GDPpc	−0.066	−0.091	0.011
	(7.591)	(8.705)	(8.449)
Unemployment	−0.872**	−0.836*	−0.859*
	(0.340)	(0.405)	(0.399)
Country Fixed Effects	yes	yes	yes
Year Fixed Effects	yes	yes	yes
Industry Fixed Effects	yes	yes	yes
Industry-Year Fixed Effects	yes	no	yes
Industry-Country Fixed Effects	no	yes	yes
N	7755	7755	7755
R^2	0.307	0.385	0.430
adj. R^2	0.254	0.228	0.230
Resid. sd	12.943	13.171	13.153

OLS Regression Results. DV = Wage*.

Cluster-robust standard errors in parentheses

[†] significant at $p < 0.10$; *$p < 0.05$; **$p < 0.01$; ***$p < 0.001$

Table 7.10. *Robustness Check: Disaggregate* LaborRights
into Law and Practice

	Model 1	Model 2
(Intercept)	8.687	8.448
	(70.125)	(70.125)
Productivity*	0.084	−0.021
	(0.165)	(0.165)
LRLaw	−0.269	
	(0.259)	
LRPractice		−0.111
		(0.259)
Productivity*:LRLaw	0.011†	
	(0.007)	
Productivity*:LRPractice		0.017*
		(0.007)
Employment	0.352	0.380
	(0.291)	(0.291)
FDI	−0.538	−0.733
	(1.955)	(1.955)
Capital/Labor	−0.382	−0.311
	(0.792)	(0.792)
PopEmployed	−1.215	−1.265†
	(0.740)	(0.740)
Polity	0.863***	0.869***
	(0.233)	(0.233)
Openness	0.985	1.647
	(4.668)	(4.668)
GDPpc	−0.027	−0.226
	(6.276)	(6.276)
Unemployment	−0.873**	−0.866**
	(0.270)	(0.270)
Country Fixed Effects	yes	yes
Year Fixed Effects	yes	yes
Industry Fixed Effects	yes	yes
N	7755	7755
R^2	0.265	0.267
adj. R^2	0.253	0.255
Resid. sd	12.953	12.937

OLS Regression Results. DV = Wage*.
Panel-corrected standard errors in parentheses
† significant at $p < 0.10$; *$p < 0.05$; **$p < 0.01$; ***$p < 0.001$

Table 7.11. *Robustness Check: Determinants of the Profit-Sharing Rate*

	Model 1
(Intercept)	−5.281
	(43.620)
Productivity*	1.778*
	(0.839)
LaborRights	−0.107
	(0.157)
Productivity*:LaborRights	0.010*
	(0.004)
Productivity*:Employment	0.033[†]
	(0.018)
Productivity*:FDI	−0.086*
	(0.039)
Productivity*:Capital/Labor	−0.036
	(0.090)
Productivity*:PopEmployed	−0.044
	(0.105)
Productivity*:Polity	−0.001
	(0.006)
Productivity*:Unemployment	−0.003
	(0.006)
Country Fixed Effects	yes
Year Fixed Effects	yes
Industry Fixed Effects	yes
N	7755
R^2	0.268
adj. R^2	0.256
Resid. sd	12.927

OLS Regression Results. DV = Wage*.

Panel-corrected standard errors in parentheses

The model includes the constituent terms of each interaction, but for presentation purposes only the interaction coefficients are presented.

[†] significant at $p < 0.10$; *$p < 0.05$; **$p < 0.01$; ***$p < 0.001$

Table 7.12. *Robustness Check: OECD and Developing Countries*

	Model 1	Model 2	Model 3
(Intercept)	5.639	29.632	−228.768*
	(69.145)	(98.060)	(102.750)
Productivity*	0.109	−0.136	0.118
	(0.110)	(0.193)	(0.098)
LaborRights	−0.093	0.212	−0.123
	(0.164)	(0.211)	(0.188)
Productivity*:LaborRights	0.009*	0.016**	0.008*
	(0.004)	(0.006)	(0.004)
Employment	0.361	−0.386	0.121
	(0.300)	(0.349)	(0.435)
FDI	−0.594	2.124	9.421*
	(1.963)	(2.212)	(4.308)
Capital/Labor	−0.116	0.137	−0.077
	(0.251)	(0.406)	(0.224)
PopEmployed	−1.221	−0.757	−0.486
	(0.759)	(1.112)	(0.747)
Polity	0.852***	1.633***	0.025
	(0.234)	(0.325)	(0.265)
Openness	1.360	0.577	−4.010
	(4.859)	(5.716)	(6.002)
GDPpc	−0.262	−8.183	4.905
	(6.257)	(7.951)	(5.241)
Unemployment	−0.866**	−0.110	
	(0.273)	(0.318)	
PLP			0.131
			(0.395)
Country Fixed Effects	yes	yes	yes
Year Fixed Effects	yes	yes	yes
Industry Fixed Effects	yes	yes	yes
N	7755	4550	3389
R^2	0.266	0.410	0.177
adj. R^2	0.254	0.399	0.157
Resid. sd	12.942	9.883	14.605

OLS Regression Results. DV = Wage*.
Panel-corrected standard errors in parentheses
[†] significant at $p < 0.10$; *$p < 0.05$; **$p < 0.01$; ***$p < 0.001$

Table 7.13. *117 Countries in Dataset*

Afghanistan, Albania, Algeria, Argentina, Armenia, Australia, Austria, Azerbaijan, Bahamas, Bangladesh, Barbados, Belgium, Belize, Bolivia, Bosnia and Herzegovina, Botswana, Brazil, Bulgaria, Burundi, Cameroon, Canada, Central African Republic, Chile, China, Colombia, Costa Rica, Cote d'Ivoire, Croatia, Cuba, Cyprus, Czech Republic, Czechoslovakia, Denmark, Ecuador, El Salvador, Eritrea, Estonia, Fiji, Finland, France, Gabon, Germany, Ghana, Greece, Guatemala, Honduras, Hungary , Iceland, India, Indonesia, Iraq, Ireland, Israel, Italy, Jamaica , Japan, Jordan, Kazakhstan, Kenya, Korea, Kuwait, Latvia, Lithuania, Luxembourg, Macedonia, Madagascar, Malawi, Malaysia, Malta, Mauritius, Mexico, Moldova, Mongolia, Morocco, Mozambique, Myanmar, Nepal, Netherlands, New Zealand, Niger, Nigeria, Norway, Oman, Pakistan, Panama, Papua New Guinea, Peru, Philippines, Poland, Portugal, Qatar, Romania, Russia, Rwanda, Senegal, Seychelles, Singapore, Slovenia, South Africa, Spain, Sri Lanka, Suriname, Swaziland, Sweden, Syrian Arab Republic, Tanzania, Thailand, Tonga, Trinidad and Tobago, Tunisia, Turkey, Ukraine, United Kingdom, United States, Uruguay, Venezuela, and Zimbabwe.

Table 7.14. *46 Countries Missing Data and Dropped from Full Model*

Afghanistan, Albania, Argentina, Armenia, Bahamas, Barbados, Belize, Bosnia and Herzegovina, Burundi, Central African Republic, China, Costa Rica, Cuba, Czechoslovakia, Eritrea, Estonia, Ghana, Honduras, Iceland, Iraq, Jamaica, Kazakhstan, Luxembourg, Macedonia, Madagascar, Malawi, Malta, Mauritius, Moldova, Mongolia, Mozambique, Myanmar, Nepal, Nigeria, Oman, Papua New Guinea, Qatar, Russia, Rwanda, Senegal, Seychelles, South Africa, Suriname, Syrian Arab Republic, Tonga, and Trinidad and Tobago.

8

Conclusion

The assumption of many political economists that the interests of these two classes are identical, that the employer is best able to judge what is expedient, and that therefore the employee should trust his interests to him, assured that if he takes excessive profits they will, under the action of economical forces, be restored speedily and surely in increased wages, is both absurd and dangerous. The tendency of these economical forces under present conditions is the perpetuation and deepening of industrial injustice.   Joseph D. Weeks, 1886

For at least the past thirty years, scholars of international trade have assumed that the benefits of international trade policy are automatically shared between capital and labor.[1] Based on this assumption, canonical works in the field argue that trade policy reform is often driven by a harmonious coalition of capital and labor in favor of the same international trade policy. In direct contrast, this book demonstrated that this conventional wisdom is based on a flawed understanding of history that systematically ignores major instances of class conflict. Workers often disagree with their employers concerning international trade policies that benefit their own industry of employment. Indeed, they commonly argue that trade policy reforms will increase profits for their employers without leading to increased wages for themselves. Although such worker concerns have shaped trade policy debates for the past 200 years, they cannot be explained by the traditional theories that dominate research in political economy. In short, how are we to understand when workers and their employers will actually share the same international trade policy preference?

This book brings domestic labor markets and class conflict back into the political economy of international trade. It argued that labor's trade

---

[1] Gourevitch 1986; Rogowski 1989; Scheve and Slaughter 2001; Hiscox 2002; Mansfield and Mutz 2009.

policy preferences depend on a previously omitted factor: the presence or absence of "profit-sharing institutions." Profit-sharing institutions are defined as a set of rules that govern wage negotiations and create a credible link between an increase in profits and an increase in workers' wages. When profit-sharing institutions are in place, I predict that workers will be more likely to agree with their employers concerning international trade policy. However, when profit-sharing institutions are absent, I predict that workers will be more likely to disagree with their employers concerning trade policy.

Profit-sharing institutions help us understand variation in workers' trade policy preferences that cannot be explained by the neoclassical models traditionally used in the field. According to the Heckscher-Ohlin model, a trade policy that benefits labor-intensive industries automatically increases workers' wages. Although this model can predict class conflict under certain circumstances, scholars repeatedly use this model to predict capital-labor agreement in prominent historical cases that were actually characterized by widespread worker dissent. According to the Ricardo-Viner model, a trade policy that benefits a specific industry automatically leads to increases in both profits and wages. This approach is used by scholars to predict that capital and labor employed in the same industry will always share the same trade policy preferences. Simply put, this popular model describes a world in which class conflict is theoretically impossible.

This book presented rigorous qualitative and quantitative evidence in support of my theory. Chapter 4 began by exploring trade politics in the United States during the late nineteenth century. It presented a structured, focused comparison of profit-sharing institutions and workers' trade policy preferences in the American steel and textile industries. The analysis described the origin and evolution of profit-sharing institutions in each case, and demonstrated that profit-sharing institutions make workers more likely to share the same trade policy preferences as their employers. In direct contrast to the conventional wisdom concerning this period, I demonstrated that labor unions often doubted the benefit of high tariffs, arguing that tariffs protected capital in the product market while leaving workers unprotected in the labor market. These unions only shared the same trade policy preferences of their employers when profit-sharing institutions were in place. This chapter drew on extensive archival research of labor union publications and local newspapers from the end of the nineteenth century in order to trace the evolution of workers' trade policy preferences.

Chapter 5 went a step further, and argued that profit-sharing institutions had an important impact on American trade policy outcomes. This chapter examined the renewal of the Reciprocal Trade Agreements Act in 1945, and demonstrated the important role played by the free trade demands of the Congress of Industrial Organizations (CIO). Although the CIO did not support free trade in the 1930s, the pro-labor legislation of the New Deal gave rise to profit-sharing institutions that contributed to the CIO's endorsement of free trade in the 1940s. With profit-sharing institutions in place, labor joined capital and formed a cross-class coalition that successfully lobbied the U.S. Senate in favor of free trade. In addition to demonstrating the importance of workers' trade policy preferences, this chapter contributed to a popular debate concerning American trade liberalization after World War II. Chapter 6 demonstrated the generalizability of my theory beyond the American case, by exploring trade politics in Britain and Argentina. Just like American workers in the late nineteenth and mid-twentieth centuries, British workers in the 1840s and Argentine workers in the 1930s argued that trade policy reforms increased profits for capital without increasing wages for labor. Last, Chapter 7 used quantitative data from over one hundred countries to rigorously test a critical step in my theory's causal logic. It demonstrated that when workers lack bargaining power, they are completely unable to capture a share of increased profits in the form of wages.

BEYOND THE HISTORY OF INTERNATIONAL TRADE

My theory of profit-sharing institutions has relevance far beyond the historical case studies presented above. Future research based on my theory should extend these findings in two different analytical directions. First, my theory promises to help scholars understand the political economy of trade in contemporary developing countries. The rapid industrialization and lack of labor protections that characterized Britain, the United States, and Argentina in previous centuries are now on clear display throughout the developing world. Just as workers in my historical cases disagreed with their employers concerning the trade policies that benefited their industries, we should expect workers in today's developing countries to disagree with their employers concerning the benefits of free trade. Second, my theory promises to help scholars understand domestic politics surrounding economic issue areas well beyond international trade. My theory's focus on the relationship between profits and wages promises to further our understanding of the political economy of any economic policy that influences an industry's profitability, including international economic policies such as foreign direct investment, monetary policy, and immigration, as well as domestic economic policies related to education and privatization. The remainder of this chapter briefly demonstrates these two promising avenues for future research.

Political Economy of Trade in Developing Countries

Although much of this book has focused on historical case studies, my theory of profit-sharing institutions has clear contemporary relevance. As demonstrated in Chapter 7, the gap between trade policy and workers' wages is alive and well in developing countries that do not protect labor rights. In countries with the worst violations of labor rights, such as Malaysia and Colombia, free trade policies that benefit export-oriented industries are unlikely to increase workers' wages at all. Based on this lack of profit sharing, workers and unions throughout the developing world have frequently disagreed with their employers concerning the benefits of free trade, which tends to increase exports and profits, without increasing workers' wages.

For example, consider the trade policy preferences of Mexican workers during the negotiations of the North American Free Trade Agreement (NAFTA) in the early 1990s. According to the neoclassical approach, trade liberalization between the U.S. and Mexico would benefit Mexican workers by increasing demand for labor south of the border.[2] What position did Mexican workers and unions take on NAFTA? It depends where we look, and whether or not labor unions were closely aligned with the government. The main labor federation, the *Confederación de Trabajadores de México* was closely aligned with Mexico's long-dominant ruling party, the *Partido Revolucionario Institucional*, and consistently supported the government's pro-NAFTA position. This coalition of labor and the state was joined by export-oriented Mexican businesses that sought to increase trade with the United States.[3]

However, Mexican labor unions unaffiliated with the state argued that the agreement would increase the profitability of labor-intensive, export industries without increasing workers' wages. According to the *Frente Auténtico del Trabajo*, workers would fail to benefit from the agreement unless mechanisms were put into place that would ensure that wages increased along with productivity gains.[4] The *Frente* joined with other Mexican labor unions, peasant organizations, and indigenous groups to form the Mexican Action Network on Free Trade, which formally

---

[2] Brown et al. 1992. According to the H-O model, all Mexican workers stood to gain from NAFTA. According to the R-V model, only Mexican workers in export-oriented industries stood to gain.

[3] Poitras and Robinson 1994.

[4] de la Garza Toledo 1994.

opposed NAFTA.[5] At the heart of these workers' disagreement with employers and the state was the insight that trade policy reforms can increase profits without increasing wages for workers.

In 2007, Peruvian labor unions expressed similar concerns regarding the extension of NAFTA through a U.S.-Peru Free Trade Agreement. In a letter to Democrats in the U.S. Congress, Peruvian labor union leaders explained that "we write today to ask that your concern for workers guide your decisions regarding the FTA, and that you vote 'no' to the expansion of the North American Free Trade Agreement to Peru."[6] The letter, which was signed by the Secretary General of the *Central Unitaria de Trabajadores del Perú* and the Secretary of International Relations of the *Confederación General de Trabajadores del Perú*, argued that without increased protection of labor rights, "the situation is still far from hopeful for Peruvian workers." However, as these labor leaders lamented, "the problem is that those who support the FTA in Peru are the same ones that oppose labor reform in Peru."[7] Two years later, the same unions warned that, "In the face of the Peruvian government's rush to seek implementation of the FTA ... [we] urge the government to slow down and protect the rights of working people. The best way to do this would be to pass a new General Labor Law."[8]

Worker skepticism about the benefits of free trade and export-led growth can also be seen in Bangladesh, where 200,000 workers in the ready-made garment (RMG) sector went on strike in September 2013. These workers argued that despite the growing profitability of their industry, their wages were falling behind the cost of living. As Sirajul Islam Rony, a leader of Bangladesh's National Garment Workers, explained, "The industry is the top foreign-currency earner in the country, but the workers are not getting the benefits. If the owners don't listen to our demands, there will be more unrest in the garment sector."[9] Whereas the neoclassical approach would predict that the wages paid to Bangladeshi workers would automatically increase along with the profitability of the RMG sectors, the reality appears to be playing out quite differently. According to MA Taslim, the chairman of the Economics Department of Dhaka University, "The wages of the RMG workers are not increasing in tandem with the increase in production and export earnings in the sector."[10] Or, as Nazma Akter, President of the Garment-Worker

5 MacDonald 2003; Hathaway 1997.
6 www.citizen.org/documents/PeruvianLaborLetter-082007.pdf
7 www.citizen.org/documents/PeruvianLaborLetter-082007.pdf
8 *Washington Office on Latin America,* January 16, 2009.
9 *Wall Street Journal,* September 22, 2013.
10 *The Daily Star,* October 1, 2013.

Federation, lamented, "The garment factory owners sell the products abroad at a high price, but we get low wages. This can't be justified."[11]

Such workers' concerns were brought to the fore in the aftermath of the Rana Plana factory collapse, which killed over 1,000 workers in April 2013. Following this industrial accident, the U.S. suspended Bangladesh's trade benefits under the Generalized System of Preferences (GSP), a program that grants developing countries preferential access to the U.S. market. As might be expected, Bangladeshi manufacturers were deeply opposed to the U.S. decision and pushed for the unconditional reinstatement of GSP. According to Atiqul Islam, President of the Bangladesh Garment Manufacturers and Exporters Association, "I can see no logical reason for this. We are not clear why it took such a decision. The U.S. says we need to improve working conditions. We did that ... What they are saying about working conditions and labour standards is not right."[12] Bangladeshi manufacturers dismissed concerns about Bangladeshi labor standards and sought duty-free access for garments to the U.S. market.[13]

In contrast, Bangladeshi labor unions in the RMG sector disagree with their employers concerning GSP, and have taken a very different approach. Rather than demand increased market access, Bangladeshi workers requested that the U.S. require several pro-labor reforms *before* GSP is reinstated. These demands were delivered by Kalpona Akter, the Executive Director of the Bangladesh Center for Worker Solidarity, in testimony before the U.S. Senate Foreign Relations Committee in February 2014. According to Akter, the U.S. should not reinstate GSP until workers are free to exercise their collective bargaining rights, Bangladesh reforms its labor laws so that they meet the ILO standards, and unsubstantiated charges against labor leaders are dismissed, among other demands.[14] In short, doubts about the link between trade policy and wages has led to growing disagreement between Bangladeshi workers and their employers. Whereas manufacturers in the RMG sector see GSP, increased market access, and exports as immediately beneficial, workers appear to disagree and are withholding support for free trade until conditions in the labor market improve.

Implications Beyond International Trade

My theory of profit-sharing institutions has important implications for the study of political economy issue areas well beyond international trade.

---

[11] *World Policy Blog*, June 27, 2013.
[12] "U.S. Decision to Suspend GSP Illogical," *Priyo News*, June 29, 2013.
[13] "BGMEA Expects GSP Restoration," *bdnews24.com*, November 18, 2013.
[14] www.foreign.senate.gov/imo/media/doc/Akter_Testimony.pdf

My theory's basic insight – that the link between economic policy and workers' wages depends on domestic labor market institutions – is easily generalizable to international political economy topics such as foreign direct investment, exchange rates, and immigration policy.[15] The causal logic linking all of these economic policies to workers' wages includes the assumption of full employment and the prediction that an increase in the marginal revenue product of labor automatically leads to an increase in workers' wages. Just as profit-sharing institutions increase capital-labor agreement concerning international trade policy, such institutions should have a similar influence on cross-class cooperation concerning other economic policies.

My theory of profit-sharing institutions also has implications for domestic policy debates concerning issues as diverse as education reform and the privatization of industry. In these debates, the link between policy reform and wages is only slightly different: policy increases worker productivity, which increases the marginal revenue product of labor, which automatically increases workers' wages. Since at least Thatcher's Britain, politicians and scholars have regularly argued that privatization of industry would increase worker productivity, and therefore, workers' wages.[16] These arguments were commonly applied to post-socialist economies in the 1990s and continue to dominate debate on the ownership of industry in contemporary developing countries.[17] For example, consider the ongoing debate in Mexico concerning the privatization of PEMEX, the state-owned oil enterprise. According to Mexican President Enrique Peña Nieto, "This is the final goal ... that our economic policies are pushing for: That families can earn more, have better incomes, by being more productive."[18]

The assumption that an increase in productivity will automatically increase wages can also be found in debates surrounding education reform and income inequality. In general, the argument holds that increased education spending will increase the productivity of low-skilled workers, automatically increase their wages, and therefore reduce income inequality. This argument shapes the World Banks' proposals for reducing income inequality in Latin America, where they advocate education reform but make no reference to improving the protection

---

[15] On foreign direct investment, see Jensen and Rosas 2007; on exchange rate policy, see Frieden 1991; on immigration, see Peters 2015.

[16] Kornberg and Mishler 1988; Denisova et al. 2009.

[17] Estrin et al. 2009; Boix 1997.

[18] Alexandra Alper and Pablo Garibian, "Analysis: Mexico Bets on Reforms to Boost Wages, But No Quick Fix," *Reuters*, August 4, 2013.

of workers' rights.[19] Similarly, President Obama's new "middle-class economics" proposes to reduce income inequality through increased education spending, and other measures, without attention to protecting the rights of American workers.[20] While increased education spending is likely part of the solution to income inequality, increasing productivity without attention to workers' rights threatens to increase profits without increasing workers' wages.

Normative Implications

In addition to helping us understand trade policy outcomes, the trade policy preferences of workers explored in this book also have important normative implications. In short, the accepted wisdom in the field systematically exaggerates the benefits that workers receive from trade policy reforms that benefit their industry. Throughout the past two centuries, workers have explicitly denied that they receive the benefits predicted by the neoclassical models of international trade. While this mismatch between theory and reality is troubling in its own right, this gap takes on new meaning when we move to the world of policy advice and implications. Most importantly, the neoclassical trade models discussed in this book serve as the foundation for an extremely optimistic, and unfortunately naive, understanding of how contemporary globalization impacts the world's poor.

Trade liberalization in the developing world, where respect for labor rights is often quite low, is likely to deliver much lower wage increases than those predicted by the Heckscher-Ohlin or Ricardo-Viner models. Although trade liberalization is likely to increase productivity in labor-intensive industries,[21] potential wage increases are likely to be competed away by labor surpluses associated with unemployment and migration from rural areas.[22] A growing body of evidence now shows that international trade is associated with stagnant incomes and rising inequality in the world's least developed countries.[23] The prospect of trade liberalization increasing wages in developing countries is further dampened by development strategies that jointly pursue liberalization of

---

[19] Augusto de la Torre, Eduardo Levy Yeyati, Guillermo Beylis, Tatiana Didier, Carlos Rodríguez Castelán, and Sergio Schmukler, 2014. "Inequality in a Lower Growth Latin America." LAC Semiannual Report (October), World Bank, Washington, DC.

[20] Council of Economic Advisers, *Economic Report of the President* (Washington, D.C.: Government Printing Office, 2015).

[21] Krishna and Mitra 1998.

[22] Lewis 1954.

[23] Goldberg and Pavcnik 2004, 2007; Topalova and Khandelwal 2011.

trade policy alongside liberalization of the labor market.[24] To the extent that trade policy reform goes hand-in-hand with the deregulation of the labor market, workers will be left without the institutional protections that increase their ability to capture a share of increased prosperity. Such neoliberal reform is often advocated specifically because of the benefits that workers are predicted to receive from trade liberalization. Therefore, it is troubling that jointly pursued labor market reforms directly undermine the optimistic predictions concerning the effect of trade liberalization on wages. It seems ill-advised to propose policy reform *on behalf of* a group that may not actually benefit from the proposed policy change.

While the Bangladeshi case is still unfolding, this simple example should serve as a reminder of the actual distributional consequences of globalization. While thirty years of political economy scholarship has suggested that the spreading of markets will be like a rising tide that automatically lifts all boats, it is time to re-examine how domestic institutions determine who wins and who loses from economic policy changes. While the neoclassical trade models provide a morally attractive narrative – that free trade will disproportionately benefit the world's most poor – scholars ought to re-examine the conditions under which such laudable goals can be accomplished. It is my hope that the theory of profit-sharing institutions inspires scholars to provide a more accurate understanding of the distributional consequences of the modern world economy and to develop theories that help foster economic development that is shared more equitably with workers throughout the world.

[24] Rodrik 2011.

References

Acemoglu, D. and J. Robinson (2006). *Economic Origins of Dictatorship and Democracy.* Cambridge University Press.

Acemoglu, D. and J. A. Robinson (2008). Persistence of Power, Elites, and Institutions. *American Economic Review* 98(1), 267–293.

Adserà, A. and C. Boix (2002). Trade, Democracy, and the Size of the Public Sector: The Political Underpinnings of Openness. *International Organization* 56(2), 229–262.

Ahlquist, J. S., A. B. Clayton, and M. Levi (2014). Unionization and Workers' Attitudes toward International Trade: The ILWU puzzle. *International Organization* 68(1), 33–75.

Alexander, C. O. (1993). The Changing Relationship Between Productivity, Wages and Unemployment in the UK. *Oxford Bulletin of Economics and Statistics* 55(1), 87–102.

Alexander, R. J. (1962). *Labor Relations in Argentina, Brazil, and Chile.* McGraw-Hill.

Alt, J. E. and M. Gilligan (1994). The Political Economy of Trading States: Factor Specificity, Collective Action Problems and Domestic Political Institutions. *Journal of Political Philosophy* 2(2), 165–192.

Amalgamated Association of Iron and Steel Workers (1890). *Proceedings of the Sixteenth Annual Convention of the National Lodge.* Allied Printing.

Amalgamated Association of Iron and Steel Workers (1894). *Proceedings of the Twentieth Annual Convention of the National Lodge.* Allied Printing.

American Federation of Labor (1909). *Report of the Proceedings of the Twenty-Ninth Annual Convention of the American Federation of Labor.* Washington DC: The Law Reporter Printing Company.

American Manufacturers Export Association (1935). *Foreign Trade and Domestic Markets.* American Manufacturers Export Association.

Anderson, G. M. and R. D. Tollison (1985). Ideology, Interest Groups, and the Repeal of the Corn Laws. *Journal of Institutional and Theoretical Economics* 141, 197–212.

Archer, R. (2010). *Why Is There No Labor Party in the United States?* Princeton University Press.

Ardanaz, M., M. V. Murillo, and P. Pinto (2013). Sensitivity to Issue Framing on Trade Policy Preferences: Evidence from a Survey Experiment. *International Organization* 67(02), 411–437.

Axelrod, R. (2006). *Evolution of Cooperation*. Basic Books.

Bailey, M., J. Goldstein, and B. Weingast (1997). The Institutional Roots of American Trade Policys. *World Politics* 49(3), 309–338.

Baker, A. (2005). Who Wants to Globalize? Consumer Tastes and Labor Markets in a Theory of Trade Policy Beliefs. *American Journal of Political Science* 49(4), 924–938.

Baldwin, R. E. (1985). *Political Economy of US Import Policy*. MIT Press.

Barnard, J. (2005). *American Vanguard: The United Auto Workers During the Reuther Years, 1935–1970*. Wayne State University Press.

Barnes, D. G. (2005). *A History of the English Corn Laws, from 1660-1846*. Taylor & Francis US.

Beck, N. (2011). Of Fixed-Effects and Time-Invariant Variables. *Political Analysis* 19(2), 119–122.

Beck, N. and J. N. Katz (1995). What to Do (and Not to Do) with Time-Series Cross-Section Data. *American Political Science Review* 89(3), 634–647.

Beck, N. and J. N. Katz (1996). Nuisance vs. Substance: Specifying and Estimating Time-Series-Cross-Section Models. *Political Analysis* 6(1), 1–36.

Belman, D. L. and P. B. Voos (1993). Wage Effects of Increased Union Coverage: Methodological Considerations and New Evidence. *Industrial and Labor Relations Review* 46(2), 368–380.

Bennett, J. T. and B. E. Kaufman (2011). *What Do Unions Do?: A Twenty-Year Perspective*. Transaction Books.

Bensel, R. (2000). *The Political Economy of American Industrialization 1877–1900*. Cambridge University Press.

Bentolila, S. and G. Saint-Paul (2003). Explaining Movements in the Labor Share. *Contributions to Macroeconomics* 3(1), 1–33.

Bergquist, C. (1986). *Labor in Latin America*. Stanford University Press.

Bernstein, I. and F. F. Piven (1969). *The Turbulent Years: A History of the American Worker, 1933–1941*. Haymarket Books.

Blanchflower, D. G. and A. J. Oswald (1995). An Introduction to the Wage Curve. *The Journal of Economic Perspectives* 9(3), 153–167.

Blewett, M. H. (2000). *Constant Turmoil: The Politics of Industrial Life in Nineteenth-Century New England*. University of Massachusetts Press.

Blewett, M. H. (2009). Strikes in the Nineteenth-Century Cotton Textile Industry in the Northeast United States. In B. D. Aaron Brenner and I. Ness (Eds.), *The Encyclopedia of Strikes in American History*. Taylor & Francis, pp. 314–329.

Boix, C. (1997). Privatizing the Public Business Sector in the Eighties: Economic Performance, Partisan Responses and Divided Governments. *British Journal of Political Science* 27(04), 473–496.

Borjas, G. (2005). *Labor Economics*. McGraw-Hill Irwin.

Bosworth, B., G. L. Perry, and M. D. Shapiro (1994). Productivity and Real Wages: Is There a Puzzle? *Brookings Papers on Economic Activity* 1994(1), 317–344.

Brecher, J. (2014). *Strike!* PM Press.

Brennan, J. (2009). *The Labor Wars in Córdoba, 1955–1976: Ideology, Work, and Labor Politics in an Argentine Industrial Society*, Volume 116. Harvard University Press.

Brennan, J. P. (1998). *Peronism and Argentina*. Rowman & Littlefield.

Brock, W. A. and S. P. Magee (1978). The Economics of Special Interest Politics: The Case of the Tariff. *The American Economic Review 68*(2) May, 246–250.

Brody, D. (1960). *Steelworkers in America: The Nonunion Era*. University of Illinois Press.

Brody, D. (1993). *Workers in Industrial America: Essays on the Twentieth Century Struggle*. Oxford University Press.

Brooks, R. R. R. (1935). *The United Textile Workers of America*. Ph.D. thesis, Yale University.

Brown, D. K., A. V. Deardorff, and R. M. Stern (1992). A North American Free Trade Agreement: Analytical Issues and a Computational Assessment. *The World Economy 15*(1), 11–30.

Buchanan, P. G. (1985). State Corporatism in Argentina: Labor Administration Under Perón and Onganía. *Latin American Research Review 20*(1), 61–95.

Bureau of Labor of the State of New Hampshire (1894). *Annual Report*, Volume 2. Republican Press Association.

Burgoyne, A. (1979). *The Homestead Strike of 1892*. University of Pittsburgh Press.

Camargo, H. (2007). *La Union Industrial Argentina, 120 Anos Defendiendo la Produccion Nacional, 1887–2007*. Baires Print S.A.

Cameron, D. R. (1978). The Expansion of the Public Economy: A Comparative Analysis. *American Political Science Review 72*(04), 1243–1261.

Campbell, J. (1840). *An Examination of the Corn and Provision Laws, from their First Enactment to the Present Period*. A. Heywood.

Capozzola, C. (2002). The Only Badge Needed is Your Patriotic Fervor: Vigilance, Coercion, and the Law in World War I America. *The Journal of American History 88*(4), 1354–1382.

Chase, K. (2008). Moving Hollywood Abroad: Divided Labor Markets and the New Politics of Trade in Services. *International Organization 62*(4), 653–687.

Chase, K. A. (2003). Economic Interests and Regional Trading Arrangements: The Case of NAFTA. *International Organization 57*(1), 137–174.

Chaudoin, S., H. V. Milner, and X. Pang (2015). International Systems and Domestic Politics: Linking Complex Interactions with Empirical. Models in International Relations. *International Organization 69*(02), 275–309.

Cohen, M. (2007). "The Ku Klux Government": Vigilantism, Lynching, and the Repression of the IWW. *Journal for the Study of Radicalism 1*(1), 31–56.

Collier, R. and D. Collier (1991). *Shaping the Political Arena*. Princeton University Press Princeton.

Collier, R. B. and S. Handlin (2009). *Reorganizing Popular Politics: Participation and the New Interest Regime in Latin America*. Penn State Press.

Commons, J. R., D. J. Saposs, H. L. Sumner, E. B. Mittelman, H. E. Hoagland, J. B. Andrews, S. Perlman, D. D. Lescohier, E. Brandeis, and P. Taft (1918). *History of Labor in the United States*, Volume 2. The Macmillan Company.

Congress of Industrial Organizations (1941). *Daily Proceedings of the Fourth Constitutional Convention of the Congress of Industrial Organizations*. Congress of Industrial Organizations.

de la Garza Toledo, E. (1994). Mexican Labor Unions Facing the Free Trade Agreement (NAFTA). Presented at Conference on International Trade

Unionism at the Current Stage of Economic Globalization and Regionalization, Saitama University, Japan.

Denisova, I., M. Eller, T. Frye, and E. Zhuravskaya (2009). Who Wants to Revise Privatization? The Complementarity of Market Skills and Institutions. *American Political Science Review* 103(02), 284–304.

Dennis, M. (2014). *Blood on Steel: Chicago Steelworkers and the Strike of 1937*. JHU Press.

Destler, I. M. (2005). *American Trade Politics*. Peterson Institute.

Dicey, A. V. (1904). The Combination Laws as Illustrating the Relation between Law and Opinion in England during the Nineteenth Century. *Harvard Law Review* 17(8), 511–532.

Donohue, P. (1992). Free Trade Unions and the State: Trade Liberalization's Endorsement by the AFL–CIO, 1943–1962. *Research in Political Economy* 13, 1–73.

Ehrlich, S. D. (2010). The Fair Trade Challenge to Embedded Liberalism. *International Studies Quarterly* 54(4), 1013–1033.

Ehrlich, S. D. and C. Maestas (2010). Risk Orientation, Risk Exposure, and Policy Opinions: The Case of Free Trade. *Political Psychology* 31(5), 657–684.

Eichengreen, B. (1991). The Eternal Fiscal Question: Free Trade and Protection in Britain, 1860–1929. *Working Paper No. 91–171*, Department of Economics, University of California at Berkeley.

Erickson, C. (1952). *The Recruitment of European Immigrant Labor for American Industry from 1860 to 1885*. Ph.D. thesis, Cornell University.

Estrin, S., J. Hanousek, E. Kočenda, and J. Svejnar (2009). The Effects of Privatization and Ownership in Transition Economies. *Journal of Economic Literature* 47(3), 699–728.

Fall River Mule Spinners' Association (1894). *Handbook for Cotton Mule Spinners' Associations*. Fall River Mule Spinners' Association.

Farhang, S. and I. Katznelson (2005). The Southern Imposition: Congress and Labor in the New Deal and Fair Deal. *Studies in American Political Development* 19(01), 1–30.

Fearon, J. D. (1995). Rationalist Explanations for War. *International Organization* 49(3), 379–414.

Federation of Organized Trades and Labor Unions (1882). *Report of the Second Annual Session of the Federation of Organized Trades and Labor Unions of the United States and Canada*.

Fink, L. (1988). The New Labor History and the Powers of Historical Pessimism: Consensus, Hegemony, and the Case of the Knights of Labor. *The Journal of American History* 75(1), 115–136.

Foner, E. (1984). Why is There no Socialism in the United States? In *History Workshop Journal*, Volume 17, Oxford University Press, pp. 57–80.

Foner, P. (1998). *History of the Labor Movement in the United States*, Volume 2. International Publishers Company.

Freeman, R. B. and J. L. Medoff (1984). What Do Unions Do? *Industrial & Labor Relations Review* 38, 244.

Frieden, J. (1988). Sectoral Conflict and Foreign Economic Policy, 1914–1940. *International Organization* 42(01), 59–90.

Frieden, J. (1999). Actors and Preferences in International Relations. In D. Lake and R. Powell (Eds.), *Strategic Choice and International Relations*. Princeton University Press.

Frieden, J. A. (1991). Invested Interests: The Politics of National Economic Policies in a World of Global Finance. *International Organization* 45(4), 425–451.

Friedman, M. (1907). *The Pinkerton Labor Spy*. Wilshire Book Company.

Galenson, W. (1960). *The CIO Challenge to the AFL: A History of the American Labor Movement, 1935–1941*. Harvard University Press.

Garraty, J. (1968). *Labor and Capital in the Gilded Age*. Little, Brown.

George, A. L. and A. Bennett (2005). *Case Studies and Theory Development in the Social Sciences*. MIT Press.

Giavazzi, F. and G. Tabellini (2005). Economic and Political Liberalizations. *Journal of Monetary Economics* 52(7), 1297–1330.

Gilens, M. (2012). *Affluence and Influence: Economic Inequality and Political Power in America*. Princeton University Press.

Gilligan, M. J. (1997). *Empowering Exporters: Reciprocity, Delegation, and Collective Action in American Trade Policy*. University of Michigan Press.

Gilman, N. P. (1904). *Methods of Industrial Peace*. Houghton, Mifflin.

Gilpin, R. (1983). *War and Change in World Politics*. Cambridge University Press.

Goldberg, P. K. and N. Pavcnik (2004). Trade, Inequality, and Poverty: What Do We Know? Evidence from Recent Trade Liberalization Episodes in Developing Countries. In *Brookings Trade Forum*, JSTOR, pp. 223–269.

Goldberg, P. K. and N. Pavcnik (2007). Distributional Effects of Globalization in Developing Countries. *Journal of Economic Literature* 45(1), 39–82.

Goldstein, J. (1993). *Ideas, Interests, and American Trade Policy*. Cornell University Press.

Goldstein, J. and R. Gulotty (2014). America and Trade Liberalization: The Limits of Institutional Reform. *International Organization* 68(02), 263–295.

Gordon, C. (1994). *New Deals: Business, Labor, and Politics in America, 1920–1935*. Cambridge University Press.

Gourevitch, P. (1986). *Politics in Hard Times: Comparative Responses to International Economic Crises*. Cornell University Press.

Green, D. P., S. Y. H. Kim, and D. Yoon (2001). Dirty Pool. *International Organization* 55(02), 441–468.

Greene, J. (1998). *Pure and Simple Politics: The American Federation of Labor and Political Activism, 1881–1917*. Cambridge University Press.

Greenfield, H. I. (1959). *Sliding Wage Scales: A Theoretical and Historical Evaluation*. Columbia University.

Greenstone, J. D. (1969). *Labor in American Politics*, Volume 618. Knopf New York.

Guisinger, A. (2009). Determining Trade Policy: Do Voters Hold Politicians Accountable? *International Organization* 63(03), 533–557.

Hacker, J. S. and P. Pierson (2011). *Winner-Take-All Politics: How Washington Made the Rich Richer–and Turned Its Back on the Middle Class*. Simon and Schuster.

Haggard, S. and L. Tiede (2011). The Rule of Law and Economic Growth: Where Are We? *World Development* 39(5), 673–685.

Hainmueller, J. and M. J. Hiscox (2006). Learning to Love Globalization: Education and Individual Attitudes Toward International Trade. *International Organization* 60(02), 469–498.

Hall, R. E. and E. P. Lazear (1984). The Excess Sensitivity of Layoffs and Quits to Demand. *Journal of Labor Economics* 2(2), 233–257.

Hall, S. G. (1986). An Application of the Granger & Engle Two-Step Estimation Procedure to United Kingdom Aggregate Wage Data. *Oxford Bulletin of Economics and Statistics* 48(3), 229–239.

Hansen, J. M. (1991). *Gaining Access: Congress and the Farm Lobby, 1919–1981*. University of Chicago Press.

Harring, S. L. and L. M. McMullin (1975). The Buffalo Police 1872–1900: Labor Unrest, Political Power and the Creation of the Police Institution. *Crime and Social Justice* (4), 5–14.

Harris, J. R. and M. P. Todaro (1970). Migration, Unemployment and Development: A Two-Sector Analysis. *The American Economic Review* 60(1), 126–142.

Harvey, A. C. (1980). On Comparing Regression Models in Levels and First Differences. *International Economic Review* 21(3), 707–720.

Hathaway, D. (1997, April). Mexico's Frente Auténtico del Trabajo: Organizing Beyond the PRI and Across Borders. Latin American Studies Association Conference, Guadalajara.

Hattam, V. C. (1993). *Labor Visions and State Power: The Origins of Business Unionism in the United States*. Princeton University Press New Jersey.

Hayes, B. (1984). Unions and Strikes with Asymmetric Information. *Journal of Labor Economics* 2(1), 57–83.

Helpman, E., M. J. Melitz, and S. R. Yeaple (2004). Export versus FDI with Heterogeneous Firms. *The American Economic Review* 94(1), 300–316.

Hicks, R., H. V. Milner, and D. Tingley (2013). Trade Policy, Economic Interests, and Party Politics in a Developing Country: The Political Economy of CAFTA-DR. *International Studies Quarterly* 58, 106–117.

Hiscox, M. J. (1999). The Magic Bullet? The RTAA, Institutional Reform, and Trade Liberalization. *International Organization* 53(4), 669–698.

Hiscox, M. J. (2001). Class Versus Industry Cleavages: Inter-Industry Factor Mobility and the Politics of Trade. *International Organization* 55(01), 1–46.

Hiscox, M. J. (2002). *International Trade and Political Conflict: Commerce, Coalitions and Mobility*. Princeton University Press.

Hoagland, H. (1917). Trade Unionism in the Iron Industry: A Decadent Organization. *The Quarterly Journal of Economics* 31(4), 674–689.

Hogg, J. (1943). *The Homestead Strike of 1892*. Ph.D. thesis, Department of History, University of Chicago.

Horowitz, J. (1990). *Argentine Unions, the State, and the Rise of Perón, 1930–1945*. Institute of International Studies, University of California, Berkeley.

Horowitz, J. (2010). *Argentina's Radical Party and Popular Mobilization, 1916–1930*. Penn State Press.

International Association of Machinists (1893). *Journal of the International Association of Machinists*, Volume 9.

Irwin, D. A. and R. S. Kroszner (1999). Interests, Institutions, and Ideology in Securing Policy Change: The Republican Conversion to Trade Liberalization After Smoot-Hawley. *The Journal of Law and Economics* 42(2), 643–674.

Jacoby, S. M. (1998). *Modern Manors: Welfare Capitalism Since the New Deal*. Princeton University Press.

James, D. (1993). *Resistance and Integration: Peronism and the Argentine Working Class, 1946–1976*, Volume 64. Cambridge University Press.

Jarrett, J. (1882). Protection and Free Trade in their Relations to Wage Earners and Commerce. *The American Journal of Politics 1*, 528–545.

Jensen, N. M. and G. Rosas (2007). Foreign Direct Investment and Income Inequality in Mexico, 1990–2000. *International Organization 61*(3), 467–487.

Johnson, B. C. (1976). Taking Care of Labor. *Theory and Society 3*(1), 89–117.

Kappner, T. M. (1985). *The Political Economy of Populist-Nationalism in Argentina 1943–55: Peronism as a Transitional Stage in the Development of a Dependent Industrial Economy*. Ph.D. thesis, City University of New York.

Katz, L. F., L. H. Summers, R. E. Hall, C. L. Schultze, and R. H. Topel (1989). Industry Rents: Evidence and Implications. *Brookings Papers on Economic Activity. Microeconomics 1989*, 209–290.

Katzenstein, P. J. (1985). *Small States in World Markets: Industrial Policy in Europe*. Cornell University Press.

Keohane, R. (1984). *After Hegemony: Cooperation and Discord in the World Political Economy*. Princeton University Press.

Keynes, J. M. (1936). *The General Theory of Employment, Interest and Money*. Palgrave Macmillan.

Keyserling, L. (1945). *Why the Wagner Act?* Bureau of National Affairs.

Klein, N. (2012). Real Wage, Labor Productivity, and Employment Trends in South Africa: A Closer Look. *International Monetary Fund*.

Knight, J. (1992). *Institutions and Social Conflict*. Cambridge University Press.

Knowles, A. K. (2013). *Mastering Iron: The Struggle to Modernize an American Industry, 1800–1868*. University of Chicago Press.

Kohli, A. (2004). *State-Directed Development: Political Power and Industrialization in the Global Periphery*. Cambridge University Press.

Koremenos, B., C. Lipson, and D. Snidal (2001). The Rational Design of International Institutions. *International Organization 55*(04), 761–799.

Kornberg, A. and W. Mishler (1988). *The Resurgence of Conservatism in Anglo-American Democracies*. Duke University Press.

Korpi, W. (2006). Power Resources and Employer-Centered Approaches in Explanations of Welfare States and Varieties of Capitalism: Protagonists, Consenters, and Antagonists. *World Politics 58*(02), 167–206.

Korzeniewicz, R. P. (1989). Labor Unrest in Argentina, 1887–1907. *Latin American Research Review* 24(3), 71–98.

Krause, P. (1992). *The Battle for Homestead, 1880–1892: Politics, Culture, and Steel*. University of Pittsburgh Press.

Krishna, P. and D. Mitra (1998). Trade Liberalization, Market Discipline and Productivity Growth: New Evidence from India. *Journal of Development Economics 56*(2), 447–462.

Krooth, R. (2004). *A Century Passing: Carnegie, Steel and the Fate of Homestead.* University Press of America.

Krueger, A. B. and L. H. Summers (1988). Efficiency Wages and the Inter-industry Wage Structure. *Econometrica* 56(2), 259–293.

Krueger, A. O. (2004). Wilful Ignorance: The Struggle to Convince the Free Trade Skeptics. *World Trade Review* 3(03), 483–493.

Kuruvilla, S. (1996). Linkages Between Industrialization Strategies and Industrial Relations/Human Resource Policies: Singapore, Malaysia, the Philippines, and India. *Industrial and Labor Relations Review* 49(4), 635–657.

Lake, D. (2004). *The Oxford Handbook of Political Economy*, Chapter International Political Economy: A Maturing Interdiscipline. Oxford University Press.

Lauderbaugh, R. A. (1976). Business, Labor, and Foreign Policy: US Steel, the International Steel Cartel, and Recognition of the Steel Workers Organizing Committee. *Politics & Society* 6(4), 433–457.

Layard, R., S. Nickell, and R. Jackman (2005). *Unemployment: Macroeconomic Performance and the Labour Market.* Oxford University Press.

Levy, F. and P. Temin (2010). Institutions and Wages in Post-World War II America. In C. Brown, B. J. Eichengreen, and M. Reich (Eds.) *Labor in the Era of Globalization.* Cambridge University Press.

Lewis, W. A. (1954). Economic Development with Unlimited Supplies of Labour. *The Manchester School* 22(2), 139–191.

Lichtenstein, N. (2003). *Labor's War at Home: The CIO in World War II.* Temple University Press.

Lipset, S. (1959). Some Social Requisites of Democracy: Economic Development and Political Legitimacy. *The American Political Science Review* 53(1), 69–105.

López-Córdova, J. and C. Meissner (2005). The Globalization of Trade and Democracy, 1870–2000. Technical report, National Bureau of Economic Research.

Lusztig, M. (1995). Solving Peel's Puzzle: Repeal of the Corn Laws and Institutional Preservation. *Comparative Politics* 27(4), 393–408.

MacDonald, I. T. (2003). NAFTA and the Emergence of Continental Labor Cooperation. *American Review of Canadian Studies* 33(2), 173–196.

MaCurdy, T. E. and J. H. Pencavel (1986). Testing Between Competing Models of Wage and Employment Determination in Unionized Markets. *The Journal of Political Economy* 94(3), 3–39.

Magee, S. P. (1994). Three Simple Tests of the Stolper-Samuelson Theorem. In A. Deardorff and R. Stern (Eds.), *The Stolper-Samuelson Theorem: A Golden Jubilee*, Volume 185. University of Michigan Press.

Mansfield, E. D. and D. C. Mutz (2009). Support for Free Trade: Self-Interest, Sociotropic Politics, and Out-Group Anxiety. *International Organization* 63(3), 425–457.

Marcus, I. M., J. Bullard, and R. Moore (1987). Change and Continuity: Steel Workers in Homestead, Pennsylvania, 1889–1895. *Pennsylvania Magazine of History and Biography*, 61–75.

Margalit, Y. (2012). Lost in Globalization: International Economic Integration and the Sources of Popular Discontent. *International Studies Quarterly* 56(3), 484–500.

Massachusetts Bureau of the Statistics of Labor (1894). *Twenty-fifth Annual Report*. Wright and Potter Printing Company.

Mayda, A. M. and D. Rodrik (2005). Why are Some People (and Countries) More Protectionist than Others? *European Economic Review* 49(6), 1393–1430.

McCabe, D. A. (1912). *The Standard Rate in American Trade Unions*. Johns Hopkins Press.

McCabe, D. A. (1932). *National Collective Bargaining in the Pottery Industry*. Number 16. Johns Hopkins Press.

McCallum, J. K. (2013). *Global Unions, Local Power: The New Spirit of Transnational Labor Organizing*. Cornell University Press.

McCord, N. (2005). *The Anti-Corn Law League, 1838–1846*, Volume 50. Taylor & Francis US.

McKinley, W. (1893). *Speeches and Addresses of William McKinley: From his Election to Congress to the Present Time*. D. Appleton and Company.

McNeill, G. (1887). *The Labor Movement*. The M.W. Hazen Co.

Mearsheimer, J. J. (1994). The False Promise of International Institutions. *International Security* 19(3), 5–49.

Melitz, M. J. (2003). The Impact of Trade on Intra-Industry Reallocations and Aggregate Industry Productivity. *Econometrica* 71(6), 1695–1725.

Menendez, I. and D. Rueda (2015). Labor Market Institutions and Economic Performance. In J. Gandhi and R. Ruiz-Rufino (Eds.), *Routledge Handbook of Comparative Political Institutions*. Routledge.

Midford, P. (1993). International Trade and Domestic Politics: Improving on Rogowski's Model of Political Alignments. *International Organization* 47(4), 535–564.

Milner, H. and K. Kubota (2005). Why the Move to Free Trade? Democracy and Trade Policy in the Developing Countries. *International Organization* 59(01), 107–143.

Montgomery, D. (1989). *The Fall of the House of Labor: The Workplace, the State, and American Labor Activism, 1865–1925*. Cambridge University Press.

Morley, J. (1883). *The Life of Richard Cobden*. Roberts Brothers.

Mosley, L. (2010). *Labor Rights and Multinational Production*. Cambridge University Press.

Murmis, M. and J. C. Portantiero (2004). *Estudios sobre los orígenes del peronismo*, Volume 1. Siglo XXI de España Editores, SA.

National Association of Wool Manufacturers (1883). *Bulletin of the National Association of Wool Manufacturers: A Quarterly Journal Devoted to the Interests of the National Wool Industry*, Volume 13. University of North Carolina Press.

National Brotherhood of Operative Potters (1915). *Twenty-Fifth Annual Convention of the National Brotherhood of Operative Potters*. The Potters Herald Print.

National War Labor Board (1942). *Directive Orders and Opinions of the National War Labor Board in the "Little Steel" Case*. United States Government Printing Office.

North, D. C. (1990). *Institutions, Institutional Change and Economic Performance*. Cambridge University Press.

Northrup, H. R. (1946). A Critique of Pending Labor Legislation. *Political Science Quarterly* 61(2), 205–221.

Norwood, S. H. (2002). *Strikebreaking & Intimidation: Mercenaries and Masculinity in Twentieth-Century America*. University of North Carolina Press.

Oatley, T. (2011). The Reductionist Gamble: Open Economy Politics in the Global Economy. *International Organization 65*(02), 311–341.

O'Brien, R. M. (2007). A Caution Regarding Rules of Thumb for Variance Inflation Factors. *Quality & Quantity 41*(5), 673–690.

Olson, M. (1965). *The Logic of Collective Action: Public Goods and the Theory of Groups*. Harvard University Press.

O'Rourke, K. and A. Taylor (2006). Democracy and Protectionism. NBER Working Paper No. 12250.

O'Rourke, K. and A. Taylor (2006). Democracy and Protectionism. *Working Paper, Department of Economic, University of California David*.

O'Rourke, K. H., R. Sinnott, J. D. Richardson, and D. Rodrik (2001). The Determinants of Individual Trade Policy Preferences: International Survey Evidence [with comments and discussion]. *Brookings Trade Forum*, 157–206.

Orren, K. (1991). *Belated Feudalism*. Cambridge University Press.

Oswald, A. J. (1982). The Microeconomic Theory of the Trade Union. *The Economic Journal 92*(367), 576–595.

Owen, E. (2015). The Political Power of Organized Labor and the Politics of Foreign Direct Investment in Developed Democracies. *Comparative Political Studies 48*(13), 1746–1780.

Pastor, R. (1983). The Cry-and-Sigh Syndrome: Congress and trade policy. In *Making Economic Policy in Congress*, American Enterprise Institute for Public Policy Research Washington, DC, pp. 158–195.

Perlman, S. (1922). *A History of Trade Unionism in the United States*. The Macmillan Company.

Peters, M. E. (2015). Open Trade, Closed Borders Immigration in the Era of Globalization. *World Politics 67*(01), 114–154.

Plümper, T. and V. E. Troeger (2007). Efficient Estimation of Time-Invariant and Rarely Changing Variables in Finite Sample Panel Analyses with Unit Fixed Effects. *Political Analysis 15*(2), 124–139.

Poitras, G. and R. Robinson (1994). The Politics of NAFTA in Mexico. *Journal of Inter-American Studies and World Affairs 36*(1), 1–35.

Polanyi, K. (1944). *The Great Transformation: The Political and Economic Origins of our Time*. Beacon Press.

Powell, R. (1991). Absolute and Relative Gains in International Relations Theory. *The American Political Science Review 85*(4), 1303–1320.

Rees, J. (2007). Sons of Vulcan. In E. Arnese (Ed.), *Encyclopedia of U.S. Labor and Working-Class History*, Volume 1. Taylor & Francis.

Robinson, C. and R. E. Schumacker (2009). Interaction Effects: Centering, Variance Inflation Factor, and Interpretation Issues. *Multiple Linear Regression Viewpoints 35*(1), 6–11.

Robinson, J. S. (1920). *The Amalgamated Association of Iron, Steel and Tin Workers*. Johns Hopkins Press.

Rodrik, D. (1995). Political Economy of Trade Policy. *Handbook of International Economics 3*(4), 1457–1494.

Rodrik, D. (2011). *The Globalization Paradox: Democracy and the Future of the World Economy*. WW Norton & Company.

Rogowski, R. (1987). Political Cleavages and Changing Exposure to Trade. *The American Political Science Review* 81(4), 1121–1137.

Rogowski, R. (1989). *Commerce and Coalitions: How Trade Affects Domestic Political Alignments*. Princeton University Press.

Rose, N. L. (1987). Labor Rent Sharing and Regulation: Evidence from the Trucking Industry. *The Journal of Political Economy* 95(6), 1146–1178.

Rosen, S. (1969). Trade Union Power, Threat Effects and the Extent of Organization. *The Review of Economic Studies* 36(2), 185–196.

Rosenfeld, J. (2014). *What Unions No Longer Do*. Harvard University Press.

Rudra, N. (2002). Globalization and the Decline of the Welfare State in Less-Developed Countries. *International Organization* 56(2), 411–445.

Rudra, N. (2005). Globalization and the Strengthening of Democracy in the Developing World. *American Journal of Political Science* 49(4), 704–730.

Rudra, N. (2008). *Globalization and the Race to the Bottom in Developing Countries: Who Really Gets Hurt?* Cambridge University Press.

Rupert, M. (1995). *Producing Hegemony*. Cambridge University Press.

Sanders, E. (1999). *Roots of Reform: Farmers, Workers, and the American State, 1877–1917*. University of Chicago Press.

Scheve, K. F. and M. J. Slaughter (2001). What Determines Individual Trade-Policy Preferences? *Journal of International Economics* 54(2), 267–292.

Schonhardt-Bailey, C. (2006). From the Corn Laws to Free Trade: Interests, Ideas, and Institutions in Historical Perspective. The MIT Press.

Schumpeter, J. A. (1994). *History of Economic Analysis*. Routledge.

Segal, M. (1956). Interrelationship of Wages Under Joint Demand: The Case of the Fall River Textile Workers. *The Quarterly Journal of Economics* 70(3), 464–477.

Seidman, J. I. (1953). *American Labor from Defense to Reconversion*. University of Chicago Press.

Shapiro, C. and J. E. Stiglitz (1984). Equilibrium Unemployment as a Worker Discipline Device. *The American Economic Review* 74(3), 433–444.

Shepsle, K. A. and B. R. Weingast (1995). *Positive Theories of Congressional Institutions*. University of Michigan Press.

Shotliff, D. (1977). *The History of the Labor Movement in the American Pottery Industry: The National Brotherhood of Operative Potters – International Brotherhood of Operative Potters, 1890–1970*. Ph.D. thesis, Kent State University.

Silver, B. J. (2003). *Forces of Labor: Workers' Movements and Globalization Since 1870*. Cambridge University Press.

Silvia, P. T. J. (1973). The Spindle City: Labor, Politics, and Religion in Fall River, Massachusetts, 1870–1905. *ETD Collection for Fordham University*, AAI7402761.

Slater, D. (2009). Revolutions, Crackdowns, and Quiescence: Communal Elites and Democratic Mobilization in Southeast Asia. *American Journal of Sociology* 115(1), 203–254.

Smith, A. (1776). *An Inquiry into the Nature and Causes of the Wealth of Nations*.

Solberg, C. (1973). The Tariff and Politics in Argentina 1916–1930. *Hispanic American Historical Review* 53(2), 260–284.

Stiglitz, J. E. (1974). Alternative Theories of Wage Determination and Unemployment in LDCs: The Labor Turnover Model. *The Quarterly Journal of Economics* 88(2), 194–227.

Stokes, S. (2001). *Mandates and Democracy: Neoliberalism by Surprise in Latin America*. Cambridge University Press.

Stolper, W. F. and P. A. Samuelson (1941). Protection and Real Wages. *The Review of Economic Studies* 9(1), 58–73.

Strauss, J. and M. E. Wohar (2004). The Linkage Between Prices, Wages, and Labor Productivity: A Panel Study of Manufacturing Industries. *Southern Economic Journal* 70, 920–941.

Tamarin, D. (1985). *The Argentine Labor Movement, 1930–1945: A Study in the Origins of Peronism*. University of New Mexico Press.

Taussig, F. W. (1915). *Some Aspects of the Tariff Question*. Harvard University Press.

Teubal, M. (2001). From Import Substitution Industrialization to the "Open" Economy in Argentina: The Role of Peronism. *Miraculous Metamorphoses: The Neoliberalization of Latin American Populism*. Zed Books, 22–59.

Tilly, C. (1995). Globalization Threatens Labor's Rights. *International Labor and Working-Class History* 47, 1–23.

Tomlins, C. L. (1979). AFL Unions in the 1930s: Their Performance in Historical Perspective. *The Journal of American History* 65(4), 1021–1042.

Topalova, P. and A. Khandelwal (2011). Trade Liberalization and Firm Productivity: The Case of India. *Review of Economics and Statistics* 93(3), 995–1009.

Troy, L. (1957). *Distribution of Union Membership Among the States, 1939 and 1953*. NBER Books.

Turner, F. and J. E. Miguens (1983). *Juan Perón and the Reshaping of Argentina*. University of Pittsburgh Press.

Ulman, L. (1966). *The Rise of the National Trade Union: The Development and Significance of the Structure, Governing Institutions, and Economic Policies*. Harvard University Press, 1966.

United States (1885). *Committee of the Senate upon the Relations of Labor and Capital*, Volume 1. Government Printing Office.

United States (1888a). *Journal of the House of Representatives*, Volume 2529. Government Printing Office.

United States (1888b). *Testimony in Connection with the Bill H.R. 9051, To Reduce Taxation and Simplify the Laws in Relation to the Collection of the Revenue*. Government Printing Office.

United States (1890). *Tariff Hearing Before the House Ways and Means Committee*. Government Printing Office.

United States (1895). *Report on Manufacturing Industries in the United States*. Government Printing Office.

United States (1901). *Report of the Industrial Commission on Labor Organizations, Labor Disputes, and Arbitration, and on Railway Labor*, Volume 17. Government Printing Office.

United States Bureau of Labor Statistics (1936). Collective Bargaining in the Glass Industry, 1935–36. *Monthly Labor Review* 42(5).

United States Bureau of Labor Statistics (1979). *Handbook of Labor Statistics*. Number 2000. United States Government Printing Office.

U.S. House Committee on the Judiciary (1892). *Investigation of the Employment of Pinkerton Detectives in Connection with the Labor Troubles at Homestead, PA*. Government Printing Office.

van Voss, L. H., E. Hiemstra-Kuperus, and E. van Nederveen Meerkerk (2010). *The Ashgate Companion to the History of Textile Workers, 1650–2000*. Ashgate Publishing, Ltd.

Verdier, D. (1994). *Democracy and International Trade: Britain, France, and the United States, 1860–1990*. Princeton University Press.

Wakeford, J. (2004). The Productivity-Wage Relationship in South Africa: An Empirical Investigation. *Development Southern Africa 21*(1), 109–132.

Walter, R. J. (1977). *The Socialist Party of Argentina, 1890–1930*. Institute of Latin American Studies, University of Texas at Austin.

Waltz, K. N. (1979). *Theory of International Politics*. McGraw-Hill.

Weeks, J. D. (1881). *Industrial Conciliation and Arbitration in New York, Ohio, and Pennsylvania*. Rand, Avery & Company.

Weingast, B. R., K. A. Shepsle, and C. Johnsen (1981). The Political Economy of Benefits and Costs: A Neoclassical Approach to Distributive Politics. *The Journal of Political Economy 89*(4), 642.

Werner, S. and A. Yuen (2005). Making and Keeping Peace. *International Organization 59*(02), 261–292.

Weyland, K. (2002). *The Politics of Market Reform in Fragile Democracies: Argentina, Brazil, Peru, and Venezuela*. Princeton University Press.

Wolman, L. (1916). Collective Bargaining in the Glass Bottle Industry. *The American Economic Review 6*(3), 549–567.

Wright, C. D. (1893). The Amalgamated Association of Iron and Steel Workers. *The Quarterly Journal of Economics 7*(4), 400–432.

Wright, E. O. (2000). Working-Class Power, Capitalist-Class Interests, and Class Compromise. *American Journal of Sociology 105*(4), 957–1002.

Yellen, J. L. (1984). Efficiency Wage Models of Unemployment. *The American Economic Review 74*(2), 200–205.

Index